POLITICAL BEHAVIOR OF ADOLESCENTS IN CHINA

MONOGRAPHS OF THE ASSOCIATION FOR ASIAN STUDIES
Published by and available from: The University of Arizona Press
Box 3398, Tucson, Arizona 85722

XXXII. *Political Behavior of Adolescents in China: The Cultural Revolution in Kwangchow*, by David M. Raddock. 1977. $8.95 cloth; $4.50 paper.

XXXI. *Big City Government in India: Councilor, Administrator, and Citizen in Delhi*, by Philip Oldenburg. 1976. $9.50 cloth; $4.95 paper.

XXX. *The New Jerusalem: Aspects of Utopianism in the Thought of Kagawa Toyohiko*, by George B. Bikle, Jr. 1976. $8.95 cloth; $4.95 paper.

XXIX. *Dōgen Kigen–Mystical Realist*, by Hee-Jin Kim. 1975. $8.95 cloth; $4.95 paper.

XXVIII. *Masks of Fiction in DREAM OF THE RED CHAMBER: Myth, Mimesis, and Persona*, by Lucien Miller. 1975. $7.95 cloth; $3.95 paper.

XXVII. *Politics and Nationalist Awakening in South India, 1852–1891*, by R. Suntharalingam. 1974. $7.95 cloth; $3.95 paper.

XXVI. *The Peasant Rebellions of the Late Ming Dynasty*, by James Bunyan Parsons. 1970. $7.50.

XXV. *Political Centers and Cultural Regions in Early Bengal*, by Barrie M. Morrison. 1970. $7.50.

XXIV. *The Restoration of Thailand Under Rama I: 1782–1809*, by Klaus Wenk. 1968. $7.50.

XXIII. *K'ang Yu-wei: A Biography and a Symposium*, translated and edited by Jung-pang Lo. 1967. 541 pp. $14.50.

XXII. *A Documentary Chronicle of Sino-Western Relations (1644–1820)*, by Lo-shu Fu. 1966. xviii + 792 pp. $14.50.

XXI. *Before Aggression: Europeans Prepare the Japanese Army*, by Ernst L. Presseisen. 1965. O. P.

XX. *Shinran's Gospel of Pure Grace*, by Alfred Bloom. 1965. $2.50 paper.

XIX. *Chiaraijima Village: Land Tenure, Taxation, and Local Trade, 1818–1884*, by William Chambliss. 1965. $5.00.

XVIII. *The British in Malaya: The First Forty Years*, by K. G. Tregonning. 1965. O. P.

XVII. *Ch'oe Pu's Diary: A Record of Drifting Across the Sea*, by John Meskill. 1965. $4.50.

XVI. *Korean Literature: Topics and Themes*, by Peter H. Lee. 1965. O. P.

XV. *Reform, Rebellion, and the Heavenly Way*, by Benjamin B. Weems. 1964. $3.75.

XIV. *The Malayan Tin Industry to 1914*, by Wong Lin Ken. 1965. $6.50.

Earlier-published AAS Monographs

XIII. *Conciliation and Japanese Law: Tokugawa and Modern*, D. F. Henderson. Univ. Washington Press, 1965.

XII. *Maharashta Purana*, E. C. Dimock, Jr., and P. C. Gupta. East-West Center Press, 1964. O. P.

XI. *Agricultural Involution: The Process of Ecological Change in Indonesia*, C. Geertz. Univ. California Press, 1963.

X. *Bangkhuad: A Community Study in Thailand*, H. K. Kaufman. J. J. Augustin, 1959. O. P.

IX. *Colonial Labor Policy and Administration, 1910–1941*, J. N. Parmer. Augustin, 1959.

VIII. *A Comparative Analysis of the Jajmani System*, T. O. Beidelman. Augustin, 1959.

VII. *The Traditional Chinese Clan Rules*, Hui-chen Wang Liu. Augustin, 1959.

VI. *Chinese Secret Societies in Malaya*, L. F. Comber. Augustin, 1959.

V. *The Rise of the Merchant Class in Tokugawa Japan: 1600–1868*, C. D. Sheldon. Augustin, 1958. O. P.

IV. *Siam Under Rama III, 1824–1851*, W. F. Vella. Augustin, 1957. O. P.

III. *Leadership and Power in the Chinese Community of Thailand*, G. W. Skinner. Cornell Univ. Press, 1958. O. P.

II. *China's Management of the American Barbarians*, E. Swisher. Far Eastern Pubs., Yale, 1951. O. P.

I. *Money Economy in Medieval Japan*, D. M. Brown. Far Eastern Pubs., Yale, 1951. O. P.

The Association for Asian Studies: Monograph No. XXXII
Paul Wheatley, *Editor*

POLITICAL BEHAVIOR OF ADOLESCENTS IN CHINA

The Cultural Revolution in Kwangchow

David M. Raddock

Published for the Association for Asian Studies by
THE UNIVERSITY OF ARIZONA PRESS
Tucson, Arizona

About the author...

David M. Raddock received his Ph.D. from Columbia University in 1974 in the combined fields of comparative politics and political psychology. A specialist in Asian and Communist affairs, he has written on China for scholarly journals and popular periodicals. During 1976 he was in Hong Kong, on a grant from the National Endowment for the Humanities, following up on a theme from the present volume, namely the role of youth in social change in China since 1949. In 1973 he joined the faculty of social sciences at the University of Texas at Dallas.

The publication of this volume has been financed from a revolving fund that initially was established by a generous grant from the Ford Foundation to the Association for Asian Studies.

THE UNIVERSITY OF ARIZONA PRESS

Copyright © 1977
The Arizona Board of Regents
All Rights Reserved
Manufactured in the U.S.A.

I.S.B.N. 0-8165-0571-3 paper
I.S.B.N. 0-8165-0607-8 cloth
L.C. No. 76-19640

Contents

Acknowledgments   vii

1. Introduction   1
    Cultural Revolution and Adolescence
    Questions Posed
    Major Findings
    The Pool of Respondents
    Method and Interviewing Approach
    The Individual Respondents: Thumbnail Sketches

2. The Cultural Revolution: Early Stages of Student Involvement   40
    The Concept of Revolutionary Successors
    Early Stages of the GPCR in the Schools: Evolving Lines of Cleavage
    Epilogue

3. Class Background and Youth Behavior   57
    Uniform or Non-Uniform Socialization
    Early Alienation
    The Opportunistic Middle Course
    Class Background, the Politicization of the 1960s and Participation in the GPCR
    Wang Lok-ch'ao: A Case Study of the Interaction Between Pre-GPCR Ostracism and Intra-Family Dynamics
    Background and Behavior: A Summation

4. The Competitive Dynamic Between Parent and Child: The Projection of Inter-Generational Rivalry in the Family on to Political Behavior in the Great Proletarian Cultural Revolution   90
    Proving Self to Father Re-channelled
    The Vertical Father-Son Relationship: Two Brothers
    Significance of the Lo Brothers
    Father-Son Competition in the Horizontal Relationship and Political Participation: Pao Kuo-fu
    Feeling Big
    Two Extreme Cases along a Continuum of Change
    Non-Political Competition in a Proletarian Family
    Some Further Comments on the Competitive Dynamic

5. Peer Relations and Political Participation in the GPCR   138
    The Passive Red Guards
    The Active Participant
    The Non-Participant in the GPCR
    Chapter Summary

6. Youth and Authority — 154
   The Unalienated Activist: Rebel With a Cause
   One Red Peasant's Defiance of Authority: Unalienated
      but Unpolitical
   The Authority-Submissive, Passive Bystander
   Abstaining from the GPCR: Variations in the Early Alienation
      of a Bad Class Child from Authority
   Returning Full Circle to the Question of Class
7. Concluding Commentary: Changes in Family Relations and the Impact of GPCR in Developing the New Socialist Man — 174
   Norms Leading Toward a New Socialist Man
   More Open Behavioral Trends in the Home Even Prior to GPCR
   Some Questions to Ponder

Notes — 205
Bibliography — 231
Index — 237

Acknowledgments

First and foremost, I would like to thank my wife, Annette, for her loving help in preparing the dissertation which now appears before you in polished form. Apart from providing moral support and technical aid, and putting up with my temperament, Annette made a creative contribution to every phase of this work.

I am intellectually indebted to Professor Michel Oksenberg who, as advisor and skeptic, forced me to concretize my hypotheses and defend them against alternative interpretations and approaches, but who, in the final analysis, offered only the most constructive criticism of my first draft. I am grateful that he urged me to restructure my manuscript, and flattered by his comment that I have "removed all grounds for skepticism" from his mind.

At different phases of this project, numerous colleagues offered encouragement, technical suggestions, and criticism. I particularly appreciate the substantive critiques offered by Bill Parish of the University of Chicago with regard to my early proposal, and by Drs. Joseph Vollmerhausen of the Post-Graduate Center and Milton Viederman of the Columbia College of Physicians and Surgeons with regard to my findings.

Among the many others who have contributed in varying ways as the research project developed are A. Doak Barnett, Thomas Bernstein, Ai-li Chin, Myron Cohen, Lewis Edinger, Stanley Heginbotham, Roy Hofheinz, Richard Kraus, Olga Lang, Steve Levine, Klaus Mehnert, Andrew Nathan, Richard H. Solomon, Richard Sorich, Ross Terrill, C. Martin Wilbur, and the staff of the Universities Service Centre in Hong Kong.

I appreciate the financial assistance of Columbia University's East Asian Institute, the University of Texas at Dallas, and the National Endowment for the Humanities. My typist, Loretta Neubauer, took painstaking care in preparing the final draft. Their aid helped "carry [this work] through to the end."

To the thirty-five young Cantonese respondents, who are the stuff of this study and who brought China to life for me, I dedicate this work.

POLITICAL BEHAVIOR OF ADOLESCENTS IN CHINA

1. Introduction

The initial focus of the Cultural Revolution in the middle schools and universities of China tapped the energy resources of adolescence. It caught the young individual at a stage in his life when he was seeking to relate his childhood experience to an adult identity, and thus it represented a delicate interplay between psychological growth and political development. Tearing at the fabric of power and authority in school and society, the Cultural Revolution, at least for two or three psychologically important years, liberated the youth from the institutions that had bound him and had dictated his growth. By studying the individual's perceived interaction with this movement, the scholar may better understand the dynamics of youth and political participation in New China.

Although not entirely unprecedented, this study in many respects is still an *exploratory* one. First, it examines the relation of family socialization variables to the individual's attitudes toward political participation; unlike Almond and Verba's *Civic Culture* or Inkeles and Bauer's *The Soviet Citizen*, the *emphasis* is on patterns of interaction within the family rather than on the specific inculcation of politically oriented attitudes and values in the early family ambience.[1] Second, it applies principles of psychology to illuminate the subjective dimension of individual participation in a specific, well-defined political movement rather than simply in an observed, amorphous social trend or across an undefined span of time. Third, it offers hypotheses concerning the feedback into the immediate early socialization process of several generations of social ferment, revolutionary change, and the new behavioral norms since the success of the Communist revolution in China. The emphasis here is on trends toward change elicited by new environmental changes. Fourth, it seeks further insight into the relationship between objectives of the new regime and the individual's own effort to adapt to them. Fifth, it looks at the effects of adolescent alienation, particularly on those most motivated toward political or other affiliations and upward mobility, when political criteria combine with group ostracism to obstruct the fulfillment of personal social and political objectives. Finally, this study attempts to demonstrate the *universality* of the adolescent's proclivity to express ambivalent rebelliousness toward father and father-surrogate, given a relatively free milieu, in his quest for adult identity; and at the same time, to illuminate the *uniqueness* of the Maoist strategy in redirecting this energy into political channels. One is compelled to ask what problems this strategy might pose for the social integration of rebels after a political movement has ended, and whether these problems can be resolved.

CULTURAL REVOLUTION AND ADOLESCENCE

The Cultural Revolution (GPCR) was an ideal stage in front of which an audience of scholars interested in these problems of political and human behavior in the PRC could observe a relevant drama. Its youthful players could make a quick and permanent exit, act out their conflicts in an early scene only to withdraw later, play out their conflicts to the end or simply stand in the wings watching. One of the purposes of the GPCR was to have been the cultivation of a new generation of "revolutionary successors" among the educated youth of today's China. Resonating with the adolescent phase of development in the lives of this first, post-revolutionary generation of young people, it provided, at least during the zenith of spontaneity and release from authority in summer 1966-early 1967, a fluid milieu for the individual to apply experiences learned in the home to the quest for an adult social identity; it gave rise to a relatively institutionally free environment for the resolution of family conflicts.

The GPCR drew on the revolutionary potential of young people previously excluded from active political role-playing, and awakened some of those people already in the Communist Youth League (YCL) to whom politics had been important but perhaps ritualized and routinized. Although many former YCL members, faced now with the disbanding of their organization and with a narcissistic loss of identity from the delegitimating attacks on their "consecrators," may have withdrawn from political involvement or retreated into cynicism,[2] others must have reconstructed a mazeway that allowed them to sustain and build on their political identities through participation in the GPCR; for these people, the departure from the past was that they could now give their personalities some play in this process. As for the outsiders who constituted the overwhelming majority, they now had the opportunity to choose among forging a new adult identity, just getting by, or falling back on their pre-Cultural Revolution state of alienation or anti-social, bourgeois family identification. For the outsiders, *active* participation in the GPCR was a function of the need to resolve earlier family conflicts and relate behavioral syndromes acquired in the home to the adult milieu, as well as a reaction in many cases to the social ostracism they had suffered during previous years. And if some had tried actively to break from their families and join the YCL earlier and the outcome had been unsuccessful, they might already have been in a state of identity confusion which could now be worked out in social-political participation.[3]

The GPCR caught the individual at a period in his life when he was most receptive to ideas and ideologies and to the prospect of making a broad and immediate contribution to society. It offered him an opportunity to carve a niche for himself in the adult world by assuming a broader *political* function in society at large, and allowed him to apply roles learned earlier to this task.

Even before the impact of the GPCR, many adolescent students became more inquisitive in all areas and found themselves involved in free-wheeling discussions. But the GPCR introduced the politically naive to hitherto undisclosed information (not always accurate) about events, processes, and personalities which they had never dared to question, and it gave adolescents the opportunity to broaden their vision through travel to other parts of China during the *exchange of experiences* or "great link up" *(ta ch'uan-lien)*.

Wall posters *(ta-tzu-pao)* and Red Guard newspapers, initiated by groups or individuals, dealt with subjects previously taboo. They cut into the lives of important and respected political figures and pretended to explain elements of the political process and political events as much a mystery to the Chinese student since "Liberation" as the "forbidden city" had been to the commoners under the dynastic system.[4]

The young person was encouraged to assert his own personality in rebellion against authority, to seek an adult social identity in a political context, and to select freely the company of peers who would mirror the identities

4 *Introduction*

he was testing for himself. As the Cultural Revolution unraveled in the schools, the formation of adolescent cliques and the ostracism of adolescent adversaries could assume political significance. For the analyst interested in the interaction of personality with the social environment, the behavior of youths in summer 1966 could provide insight into the changes in early socialization which had occurred in China, questions of political participation, and the strengths and weaknesses of social integration for the first generation of Chinese born and reared since the revolution.

QUESTIONS POSED

My assumption prior to going into the field was that adolescents deeply motivated to participate or avoid participation in a political movement of the magnitude of the GPCR--rooted in the schools, lasting nearly four years, and affecting a plethora of institutions and geographical entities in China--in this forum, could well express their early acquired personality patterns and reveal elements in their child socialization that were relevant to their attitude toward political participation. After all, the movement hit them just as they were rounding the corner of childhood and beginning to think of their place in an adult society. The central question then became just what common denominators could be found in early family interaction, socialization in the home, and the resolution of family conflict in adolescence that might bear, first, on the individual's decision to engage in the GPCR and, second, on the depth and emotional hue of that participation.

As the interviews in the field progressed, the testimony of the informants began to expand the fabric of questions to which this study is directed. Among the queries which came to constitute the themes of this project were:

What was the key family relationship in the socialization of the Chinese male child?

What bearing did the father-son relationship have on attitudes toward authority?

How were the attitudes expressed in the adolescent years inside and outside the home?

Under what circumstances could the father-son relationship be resolved through conflict with father manifested in political activity?

If a son rebelled against father and father-surrogates[5] in the GPCR, was such rebellion an extension of similarly overt protest in the past at home and/or at school?

Did rebelliousness against school authorities clearly manifest itself in obvious transferences from father to *specific* authority figures, or were they the mere outbursts of suppressed personalities?

If the former, did such rebelliousness not presuppose considerable Ego autonomy vis-à-vis parents prior to adolescence? And would this development not represent a departure from the image of the authority-dependent, filial child of "traditional" Chinese society?

Could new behavioral norms since "Liberation," in combination with social ferment and intellectual protest against Confucian morality over two or three generations, affect the family socialization process (particularly in the more modern and enlightened cities), creating a continuum of change from the traditional authority-dependent father-son relationship at one extreme to a more one-to-one relationship at the other?

In fact, to just what extent was the most "traditional" case in my sample suppressed or repressed, just how widespread has been the expression of hostility on the part of children toward parents in New China, what forms has it taken, and is the dire underrepresentation of severely suppressed children in the sample indicative of a trend toward further change from the vertical to the horizontal, intergenerational relationship?

Do the extent and circumstances of the suppression of hostility in the home affect political behavior, in what manner, and under what conditions?

If rebelliousness toward father and father-surrogates

6   *Introduction*

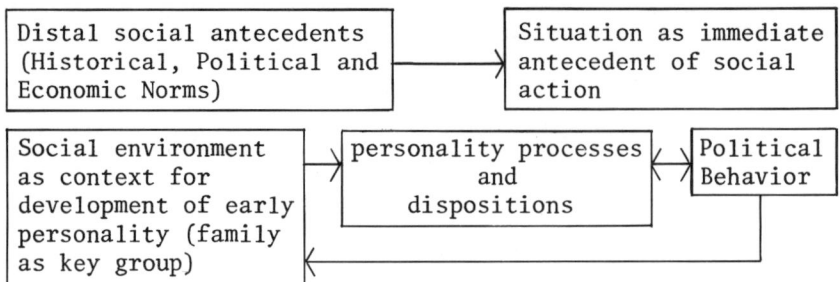

Fig.1.1. Based on a more complex model in M. Brewster Smith, "A Map for the Analysis of Personality and Politics," *Journal of Social Issues*, Vol. 24, No. 3 (1968), 25.

can stem from the ambivalent feelings of sons in *both* relatively authoritarian homes and relaxed, father-son relationships, do the forms of rebellion vary? Are they more or less acute, more or less salient, and more or less likely to be successfully realized in the course of political activities? Why?

How relevant are the father's own political values in influencing a son to choose a political course to rebellion?

If competition generated from a horizontal father-son relationship is more acute and more likely to be satisfied in political activity, what are the reasons?

Does a youth emerging from a more horizontal relationship with his parents develop a greater sense of *trust* than from an authority-dependent relationship, and is there a positive correlation between trust and group affiliation or mistrust and social isolation? What are the implications of an individual's general trust of others for political participation?

Even in focusing on the family's groundwork effect on the psychological dimension of political behavior among adolescents, it would be specious not to consider *all* intervening psychological variables in the social environment, from the setting in primary school onward to the outset of the GPCR in middle school and universities. For this purpose, I chose to work within M. Brewster Smith's schematic model (see Fig.1.1). Throughout this work references are made to the interaction of the individual and his family with the social environment. For instance, an obvious question for a political socialization study of the PRC is whether a correlation is indicated between a parent's political behavior and a son's attitude toward engaging in politics. Or alternatively, whether a more pertinent factor in a child's political behavior would be the unconscious parental-son relationship and the weight it gave to parental opinions and influence in one direction or the other. Simultaneously, however, one must also determine to just what extent negative or positive reinforcement from the social environment could have influenced a youth's response to his parent's socialization. Would a young person, for example, seeking to break from a "politically backward" father be driven back on an identity with father because of a hostile, unwelcoming social environment in the schools? Or conversely, would peer pressures in the immediate environment be sufficiently strong either to abet a youth's defiance of family or simply draw him into political action regardless of his attitudes toward family?

Indeed, we begin this study with a discussion of the psychological influences of the environment. Apart from the effect of political education at school and the general influence of peers, questions of alienation arising from class background in early childhood or in adolescence during the politicization prior to/and at the outset of the GPCR are examined at considerable length for their psychological and political impact on the individual.

Of considerable importance to investigating the behavior of adolescents prior to/and during the GPCR is the question of whether group ostracism, *given political content*, could create a large *outgroup* in the schools with both anti-social and politically revolutionary or iconoclastic intentions. Would a large group excluded from the political process on the basis of similar criteria band together and be less receptive to compromise when later admitted into the political process? And reflecting the complementary effect of early family interaction on later social behavior, would those of the ostracized individuals, psychologically most predisposed in adolescence to expressing keen generational competition through upwardly mobile activities, be most likely to use their sudden *outgroup* status as a springboard for their discontent?

Although I hope to further illumine in this work the motivation of the political behavior of adolescents in China, the study of necessity must be limited in scope. Thus, while I attempt to examine the psychological dimension of political behavior, I make no pretense of dealing adequately with, much less denying, the influence on the political participation of youth in the schools of other variables like sex, age, timing, opportunistic upward mobility, bureaucratic position in the student hierarchy or frustration over bad grades. Nevertheless, I do try to treat these variables at least in a peripheral manner, and, in many cases, do show that they are *complementary* to the dimension of behavior which I happen to be examining.

Yet I would like to comment, at the outset, on some of these alternate interpretations. Whereas high-level position in the student bureaucratic hierarchy might have been an indicator of active participation on the part of the individual in the more ritualized political movements in the past, it did not appear to work this way in the GPCR once the YCL and Student Associations were disbanded and the academic, hierarchical, organizational structure shattered. Class leaders *(pan-kan)*, however, who might have derived their status as much from the respect and affection of their peers as from the sanction of the authorities, seemed to be in a good position for collective participation and the assumption of group leadership. Also, an effort to determine the accuracy, quantitatively and qualitatively, of Neale Hunter's indication of a possible correlation between poor students and active GPCR participants was unsuccessful.[6] In my sample, there was no such relationship. Perhaps, this result stems from a key bias in my sample--the majority were from educated families-- and the incidence of poor academic performance being lower among this social group. But among those with bad grades, there was no more, and perhaps less, of a proclivity toward active participation in the GPCR.

I should like to apologize for the fact that the logistics and resources of this study only permitted me to work with male respondents. I would have liked to explore further Neale Hunter's observation at his school in Shanghai that girls were more active than boys.[7] Although the spokesmen for the regime and even a few of my respondents stress the similarities in behavior between sexes, from second-hand testimony of refugees and my own reading of the literature on political movements since "Liberation," I cannot help noticing the egregious examples of unfilial and politically zealous behavior among females, and venturing the hypothesis that young adolescent girls, perhaps because of their traditionally low and suppressed status in the family before "Liberation" and because parental treatment now still lags behind the new norms supporting equality of the sexes, have a greater propensity for anti-filial rebellion and more of a need for an identity alternate to the family than do boys.[8] I hope that in the future, someone, if not myself, will have an opportunity to explore the research potential in this area.

MAJOR FINDINGS

Just what then has been the essential thrust of this study? What new light has been shed on the nature of political participation in the GPCR? First, it is significant in the GPCR that an individual had a choice of whether or not to participate or just how much to commit himself. He did not explode emotionally in the absence of authority or in the call to attack authorities, but made a choice regarding his actions. Basically, in examining an individual's decision to participate at the early stage of the GPCR in 1966, we are dealing with a question of political choice, loosely analogous to how one casts a vote in our own political system.

A number of voter studies done in the late 1950s in the United States suggested that emotional factors could be involved in a person's choice in the voting booth. One does not always respond on a conscious basis to either the issues involved in an election campaign or one's own group affiliation, and one's own personality is susceptible to deliberate manipulation in electioneering.[9] Franz Alexander suggests that the deviant voter might be responding to a large number of coexisting motivations of which he is only partly aware, ranging from a desire to show his own independence to rebellion against authority.[10] Clearly, however, the American voter's commitment need not go beyond the momentary casting of a secret ballot. For the Chinese trying to decide whether to assume an active role in the GPCR, what faction to join, whether to tag along with his group or whether to abstain from participation, the choice could literally be a life and death one. A choice was forced upon him, and it was one which involved responsibilities, going far beyond the decision itself, which could influence his own life and the lives of those about him in a manner which might be directly related to his decision. Since the choice for the Chinese could involve great personal commitment, it might be expected that subjective and emotional variables would be brought into play. What this study demonstrates is that the emotional dynamics of political participation in the GPCR were not irrational responses to a lack of direction from above or to the unknown which lay ahead, but directed responses aimed at meeting certain emotional needs through specific courses of action and the choice of specific targets.

Yet among what one might consider an unassortable array of emotional factors in the choices surrounding participation in the GPCR, one key variable stands out. Among those interviewed, a major factor in the decision to participate in the GPCR was the interaction between father and son. Apparently more important than the conscious values inculcated in home and school was the unconscious identification with or rebellion against a father. The Cultural Revolution's call to attack authority resonated with this dynamic in the intra-family relationship.

The glaring predominance of this factor in the political behavior of students during the GPCR stems from the fact that as adolescents they were all at a crucial stage in their personal histories. Involved in tracing a continuity between child and adult roles, their relationship with their parents and authority in general played an important part in their behavior. The Cultural Revolution offered them an opportunity, so they thought, to make a great leap from childhood to adulthood and to express themselves more overtly against the existing authorities. The data show that student attacks on authorities often represented an extension of earlier family conflicts and an attempt to resolve them. They were not haphazard but guided by clearly definable psychological transferences from father to specific teachers and other authorities.

Of course, the individual's proclivity to direct adolescent hostility toward specific targets, indeed his ability to rebel rather than just "let loose," presupposes a certain amount of overt rebelliousness or expression of hostility earlier in childhood. The concluding chapter, in its discussion of the new communist socialization, will show how environmental norms, over several generations and particularly since the Communist Revolution, apparently have penetrated family socialization sufficiently to allow even children from the most authority-submissive family relationships to be conscious of their hostility in anger-provoking situations involving the father and sometimes to express this hostility indirectly. Not even the most submissive child has completely suppressed his hostility.

Indeed, what we observe from the data derived from our group of respondents is an apparent continuum of change from the vertical father-son relationship to a more horizontal, one-to-one relationship between father and son. The more horizontal the relationship, the greater the overt competitiveness the son displays toward father. When the father is closer to the son on the social scale or "pecking order," he makes himself more vulnerable as an object for the son to seek to replace. Furthermore, by placing his relationship with his son on a more egalitarian basis, the father is demonstrating a greater willingness to respect his son's autonomy and perhaps even to identify vicariously with his son's own achievements as the latter moves from childhood to adulthood. Thus, in our group of respondents, adolescents from horizontal relationships were the most disposed to seizing the GPCR as a channel for autonomous self-expression and rivalry with the father; and because of the father's attitude toward his son, such behavior on the part of the son was the more salient. The adolescent from a vertical home relationship could also avail himself of the GPCR as a means of self-expression, but his competition with father was not in the form of a mutually accepted rivalry but rather in the form of an act of defiance or "getting out from under" and thus less amenable to ultimate success; the son would be more likely in the end to revert to his father's identity.

Since the individuals represented in this study were all adolescents, their behavior during the GPCR was also an extension of their relations with their peers, in whom they saw their own identities mirrored; it was an extension as well of their relations with the authorities at school. But these societal relationships were at bottom an outgrowth of family socialization and of their parent's class label *(ch'eng-fen)*. Attitudes toward authority in society could depend both on the social effects of class background and on interaction with the authority of the household. Peer relations often hinged on trust and mistrust inculcated in early family socialization, as well as on the exigencies of coming from a bad class or not having a politically red (worker, peasant, PLA) class label. If the common denominator in a given peer group's attitude toward authority was the feeling that they were being held back from expressing themselves and getting ahead because of both official policy and the ostracism of their good class peers, then the members could form a mutually reinforcing, group of militants pitted against the authorities and the "children of the authorities," the original elite Red Guards or *Chu-yi Ping*.

Apart from the fact that to a large extent the behavior of my informants was a logical extension of their personal lives, it can not be reduced to a simple cause and effect reaction. The political behavior of my respondents was necessarily context-dependent. No single tie but a combination of them and their interrelationships were instrumental in shaping a person's decision concerning participation in the GPCR. What this study does is to cut through the multiple causal factors in the political behavior of youths in the GPCR and examine the underlying dynamics of personal relationships which were most likely to play a primary role in pushing individuals in one direction or another once a political channel of expression was open to them.

THE POOL OF RESPONDENTS

The foreign interviewer's first difficulty in Hong Kong is obtaining access to the vast pool of recent refugees, whether old or young, from the PRC. This situation becomes particularly frustrating as one reads reports in the newspapers that in a given year some thirty thousand youths fled from the PRC by swimming to Hong Kong. One is almost driven to think of ways to swim out to meet them. As legitimate welfare agencies become more ethical about protecting their clients, they have become also less amenable to making these people available to scholars, *even on a voluntary basis*. The Kuomintang and, to a lesser extent the American government agencies, are perhaps more cooperative, but the quality and reliability of respondents obtained from these sources are uncertain. Either the agency encourages a refugee to "talk to an American" with the implicit understanding that he will be feeding hostile information on China, or it prods frightened new arrivals who "could use the extra money"[11] to expose themselves to the interview situation. Neither approach is ideally conducive to reliable and open discussion between interviewer and respondent. Moreover, agencies do not like to be over-burdened, and even when they try to cooperate with scholars, generally will feel they have done their job after supplying two or three respondents. Unless an alternate approach is used, the pool of interviewees is likely to run dry.

With regard to my own project, having begun to tap the conventional sources of refugees, I was fortunate to gain introductions to two particular youths, one through a church-affiliated welfare organization and another through a scholar who had preceded me in Hong Kong, and to win their confidence and friendship. These people then introduced me to several of their friends, who in turn introduced me to their friends. Thus, a snowballing technique, less oriented in reality to social science approaches than to the nature of interpersonal relationships in Chinese society, developed as the primary means of recruiting respondents. Snowballing, as a social science sampling technique, has the possible drawback of limiting the diversity of the sample. But in the context in which I was working, it seemed the only practicable means of accumulating a good-sized pool of respondents. Moreover, the diversity of backgrounds, socially and psychologically, seemed quite adequate in the end. Perhaps the common bond among these youths was less a matter of shared socioeconomic status as in American society, than the sheer reality that they were all "refugees" from China and from the Cultural Revolution. The same sort of cross-class comradeship seemed to exist in the action of leaving China as in the school years well before the GPCR. For instance, an intellectual's son was able to introduce me to a three-generation worker's son, and the son of a liquidated KMT (Nationalist) General was able to introduce me to a poor peasant youth whose father was a commune brigade leader. They were all drawn together by their common experiences in the border communes prior to leaving China and by their need for each other in the strange environment of Hong Kong. The one obvious thread of homogeneity in their backgrounds was that they had all been students at the time of the GPCR, had been affected in some way by the GPCR, and had ultimately made the decision to leave China.

Nevertheless, a class bias did introduce itself into the sample and, interestingly, added a dimension to the subject of this study. Although children of workers and peasants apparently fled China in large numbers, they were most reluctant to meet with a foreigner and could not understand why someone would be interested in learning about China except for political espionage or "to make trouble." The three "proletarians" I did interview were too small a number to constitute a control group, and could only provide *impressions* concerning the universality of some of the emergent themes in this study. Children of soldiers and high-level cadres seemed to flee China in much smaller quantities and not only avoided interviewers, but apparently kept clear as well of those who associated with foreigners. Thus, the predominant groups in my sample were the children of "class enemies" (landlords, capitalists, former KMT officials and KMT military, and hooligans) and petit bourgeoisie or "ordinary, middle classers" (professionals, teachers and small

		Class		
		Enemy	Middle	Red
Red Guards	Activist	4	7	0
	Passive	4	8	1
	Abstainer	9	1	1

Fig.1.2. This chart indicates a total class breakdown of the sample and their distribution according to the dependent variables of Red Guard activism, passive Red Guard, and abstainer.

entrepreneurs)(See Fig.1.2.) A youth's class background was determined by his father's occupation in the three years prior to "Liberation" of the area in which his father had been situated. Nearly one-half of the sample fell into the "ordinary," petit-bourgeois category. Most of these youths had not experienced any class discrimination and had free intercourse with sons of revolutionary heroes and proletarians prior to the politicization of the mid-1960s. When class background began to be emphasized more heavily each year from the start of the *Ssu-Ch'ing Movement* (or Socialist Education Campaign) in 1962 onward, and when the category of stigmatized bad classers gradually expanded to include the "ordinary" middle classers by the onset of the GPCR, class assumed a special importance as a behavioral variable for these people. The nature of my group of informants, though imposing limits on cross-class generalizations, allowed me to treat bad class background as an independent variable and examine its interaction with the psychological fabric of socialization I had set out to investigate. Therefore, class alienation became an integral part of this study.

The pool of respondents was composed entirely of males, most from Kwangchow and some from more rural towns in Kwangtung Province, and all fell between the ages of seventeen and twenty-five at the time of interview; the mean age was twenty. In contradistinction to Solomon's sample in which only a handful of refugees (eight) had spent their formative years growing up after "Liberation" in China,[12] my entire sample was born no earlier than a year or two prior to Communist Liberation and spent their early childhoods in the post-Liberation years. Entering or deep into the adolescent growth phase in 1966,[13] all the respondents--

even one who already had just been graduated from middle school--were deeply affected by the GPCR.

For my group, the mean length of time between a respondent's departure from China and interview was approximately one year. Indeed, the majority of respondents had come to Hong Kong within a year of the interview, and this factor seemed to militate against excessive memory distortion caused by time lapse and dissonance-reduction since leaving. The very few respondents who had been in Hong Kong for only a few days or weeks were in a high state of tension and either extremely mistrustful, paralyzed in the presence of a foreign "interrogator," or conversely overly dependent on the interviewer; they were not optimal subjects for this sort of interviewing procedure. Those who were in Hong Kong for about two years (N. = 10) had a tendency to over-intellectualize, placing themselves at a great distance from the original emotional perceptions they were asked to recall; they also were inclined to rationalize their behavior in China in terms of the new situation they had adapted to in Hong Kong or were expecting to confront in migration to Taiwan or the United States. Although these latter informants could be good subjects, the interviewer had to be alert to contradictions in testimony stemming from dissonance-reduction, coordinated value judgments, and a greater overlay of avoidance techniques on the part of the respondent. After several sessions with an interviewee, the interviewer could usually break through these barriers, permitting clearer and more valid patterns to emerge. This problem will be discussed further in the section on methodology.

Thirty-seven respondents were interviewed initially. After eliminating two persons who either failed to complete the interview process or were deemed *unreliable* because of their inability to show sufficient knowledge of events and locations in China or because of deliberate efforts to deceive or distort (the latter individual was introduced by a KMT contact), the group could be broken down almost evenly, according to the dependent variable of political participation, into Red Guard active, Red Guard passive, and abstainer.[14]

The activist (N. = 11) is defined as one who assumed a position of leader or specific task-oriented responsibility in a Red Guard unit in summer 1966, and generally remained active at least through the first armed struggle between factions in early 1967. In Red Guard Activist Yang's View:

> Everyone probably wanted to be a Red Guard. The
> question was whether, after you had joined the Red
> Guards, you would dare "turn over" *(fanshen)* . . .
> that is take part in struggle. Some people . . .
> in their hearts and minds didn't have to take an
> active role . . . they could step to the rear.[15]

It was just these people who tagged along and then quickly dropped "to the rear," returning home after never having assumed positions of responsibility in waging the GPCR, who comprised the *passive* or follower category (N. = 13). The *abstainer* withdrew from school as soon as the Cultural Revolution deepened and authority crumbled in the schools in mid-summer 1966; if he had to make excuses for not participating to some of his closer peers, they generally revolved about personal ill health--mental or physical, sickness in the family or fear that his bad class family would suffer for his participation.

Little opportunity existed for interviewing parents in this study. Since most respondents fled hastily from the border areas in China after being "sent down" *(hsia-hsiang)* in the wake of the GPCR, families did not come out together. Although siblings may have fled on separate trips and may have been reunited in Hong Kong, parents were generally left behind. In only two cases did a parent join a migrant son; in one instance, an ailing mother gained legal permission to come out through Macao, and in another instance a mother had already come to Hong Kong in the 1962 migration (then, in the wake of famine and social chaos, the gateway to Hong Kong had been opened). I did interview the latter mother, but I was bent anyway on examining socialization psychoanalytically through the eyes of the children. Although the Inkeles-Bauer study of two generations of older Russian emigres in Europe was very successful in gaining insight into the changes in values and attitudes stressed in post-revolutionary Russian families and in demonstrating that radical changes could take place on this level over a relatively short period of time, it could not have dealt with the psychological dimension of human interaction in the same depth. I found Mother Huang's testimony to be revealing in this regard, but only in the light of her sons' previous testimonies. Even though she illuminated indirectly the dynamics of family relations revealed in extensive interviews with each of her three sons, Mrs. Huang was very much on her guard when it came to discussing how she had reared the children. Thus, while my study was not nearly as effective, nor was it designed to be, at gaining insight into changes in child rearing and attitude inculcation as parents perceived they manipulated them over the past generation, I do feel that I dealt with another equally interesting dynamic of behavior *underlying* changes in attitudes toward participation--the interaction of children in this generation with their parents in the last generation and with the new social environment.

In two instances, I was able to interview male siblings, attempting to shed some light on the differentials of the impact of the environment over time and of sibling-sequence socialization in a specific family, and the ways they might complement each other.

No matter what the research approach in studying China from afar, one is plagued with his own personal biases and the biases inherent in his research material. When the testimony of refugees is the primary source, the first question is how representative are the informants of the society they abandoned. However, the information they provide does represent certain patterns which, though not necessarily valid for other Chinese youths, do allow us to speculate in a more learned way about Chinese society. To deny the biases in my pool of respondents, revolving principally about the respondents' refugee status and decision to become political refugees, would be intellectual blindness. Yet at the other extreme, a reader might ask: "Given the fact that these young people chose to leave their homeland, does not their maladjustment to life there suggest a possibility that they are not representative psychologically of the other youth in China? Could not *their* childhoods therefore have been abnormal and at cross-purposes with adjusting to the standard adult society?"

My response would be that although one can not speak of these youth as representative psychologically of those who might have remained behind because they were *able to adjust to the post-Cultural Revolution phase,* one can at least argue that a psychological reaction to a traumatic and disorienting social movement in adolescence, culminating in flight to Hong Kong, is not necessarily indicative of maladjusted, psychopathic or socio-pathic behavior up to that point![16] Indeed, many youths in the group were active and enthusiastic participants in the GPCR. In other words, the childhoods of those in the group could have been, and from all indications were, normal and representative of their peers. It would be fair to say that many of these youth were *changed by* the Cultural Revolution and its consequences.

After every political and economic upheaval without exception in the history of modern China, there has been a refugee migration from south China to the colony of Hong Kong. From the Opium War to the famine and rectification campaign of 1961-1962 to the Cultural Revolution, these episodic migrations have been consistent responses to social disorders in China.[17] In 1962, when starvation was a facile explanation for the tide of refugees that swept into Hong Kong, Franz Schurmann noted that a major problem seemed to be social-psychological anomie.[18] As Kingsley Davis points out in an article on demographic responses to population pressures, people do not migrate to solve the specific problems in question, but as a response to the complexity and insecurity of the requirements for respectable adult status under changing circumstances.[19] My group of young people, most of whom swam for approximately six hours to the Hong Kong New Territories, seemed to have left mainly for this reason.

These respondents were reacting to such factors as the insecurity of a chaotic political and social environment, the absence of hierarchical authorities to bind them to the social order, the frustration of upward mobility engendered first by the cessation of regular schooling for over two years and then by the movement of youth to the countryside for a lifetime of agricultural "revolutionary" work, and to the broadening experience of travel to other parts of China during the so-called *Ch'uan-lien* of 1967.

Moreover, Hong Kong bears a special relationship, geographically and socially, to the people of Kwangtung Province. In fact, it is an appendage of Kwangtung Province where the same Cantonese dialect of Chinese is spoken. Businessmen from Hong Kong regularly visit Kwangchow; peasants in the New Territories and others who left China legally or for reasons of hardship in 1962 cross the border on holidays to visit their relatives on the other side; and trains and boats carrying produce to and from Hong Kong constitute an ineluctable link between the PRC and the British colony. Visiting relatives from Hong Kong wear their finest apparel and boast of their prosperity in Hong Kong, making their "Sunday suit" seem like work-day dress. Letters from relatives who have really done well in Hong Kong carry promises that escaping kin will be well provided for and perhaps sent abroad for study.[20] And even Hong Kong radio broadcasts can be heard in Kwangtung. Many in Kwangtung have at least one distant relative or friend in Hong Kong. From contacts of this sort, respondent Yü Ming-li concluded:

My impression of Hong Kong was that it was heaven. Because when I was in Kwangchow studying, I came into contact with a lot of schoolmates whose fathers, mothers or older brothers were in Hong Kong. They thought they understood the situation in Hong Kong very clearly.[21]

Equally important is that because of these contacts, and the long history of migration of southerners to Hong Kong, Kwangtung people do not really think of going to Hong Kong as a matter of treasonous defection, as would northerners perhaps.[22] To many, Hong Kong is still China, and the psychological break in national identity precipitated by fleeing across the border varies from person to person.

But to say that these youths are typical of a migrant population and that their exodus was predicated on an historical pattern of migration and triggered by conditions in the immediate environment is not necessarily to argue that this pool of respondents is typical of the greater populace of students. It is possible, though I do not believe likely, that many of these youths had failed to develop a resiliency to political movements that others in China had acquired; hence, they would have been more vulnerable psychologically to the GPCR.

Inferences about change in early socialization could also reflect the bias in the sample of a preponderance of youths from the metropolis of Kwangchow and the bourgeois class; in this urban, bourgeois environment, perhaps the effect of modernization and ideological "enlightenment" has been more rapid and far-reaching than in the rural, under-represented areas, where the traditional resistances to change might be expected to be greater. However, any trend toward change in one area is in itself significant, and might possibly bespeak its eventual spread to other geographical areas.

It would also be unacademic to make generalizations for the vast territory of China. Apart from the urban-rural differential just discussed, regional differences in socialization existed in the past and must also exist now. Constancy in early socialization practices throughout Kwangtung Province is uncertain. But I feel much safer in making such regional-specific generalizations, bearing in mind both the urban-rural gap and the under-representation of the proletarian majority in my group of respondents.

METHOD AND INTERVIEWING APPROACH

My research approach consisted almost entirely of firsthand, person-to-person interviews, varying in total length of time from eight to sixteen hours per respondent, composed of open-ended questions, and geared to encouraging the interviewee to free-associate whenever possible. Interviews were conducted in Mandarin Chinese which, although not the local dialect, was the language which students had to speak by the time they were in junior middle school.

Without a fluent command of Chinese, I would not have attempted this study. With language as a tool, I could conduct the interviews alone and without interference. No other person was in the room; the respondent and I sat facing each other unseparated by desk or any other barrier or status object. With the permission of the respondent, I unobtrusively recorded each interview on a small cassette set with in-built microphone; these interviews were later transcribed *verbatim* into written Chinese. The transcripts in their entirety, available but for the most part untranslated into English, are cited in the text of this dissertation according to interview session and page number.

The loosely structured interviewing format permitted closer examination of basic responses than either the written questionnaire or limited interview approaches. It often allowed the individual to produce his own indicators of socialization variables and make his *own* linkages with later behavior, political and otherwise, through the free, spontaneous flow of conversation. Indeed, the key themes of this study were first generated as hypotheses, as one would expect of empirical research in the natural sciences, in the course of the early interviewing; the pivotal theme of father-son rivalry, for instance, was not anticipated in my original dissertation proposal.

The quality of information obtained from series of in-depth interviews seemed greater than that of the data derived from questionnaires which presume the validity of the questions posed *per se* and attempt to show direct correlations between variable A and variable B. Although high statistical correlations can be significant when *pretested* questions are administered to large samples, they can be Procrustean, specious, and misleading when administered to small ones.

It seemed all the more appropriate to use the open-ended approach because of the possibility that specific questions were apt to be misinterpreted due either to a low level of education, inadequate phrasing of the questions, or cultural misunderstandings arising from bad fit between the questions and the informant's frame of reference. No one speaks to this problem better than one of my respondents himself who, in response to questions he felt rather rigid during the first interview, stated:

> I know that in the question you raised, you want only one answer. That's impossible. For example, there is a small animal. You want to catch it. But it can run away on four sides. Only if you block three sides, can you catch it as it runs away. My meaning is that in the question you just raised, if you merely expect a "yes" or "no" answer, that's very tough. Because you must understand the various sides. Only later can you pull it together.[23]

Of course, I realized then that I had been rushing this respondent because of my mood that day, but I was also pleased at the prospects for data to be derived from encouraging this sort of introspective person to feel relatively unrestricted in his response to basic lines of questioning.

Contrast the open-ended interviewing approach to the questionnaire Solomon used as the core of his own psycho-political research in Hong Kong. The informant was asked to respond on a positive=negative scale to such statements as, "For understanding the different social customs and different ways of interpersonal relations, foreign movies are worth seeing." My criticism is four-fold: 1/ The query is too broad for a proper conclusion; 2/ The average Chinese informant will not necessarily relate movies to interpersonal relations from a cognitive standpoint without the frame of reference which general, indirect discussion can provide; 3/ An answer to the statement as posed will not explain *in what manner* movies are related to the individual's personal problems and perception of others; 4/ Queries of this sort tend to reflect the hypotheses the researcher has set out to prove, leaving no room for significant adjustment. Even if these questions in Solomon's questionnaire were pre-tested in Taiwan and modified there, many significant nuances still could have been missed. Moreover, the emergent questionnaire would not necessarily have been valid for a corpus of recent emigres in Hong Kong from the PRC. By that final stage of the project, there was little chance for further change of the queries both because of the need to preserve the uniformity of the project and the psychological need on the part of the researcher to reinforce the well-formed themes stemming from the Taiwan data. I have tried to correct for all these shortcomings, while doing my best to remain on my guard against the danger, inherent in my own approach as well, of *leading* the informant into a certain range of responses.

Although my interviews were conducted loosely, they were not devoid of structure. Operating within the guidelines of set rubrics, I repeated the same lines of questioning with every respondent.[24] The structure of the interviews was coordinated with three levels of analysis: early socialization experiences, socio-political attitudes, and political action. Attention was paid to the linkages the respondents themselves made spontaneously between these various levels. Early socialization can influence directly adolescent socio-political attitudes, particularly those toward politics and participation in general, which are brought to the surface by the immediate circumstances of a politicized environment or a particular movement. In turn, political action and the denouement of events in the immediate environment will have a feedback influence on social and political attitudes, sometimes reinforcing earlier notions, sometimes leading to an emendation of earlier attitudes and sometimes creating sufficient dissonance with earlier cognitions to negate them[25] (See diagram earlier in this Chapter).

My interviewing technique was based both on my own understanding of the psychoanalytic situation and the application of Interpersonal theory to interviewing.[26] The latter theoretical approach presumes that the individual's earlier perceptions and personality problems were a result of interaction with an *other*, and therefore his problems can be explored and resolved only through an interpersonal, sharing relationship, each party playing the appropriate role. For my purposes, I did not want to be, nor did I make any pretense of being, a therapist. However, it was necessary to *share* with the respondent in order to create an open relationship in which he was free to confide in me. Moreover, the Chinese cultural principle of reciprocity in a relationship meant that if such a relationship were to be open, I could not repay a respondent's confidence merely with money or favors. Indeed, most of my respondents ultimately refused the gratuity scholars customarily give them for their time. In essence, to obtain the type of information I sought, I had to reveal something of myself and my own history to the respondent. To have maintained a "professional" distance, as some previous China scholars have advocated, would have impeded my efforts to understand the personalities of my respondents. Like an anthropologist, I had to immerse myself in their lives without denying them access to my own.

At first, I had some trepidations about the extent to which a Chinese would allow an outsider, a foreigner and an American to probe into his subjective existence. Indeed, in some instances, the first barrier I had to overcome was the interviewee's perception of me as a hostile American. "If China had not become so strong . . . ," one respondent remarked to me at our first meeting, "you most certainly would not be studying Chinese questions."[27]

But in the long run, I found that being an outsider, peripheral to the interviewee's normal daily sphere of social relations, was an advantage. The interviewee could find in me, if he wished, a repository for all the inner thoughts about the Cultural Revolution and his childhood which he had been reluctant to discuss with his most intimate friends on the mainland and in Hong Kong. Once he began to trust me, he could avail himself of the cathectic experience without it ever redounding to his disadvantage in his own community of social relations. The respondent usually ended the interview in my office, but in many instances also contacted me at other times as friend and confidante to discuss related themes and anxieties. Many of the insights into an interviewee's personality and ideas for further in-session work derived from private, informal conversations over the phone or at tea or dinner. Such research success was posited on my own attitude that the door did not close on a respondent merely because an interview in the office was over.

Moreover, my type of research seemed to them less in the nature of collecting intelligence information than the projects of other scholars. These respondents were more likely to guard themselves against and balk at a scholar asking questions about objective facts relating to policy implementation and political organization than to react negatively to one probing into their family relations and subjective perceptions of people and events.

Also, unlike Leites,[28] Slote,[29] or London[30] who respectively have done recent work in the psychological interviewing of Vietnamese internees, leftist students in Venezuela just released from prison and PRC refugees supplied to the interviewee by the Taiwan government, I was able to conduct interviews in an ambience free of the aura of prisons and interrogation, and it was objectively easier for a respondent to relax under these circumstances. As one respondent put it:

> Here there is no political oppression. I can reveal my inner thoughts. Even though there are some people who are a bit prejudiced and have developed a political point of view and their reactions might not be true to reality, at least you know they are their inner thoughts.[31]

Just how does the interviewer go about building a relationship with his respondents based on mutual confidence and open interaction of personalities? Every good interview series seems to have had some point of breakthrough. Sometimes, it occurred in the first session and sometimes not until the third or fourth. I generally began my interviewing with questions phrased in third person terms--"What does one do . . .?"--rather than intrude too quickly into the privacy of the respondent. He would answer at first by using "We" as a substitute for "I," shifting to the first person singular only after the breakthrough, and even later shifting occasionally again to the collective first person when I began to impinge on areas of personal anxiety. The breakthrough inexorably occurred after I had revealed something about my own personal history or my willingness to give of myself in the context of the respondent's discussion at the time.

For the interested reader, I would like to extrapolate from the early part of the second session with Yüan Ching-po to demonstrate further the utilization of the interpersonal interviewing approach. After I asked whether he had relatives or good friends in Hong Kong, Yüan interrupted my line of inquiry:

Yüan: I want to discuss a question with you. I don't know why since I came to Hong Kong I have had a sort of feeling of self-contempt.

Q. Have you thought about what the cause might be?

Yüan: I thought that possibly it was because in many areas, I can't measure up to Hong Kongers. For example, in the areas of knowledge and ability, in many areas I can't measure up to them . . . in social relations or, possibly more important, in the area of knowledge.

Q. Do you ever think why this is so?
Yüan: I personally can't find the cause.

Q. When you were "above" (in PRC) you didn't have this feeling of self-contempt?
Yüan: No. In China, everyone was just about the same. In Hong Kong, they have a bit of disrespect for our sort of people.

Q. Was your background that of an intellectual?
Yüan: Yes.

Q. Then why do they have no respect for you?
Yüan: . . . We are taken advantage of and browbeaten . . .

Q. I have also noticed this phenomenon. For example, when I have introduced my landlady to a few of the people I interviewed, her attitude has been unfavorable and, in appearance, disrespectful.
Yüan: Yes. They call us Mainland bugs *(ta-lu-tzu)* . . . That is why among the people I know I do not dare reveal my identity.

Q. But you ought to realize that those Hong Kongers don't have the right not to respect you.
Yüan: Everyone is Chinese. Why don't they respect us instead of making us feel self-contempt?

Q. I don't know how you should overcome this problem.
Yüan: Do you think I can overcome it?

Q. You ought to realize that you are Chinese, and they don't know what they are. As inhabitants of a colony, they are on the defensive . . . You are not an intellectually backward person, and China is a great nation.
Yüan: Since I came here, there's been a lot in the environment to which we were not adapted. When I had just come, I ran into a lot of situations with which I was not familiar, and I was not accustomed to the way of life here.

Q. I should think you will adapt gradually, but Hong Kong is not really an ideal society.
Yüan: Yes. Those Hong Kong people like to consider themselves something remarkable.

Q. I don't think they are.
Yüan: They are also very cold and inhumane to others.

Q. I agree with that . . . You know, as a New Yorker, at

times when I have visited the countryside, even though the people were as good as I, I considered myself something special. This was my shortcoming and yet a natural reaction. Perhaps, Hong Kongers react to you the same way. Also, one should realize that Hong Kong people have not had your rich experiences in Communist China.

Yüan: Right! I also want to do the utmost to overcome this emotion of mine, but it has been difficult.

Thus, for several minutes, we departed from the research line of inquiry to discuss an immediate emotional problem troubling the interviewee. I resisted the role of either therapist or father, and, rather than advise him what to do, I tried to give him some Ego support as a friend, and encourage him to think more highly of himself. Exchanges of this sort were important because they deepened a relationship. Also, by encouraging the respondent to treat the interview forum as an opportunity for introspection even into personality and adjustment problems unrelated to my research, I could stimulate the same sort of self-analysis and soul-searching in areas more germane to my interests.

Some obvious problems for the political scientist arising from the personal testimony approach were anticipated prior to my field work. The respondent may be elusive and may conceal certain information. His observations may be by-products of his own Ego defenses. In regard to first person data, there is no sure way to test reliability, except in those areas where the information pertains to concrete external events or can be corroborated by consulting others. I think I was fairly successful in spotting instances of distortion. Such distortions often revealed themselves through internal contradictions in the testimony. When such distortions did not seem to be consciously deliberate and apparently resulted from fuzzy recall, I probed more deeply by means of different and/or indirect questions.

This circular approach was fairly successful. First, one must pose further questions to ascertain whether the contradictions themselves do not reveal certain patterns. Second, when time lapse seems to be the factor involved, one must try to compose questions in *different* context that will lead to spontaneous, improved recall of earlier events. With luck and some insight, one can get a feeling for what the blockage might be. Third, one must recognize that this problem is an ever-present weakness of research interviewing.[32] In an instance where distortion was deliberate and consciously sustained, I discarded the case. In all instances, answers were weighed against concrete external data and the answers of other informants.

Another problem stems from the political refugee's need to rationalize his decision to leave his homeland. To a varying degree, the individual may have a need to reduce cognitive dissonance arising from a complex and long-pondered decision to leave, to eliminate the contradictory elements in his thought threatening the validity of that decision, to alter his values accordingly, and to introject these values and one-sided, totalistic cognitions into his recollection of earlier perceptions of China. Experiments since the original Festinger study of Cognitive Dissonance (1957) have shown that the further removed a subject is from the dissonance-causing object, the greater the dissonance reduction.[33] Indeed, apart from the variable of differing circumstances surrounding each respondent's decision to leave China, one can generalize that the longer a respondent in my sample was away from China, the greater was the dissonance reduction which already had taken place. The tendency to project new internalized values onto earlier percepts led one respondent, for example, to state that he always liked Liu Shao-ch'i. But when questioned further, he admitted that this perception was only a recent response to his psychological need to reject Mao Tse-tung.[34] To ascertain dissonance reduction and attempt to make the respondent aware of his own need to rationalize, I occasionally used open confrontation. Thus, I tried to get one "right-wing" respondent to explore his thinking in terms of his taking financial aid in Hong Kong from the Kuomintang. At least, he made his dissonance reduction apparent to me:

> Basically, I left purely for financial reasons. At the outset, I thought this way. Gradually, it wasn't this way. I felt my coming to Hong Kong was right and not at all with fault.[35]

I confronted another respondent, who had told me just how eager he had been to gain entry into the Youth League (YCL), with a copy of a pamphlet on the new post-GPCR, YCL reforms. Refusing to look at it, he frankly acknowledged: "If I read this type of thing again, I merely would have a burden on my thought."[36] The respondent's own awareness of his biases was the first step in breaking through them. I also used the obvious method of asking more questions, explaining

28 *Introduction*

contradictions and probing more deeply. The more radical technique of confrontation through the introduction of dissonance-causing material could be anxiety-provoking, but was necessary to my getting at the truth, and in the long run, with proper Ego support, was helpful to the respondent in maintaining objectivity and not swinging to an opposite political pole.

In discussing the problems of interviewing, I would be remiss in not mentioning my own shortcomings and inadequacies. Much of my hard-core training was acquired in the field, and necessarily predicated on a few early mistakes. At first, for instance, I was quick to look for Freudian slips and often, *though not always*, ultimately discovered that the slips were not slips at all but garbled Cantonese substitutes for Mandarin words. Once, I pressed too hard in an area of anxiety for the interviewee and nearly lost him as a respondent.

Any social science researcher, whatever his methodology, will inexorably project something of his subjective personality into his formulations and collection of data. As to whether, in the interpersonal interview setting, I may have intruded my *self* into the questions and data, I can only try to assure the reader that I did my best to stand aside and examine my own feelings and interpretations introspectively and, whenever possible, subject my hypotheses and data to the scrutiny of other scholars and people more removed from the material than I.

THE INDIVIDUAL RESPONDENTS: THUMBNAIL SKETCHES

Chai Cheng-li: Arrived Hong Kong November 1969, interviewed 1971-72; Age 25; Born 1946, grew up in Kwangchow; *Education:* officially, third year university, actually first year when GPCR erupted; *Class Background:* Worker (Red): Father had little formal education, but self-taught skilled worker (eight level); mother educated and a middle school teacher; Chai's family on paternal side was three-generation worker; *GPCR Activity*--abstained, after trailing along with *Chu-yi Ping* at very outset (actual sympathy was with *Hung Ch'i)*; father was active *Tung Feng* and member of work team sent to his university in 1968.

In accordance with mother's wishes, Chai took an interest in Chinese literature and majored in the subject at university. Chai contributed to various periodicals in Hong Kong, took pride in his writing style, and often lectured the interviewer. Even

sought interviewer out in spare time to engage him
in philosophical debates.

Chang Hsin: Arrived Hong Kong late 1970 and interviewed in
early 1972; Age 25; Born in 1948 in small village in Kwangtung province; *Education:* upper middle school graduate;
Class Background: poor peasant; father was educated through
equivalent of primary school and mother is illiterate;
father's occupation--village primary school teacher; *GPCR
Activity*--passive Red Guard; sent down to countryside in
1969.

Aggressive and mistrustful, was doing his friend a
favor by seeing me.

Ch'en Ling-ping: Arrived in Hong Kong in 1969, interviewed
1971; Age 22; Born and raised in Kwangchow; *Education:*
middle school graduate; *Class Background:* capitalist
("enemy"); father was a businessman before Liberation and
a medical doctor after Liberation; though trained first in
"eastern medicine" his father had gone into business after
medical school; father "struggled in" Four Olds, retired
two years before GPCR; Paternal grandfather *Hsiu ts'ai*
degree holder; mother, educated through first years of
middle school, died when Ch'en was age six; one older
brother; *GPCR Activity*--Non-Red Guard, sent down to countryside in 1969.

Ch'en was a very confident young man. Attending a
KMT-sponsored, private college in Hong Kong, he also
had wealthy relatives in Hong Kong and was well-
adjusted to the new environment.

Ch'iao Kuo-hsiung: Arrived in Hong Kong early 1970, interviewed mid-1971; Age 20; Born and raised in Kwangchow;
Education: lower middle school 2 (one of the elite middle
schools in Kwangchow); *Class Background:* Professional
(petit-bourgeois) or middle; father's education middle
school equivalent; father left family and PRC when Kuo-
hsiung was age two, whereupon mother divorced the father;
mother, struggled in "Four Olds," had been educated through
the first years of middle school and was a teacher; *GPCR
Activity*--Passive Red Guard; sent to countryside in 1969.

Ch'iao was extremely touchy about the very mention
of his father, whom he had come to detest both for
running out on his mother and for the bad politics
he symbolized. Although his father apparently was
in Hong Kong or Taiwan, Ch'iao had no intention of
trying to locate him. Ch'iao considered himself

inner-directed and independent, and sought the
interviewer's acquiescence in his opinion that
life in China during the GPCR had made him maturer
than his years.

Chou Chung-wang: Arrived Hong Kong July 1970, interviewed
in 1971; Age 25; Born in 1946 in small city in northeast
Kwangtung and raised in Kwangchow after age 6; *Education:*
to third year of university; *Class Background:* Professional
(middle); father university educated and studied theology
in Germany, mother went through lower middle school education; father was a Christian minister before Liberation
and later a University teacher; Paternal grandfather *Hsiu
Ts'ai* degree holder and landlord; three older brothers,
three older sisters (one in Hong Kong), and one younger
sister; *GPCR Activity*--Red Guard - passive (*Hung Ch'i*),
propaganda work, retired during the armed struggle; sent
down to countryside "Christmas" 1969.
  Soft-spoken and slightly effeminate. Took pride
in his intellectual heritage and his own skills
in Chinese painting.

Chu Nan-po: Arrived Hong Kong 1971, interviewed late 1971-
early 1972; Age 21; Born in Kwangchow and raised there;
Education: second year upper middle school; *Class Background:* Professional (petit-bourgeois or middle); father
educated through upper middle school, KMT postal official
before Liberation, continued as postal official after
Liberation; mother attended lower middle school; youngest
and favorite child of father - two sisters and one brother;
GPCR Activity--Red Guard - active (*Hung Ch'i*), organized own
unit at early stage, later responsible for organization and
propaganda, and one of three platoon leaders in first armed
fighting; sent down 1968; escaped by boat in 1970.
  Open, good self-insight; excellent respondent.

Fei K'o-kuan: Arrived Hong Kong March 1968, interviewed
early 1971; Age 25; Born in Ch'iaochow; *Education:* upper
middle school graduate; *Class Background:* Professional
(petit-bourgeois), "ordinary," middle; father graduated from
upper middle school and a teacher until sickness forced him
into retirement; mother attended junior middle school; *GPCR
Activity*--Passive Red Guard (*Hung Ch'i*), but withdrew and
fled PRC early.
  An impassive respondent.

Feng Chih-hsiang: Arrived Hong Kong early 1971, interviewed late 1971; Age 26; Born in 1945 in a small city in northern Kwangtung province; after 1948, raised in Kwangchow; *Education:* upper middle school graduate; *Class Background*: KMT reactionary ("enemy"); father's education in military, two-star general in KMT Army before Liberation; father left PRC with KMT army in 1948; mother taught primary school; *GPCR Activity*--abstained.
   Graduated middle school two years before the GPCR and went down to countryside. Unlike most of the others, he was no longer part of the middle school experience when the GPCR erupted, and he felt much less pressure to take part in that movement. He also had been thinking of leaving China much prior to the GPCR and of being reunited with his father in Hong Kong. Mild and open personality.

Hsieh Ting-teng: Arrived Hong Kong 1969, interviewed in 1971; Age 25, Born in 1946 in Kwangchow and raised there; *Education:* middle school graduate and attended one year as auditor at university; *Class Background:* KMT reactionary ("enemy"); father was a university graduate and KMT General, and liquidated after Liberation when Ting-teng was eight; mother was a housewife who had received a middle school education; *GPCR Activity*--abstained (but sympathized with *Hung Ch'i* faction); sent down in 1969 and became informal contact man in Hong Kong for later arrivals fleeing from his border commune.
   Poised, confident and bright. Hsieh knew Russian well and had translated articles in oceanography from Soviet journals for their Chinese counterparts. Very interested in politics, he admitted that he might well have become a Red Guard activist had his class background permitted.

Hsu Ta-liang: Arrived Hong Kong 1970, interviewed 1971; Age 20; Born in northeastern town of Kwangtung in 1951; *Education:* lower middle school 2; *Class Background:* landlord and capitalist ("enemy"); father and mother both received lower middle school education; up to "three-Anti," father in business, then worked in pharmacy and other small stores; girlfriend in China; *GPCR Activity*--Red Guard-Active (*Hung Ch'i*).
   Personality reserved.

Huang Yi: Eldest of three brothers interviewed; Arrived Hong Kong 1971; Age 22; Born in Kwangchow in 1950 (resided

in Nanking for about ten years); *Education:* upper middle
school graduate before GPCR; *Class Background:* rightist
("enemy"); father prime target at his university during
the 1957 Anti-Rightist campaign; father was a university
graduate and professor of engineering at university,
mother attended university and later became housewife;
mother left China in 1962 with infant daughter and periodi-
cally revisited China furtively; *GPCR Activity*--abstained;
sent down to countryside in 1968.

> Well-mannered, friendly boy who took great pride in
> his intellectual prowess; often played games with
> me, like showing how he could imitate Mao's hand in
> writing one of the Chairman's poems from memory, or
> writing in Russian from Voznesensky and asking me
> to translate it. Boasted that in his childhood and
> adolescence, he read a book a day in the university
> library (including some now-unobtainable classics
> and Russian novels). Became a good friend.

Huang Erh: Next youngest brother of Huang Yi; arrived Hong
Kong 1969, a few months prior to Huang Yi, and interviewed
in 1971; Age 20; Born in Kwangchow; *Education:* lower middle
school 2; *GPCR Activity*--abstained.

> Unlike his older brother, very stiff and stuffy,
> though cooperative. Reserved, proud of his English
> and his familiarity with Western customs; lived
> with missionary in Hong Kong and planned to study
> in U.S. at undergraduate level; attending Christian
> upper middle school in Hong Kong.

Huang San: The youngest of the three Huang brothers left
in the PRC with their father after their mother's departure
in 1962; Arrived Hong Kong in September 1970; interviewed
in 1971-72; Age 18; Born in 1954 in Kwangchow (lived in
Kwangchow); *Education:* lower middle school one when GPCR
erupted; *GPCR Activity*--abstained; sent down to Pao-an
December 1968.

> Low self esteem; tried to lean on interviewer as
> older brother; constantly subjected to taunts from
> his mother in Hong Kong over his being the stupidest
> of her children.

Kuang Ch'ing: Arrived Hong Kong 1969, interviewed end of
1971; Age 24; Born in 1947 in Kwangchow and raised there;
Education: upper middle school; *Class Background:* Professional (petit-bourgeois or middle); father educated in
university, studied in Japan and became upper middle school

teacher; mother educated at normal high school and became primary teacher after Liberation; *GPCR Activity*--Passive Red Guard (*Hung Ch'i*).
    Smooth and pleasant, but not prepared to reveal too much of self.

Kuo Te-en: Arrived Hong Kong 1971, interviewed two months later; Age 23; Born in 1948 in Kwangchow and raised there; *Education:* upper middle school; *Class Background:* petit-bourgeois; father educated in primary school, mother illiterate; father employed as small entrepreneur before Liberation and as factory worker afterward; father died when Kuo was age six; *GPCR Activity*--abstained.
    Introduced at early phase of interviewing project by another outgoing respondent, he himself was terse, laconic, and seemed suspicious of interviewer's motives. Never seemed to be successful breakthrough with Kuo.

Lan Wei-ying: Arrived Hong Kong October 1970, interviewed in 1971; Age 20; Born in 1951 in Kwangchow and raised there; *Education:* upper middle school one (middle school); *Class Background:* petit-bourgeois (middle); father university educated, mother unknown; father in business before Liberation, primary school teacher after Liberation, sent down to village during the Anti-Rightist campaign of 1957, then worked as administrating cadre at street station, sent to May 7 school during the GPCR; *GPCR Activity*--Red Guard activist; sent down to countryside in 1968.
    Still very adolescent; could go on for hours boasting about participation in the "gang" fights GPCR involved; spoke of joining a gang in Hong Kong (off the record).

Li Cheng: Arrived Hong Kong in 1969, interviewed 1971; Age 23; Born in 1948 in Kwangchow and raised there; *Education:* upper middle school and admitted to university before GPCR; *Class Background:* Professional (petit-bourgeois, middle, "ordinary"); father university educated and employed as physician in hospital, mother attended middle school; youngest child (two older brothers and three older sisters); *GPCR Activity*--Passive Red Guard (*Hung Ch'i*), withdrew at time of armed struggle by March 1967, sent to countryside in 1968.
    Excelled academically at one of the best middle schools in Kwangchow and won province-wide honors for his academic achievements. Extremely friendly

and extroverted now. Currently, studying in
Taiwan on fellowship--together with his long-
term girlfriend--to become a doctor; hopes to
study in U.S.

Liang Shu-ming: Arrived Hong Kong end of 1970, interviewed
1971; Age 20; Born in 1951 in outskirts of Kwangchow and
educated in Kwangchow; *Education:* upper middle school;
Class Background: KMT class enemy; father was a small
businessman and member of the KMT before Liberation; *GPCR
Activity*--passive Red Guard (*Hung Ch'i*).

Seemed rather dull. Considered Mao a genius, but
described him as tyrannical and a bit like his own
father in this sense. Frequently giggled nervously
in course of interviews.

Liu K'o-chung: Arrived Hong Kong in 1970, interviewed in
1971; Age 25; Born in 1946 in Kwangchow and raised there;
Education: lower middle school, then sent down to village
in 1964; *Class Background:* KMT class enemy; father was a
member of KMT Revolutionary committee and a military official who, despite anti-Chiang activity, was still considered class enemy; father and mother both university educated; father dead and mother lived away; cared for by
grandmother; one younger brother and sister; *GPCR Activity*--
Red Guard - passive, active in the beginning but not in
armed struggle because of class restraints.

Extroverted and a bit of a blowhard. A unique case,
Liu was already out of school and in the countryside
when the GPCR broke out. He was very outspoken at
first as a *Hung Ch'i* Red Guard when the GPCR hit his
village area; he even led a debate against capitalist-
roaders in the PLA unit. But as a member of a contingent composed almost entirely of youths from the city,
he did not allow himself to become too involved.
Prior to the GPCR, he had been made a cadre at the
village level.

Lo Ping-kok: Arrived Hong Kong May 1971, interviewed late
1971-early 1972; younger brother of Lo Ping-wen; Age 19;
Born in 1952 in Kwangchow and raised there; *Education:*
lower middle school one, then GPCR (hence considered a
graduate); *Class Background:* Capitalist (class enemy);
father died at age 72 in 1964, educated privately; two
mothers, the latter one his own, few years education;
youngest of twenty siblings (five brothers and three sisters, two of whom are in Hong Kong, still living); father

factory owner before Liberation, lost ownership in early 1950's, then became manager; *GPCR Activity*--Red Guard activist (particularly active in armed struggle); sent down late 1969.
    Affable and trusting young man.

Lo Ping-wen: Older brother of Lo Ping-kok; arrived Hong Kong September 1971, interviewed end of year; Age 24; Born in 1947 in Kwangchow; *Education:* upper middle school ("elite school"), one year of foreign languages institute at own expense; *Class Background:* capitalist (class enemy); *GPCR Activity*--abstained; sent down to the countryside in 1970.
    Suppressed child of authoritarian and aloof father.
    Open with interviewer.

Mu Chi-jui: Arrived Hong Kong June 1971, interviewed about three days after arrival; Age 19; Born in 1952 in Kwangchow and raised there; *Education:* lower middle two; *Class Background:* Professional (middle); Father a middle school graduate, was an actor and often on tour; mother died in childbirth; oldest child, one younger brother lived with widower father and grandmother who looked after children; *GPCR Activity*--Red Guard - passive (*Tung feng*); sent to countryside in 1968.
    Nervous and frightened at time of interview, yawned and twitched during first two sessions, confused and anxious after arriving in Hong Kong (complained of not being able to sleep at night); untalkative respondent. Found it difficult to recall anything prior to the GPCR, very psychologically disoriented. Found temporary, part-time work in Hong Kong textile factory. Last seen, several months after interviewing had been completed, at a bus stop; mentioned then that he could not find work and was unhappy in Hong Kong.

Nieh Li-chih: Arrived Hong Kong June 1969, interviewed mid-1971; Age 24; Born in 1947 in Kwangchow and raised there; *Education:* upper middle school, graduating as GPCR broke out; *Class Background:* Capitalist (class enemy); father educated through upper middle school one, mother through primary school; father involved in large business; *GPCR Activity*--abstained.
    Bitter about discrimination against him in China, but did not seem to have an emotional need to indict the PRC in interviewer's presence.

Pao Kuo-fu: Arrived Hong Kong March 1971, interviewed several months later; Age 24; Born in 1947 in Kwangchow and raised there; *Education:* upper middle school graduate by GPCR; *Class Background:* Professional (petit-bourgeois, middle); father was university-medical school graduate and became physician and medical researcher, and later head of hospital; mother educated through nursing school and worked at father's hospital; father became CCP branch leader at hospital and was selected once as part of delegation to Peking to meet Chairman Mao; *GPCR Activity*--Red Guard activist leader (*Hung Ch'i*).

> Helped interviewer by introducing him to an enclave of militants who were awaiting "their opportunity to return to China" (none of these agreed to *private* interview).

P'eng Te-lai: Arrived Hong Kong May 1971, interviewed summer of 1971; Age 23; Born in 1948 in Kwangchow and raised there; *Education:* upper middle school graduate; *Class Background:* Professional (middle); father and mother both university educated; father, a teacher, died in 1963; mother taught in university; three older sisters, one older brother, one younger brother; *GPCR Activity*--Red Guard - passive (*Hung Ch'i*); sent down to countryside in April 1970.

> Although introduced by good friend, hostile toward Americans in general and, *at outset*, interviewer in specific.

Shih Chi-t'ang: Arrived Hong Kong 1970, interviewed late 1971-early 1972; Age 22; Born in 1950 in Kwangchow; *Education:* upper middle school (an "elite" middle school); *Class Background:* KMT class enemy; father university educated and a military officer in KMT before Liberation, a seaman-engineer after Liberation; mother had only a couple of years' education; oldest child - two younger sisters and two younger brothers; *GPCR Activity*--left school to avoid Red Guard involvement, after limited participation early in *Hung Ch'i* prototypes, abstained from *Ch'uan-lien*, but became activist Street Committee Public Security Brigade member; father in *Tung feng* Red Guards.

> Very suspicious of people and defensively opportunistic; low trust of others. He would never commit himself to friendship.

T'ang Nai-chang: Arrived Hong Kong 1969; interviewed 1971; Age 25; Born in 1946 in Kwangchow and raised there; *Education:* second year university; *Class Background:* Rich Peasant

(middle); father educated through middle school; *GPCR Activity*--Red Guard - active (*Hung Ch'i*).
Tendency to boast and exaggerate.

Tseng K'ai-lao: Arrived Hong Kong in 1971, interviewed two weeks later; Age 18; Born in 1953 in a small Kwangtung village; *Education:* first year junior middle school in rural area; *Class Background:* poor peasant (Red); father and mother both had primary school education; Father's occupation--CCP member and brigade leader in rural Commune; *GPCR Activity*--Red Guard - passive (*Tung feng*).
Seemed to trust me because he trusted and admired city friend who introduced us. Indeed, this friend was one of the lot of Kwangchow students who, while in his village, made him feel important and a part of their group; when he was criticized later for befriending people who had fled China, he decided to join them in Hong Kong. In Hong Kong, he had great difficulty finding even part-time work. *According to our mutual friend, Mr. Tseng had returned to China before the interviewer himself returned to the United States.*

Wei Chao-fan: Arrived Hong Kong July 1969, interviewed in 1971; Age 22; Born in 1949 in suburb of Kwangchow and raised there; *Education:* upper middle school graduate; *Class Background:* petit-bourgeois; parents both died by the time he was age three (reared by his father's younger brother); lived with one older brother, and older sister and four of uncle's children; *GPCR Activity*--Red Guard - active (propaganda duties in *Hung Ch'i* group), participated in armed struggles; sent down to countryside in 1969.
Open and friendly; cynical about PRC.

Wang Lok-ch'ao: Arrived Hong Kong July 1970, interviewed 1971-72; Age 21; Born 1951 in Kwangchow and raised there; *Education:* first year upper middle school; *Class Background:* Professional (petit-bourgeois); father university educated (grandparents landlords), now occupied as engineer; mother normal middle school graduate; oldest child - younger brother and sister; *GPCR Activity*--Red Guard - active.
Having just received visa to U.S., extremely friendly and eager to cooperate. Now living with wealthy relatives and attending west coast college.

Wu Kuo-chih: Arrived Hong Kong July 1970, interviewed 1971; Age 24; Born in 1947 in Kwangchow and raised there;

Education: upper middle school graduate; *Class Background:* KMT class enemy (father had been executed as a KMT party leader); father was graduated from university, mother's education unknown; father a university professor and KMT official until he died when Kuo-chih was age three; *GPCR Activity*--Red Guard - passive (very inactive, except for his early limited association with friends in the prototypical *Mao Tse-tung Chu-yi Ping*).

Bright-eyed and vivacious, Wu looked like a character from *Red Detachment* when first met him. Extremely contemptuous of father not only because of his political history but because he regarded him as a failure and fool (his father fled to Hong Kong and, uncomfortable there, returned home, only to be executed).

Yeh Hen: Arrived Hong Kong September 1971, interviewed January-February 1972; Age 23; Born in 1948 in Kwangchow and raised there; *Education:* second year of veterinary medical high school (five-year vocational school); *Class Background:* capitalist ("enemy"); father educated at university and mother through primary five; paternal grandfather held Chü-jen degree; father was head of construction firms in Kwangchow and Hong Kong before Liberation and now in Hong Kong (left China during "Three-anti" in 1953); *GPCR Activity*--Red Guard activist (*Hung Ch'i* propaganda department); sent down in 1968, and made final decision to leave because he felt they were not making proper use of his veterinary training in the countryside and were moving him about too much.

Reunited with well-to-do father in Hong Kong, who had given him the "title" of job foreman, he seemed to be drifting without purpose.

Yang Ying-pu: Arrived Hong Kong 1968, interviewed early 1971; Age 22; Born in 1949 in Chiaochow and then moved to vicinity of Kwangchow; *Education:* middle school graduate; *Class Background:* technically "enemy," but through deception, poor peasant (Red); father fled to Taiwan with KMT and became city party official in Taiwan; Ying-pu's mother also moved to another part of the PRC and Yang was raised by his maternal grandmother, a poor peasant; *GPCR Activity*--Red Guard - active (*Hung Ch'i*).

Conducted himself like a Hong Kong businessman; tried to anticipate questions before asked, intellectualized too much when recalling early events

Introduction   39

and tended to distort in terms of current politically right-wing emotional commitments.

Yü Ming-li: Arrived Hong Kong October 1969, interviewed 1971; Age 24; Born in 1947 in Kwangchow and raised there; *Education:* upper middle school; *Class Background:* KMT class enemy; father educated at military institute (middle school level), mother at primary level; father was local army officer before Liberation, first affiliated with KMT forces and then defecting to Red Army side; father was worker cadre after Liberation; *GPCR Activity*--Red Guard - passive, but participated in armed struggle for a short while out of intense hatred for opposing *Tung Feng* faction, generally the children of good classers; sent down to countryside in November 1968.

Extroverted and introspective.

Yüan Ching-po: Arrived Hong Kong 1970, interviewed in 1971; Age 25; Born in 1946 in Kwangchow and raised there; *Education:* upper middle school graduate; *Class Background:* KMT reactionary (enemy); at pains to find permanent work in two years before the GPCR, but eventually got job in street factory; father, university graduate, died in 1966; a lawyer under KMT, retired because of ill health; *GPCR Activity*--abstained.

Though friendly, very reserved at outset; then opened up in very deep catharsis.

2. The Cultural Revolution: Early Stages of Student Involvement

The reasons for participating in the GPCR depended on the person. Some persons' brains were filled with Mao Tse-tung thought. They felt their participating was for the benefit of all China and all the Chinese people. Some also participated for the fun of it; to wear arm bands and shoot guns seemed prestigious. Thus, each individual had differing and various reasons for participating.
-- Ch'iao VI-12

We didn't merely aim at the authorities in school. We aimed at the entire society. Because at that time, entire China was concerned with the question of elitism and Class.
-- Ch'iao IV-18

For the students of the urban middle schools and universities the Cultural Revolution was indeed, as Bennett and Montaperto described it, a "happening."[1] The multifaceted explanations of why it took place and how it developed are still subjects for investigation by scholars. It would seem to have been motivated at the top, pragmatically, by a power struggle between the Mao group and the Party *apparat*, and ideologically, by a desire to smash a cancerous elitism in the bureaucracy and cultural realms, and by a vision of educating potential successors in the crucible of a truly revolutionary experience.

But this particular study focuses primarily on the phenomenon at the lower levels: students reacting to the Cultural Revolution in very subjective and personal ways. They were subjective not only in their interpretation of the principles for which they thought they were fighting, but in their dedication, in their very reasons for participating, in their manner of expression, in the concerns to which they paid heed, and in their influence upon the emerging issues which the GPCR was supposed to resolve. Secondarily, we argue that it was perhaps the genius of the Mao group to have manipulated, through political channels, what they intuitively knew to be the very personal, psychological, energizing conflicts confronting the individual adolescents.

THE CONCEPT OF REVOLUTIONARY SUCCESSORS

Already encouraged by the concept of post-revolutionary purity, the new norms supporting their autonomy in the home and general social mobility, the Chinese youth were given a cue as early as 1964 that they were to be the "revolutionary successors" and that Chairman Mao felt the fate of China and world revolution depended on their redness; they were going to be put to the test. Virtually heralding the Cultural Revolution in the schools, a major ideological article by the editorial departments of *Hung Ch'i* (the ideological journal of the Communist Party of China) and *Jenmin Jihpao* stated:

> Comrade Mao Tse-tung has pointed out that, in order to guarantee that our Party and country do not change their color, we must not only have a correct line and correct policies but must train and bring up millions of successors who will carry on the course of the proletarian revolution . . . Successors to the revolutionary cause of the proletariat come forward in mass struggles and are tempered in the great storm of revolution.[2]

And before Edgar Snow and other foreign visitors in winter 1964, Mao himself expressed his anxiety over a post-revolutionary generation which had not gone through either war or revolution; would the lack of practical revolutionary "steeling" "negate the revolution?"[3]

How then to assure the continuance of the revolution and militate against a counter-revolutionary recurrence of the pre-revolutionary intellectual and official elitism Mao had so detested? The course chosen was an obvious throwback to the experience of the May Fourth Movement, in which young intellectuals had been the vanguard of social, cultural, and political change. It was under these circumstances that Mao himself had joined a Marxist study group at Peking University, and had become one of the original members of the Chinese Communist Party (CCP). In recalling the May Fourth episode on its twentieth anniversary in 1939, Mao stated:

> What role have the youth played in the May Fourth Movement? They have in a way played the role of vanguard, and this is recognized by all the people of the country, except the diehards. What is meant by the role of vanguard? It is to take the lead, i.e., stand at the head of the revolutionary ranks.[4]

Again, as the Cultural Revolution got underway, Mao acknowledged the importance of young people as a revolutionary vanguard. Among the many phrases youth in the Cultural Revolution committed to memory was Mao's statement that "the young people are the most active and vital force in society, the most eager to learn and the least conservative in their thinking."[5] Simultaneously, however, youths were warned that past tendencies toward intellectual elitism were on trial, and that the true test of a youth's revolutionary character was integration with the broad masses of workers, peasants and soldiers.[6] Hence, young people were given a further cue that the ultimate test of their revolutionary uprightness would be productive integration with the masses. But few of the zealous participants heeded the caveats to awe-inspiring calls to revolt in the *Quotations*. Only the detached observer could have guessed that integration with the masses would mean the eventual resurrection of authority over youth and a large-scale movement of youths to the villages.

Many youths spontaneously drew the analogy between their role in the Cultural Revolution and that of the young intellectuals of the May Fourth. Chou Chung-wang's statement is particularly poignant:

> At that time, our feeling was that we had truly become revolutionary youths of our epoch. We were really engaged in discussion of national affairs and shouldering heavy responsibilities. It was as if at that time we were not only discussing the things that occurred in Kwangchow, but moreover were discussing things occurring in various places all over the country . . . *At that time we felt we were like the revolutionary youths of the May Fourth Movement, waging revolution for China's future! We felt extraordinarily proud, and extraordinarily pleased with ourselves.*[7]

The student Red Guards regarded themselves as the vanguard of the movement, as in the May Fourth period, spearheading the action and rallying the main forces of workers and peasants. According to Yeh Hen:

> It was similar to the May Fourth. In both, the student movement was the high tide. If the students had not taken the lead, then . . . (pause) . . . Any revolutionary movement must have a front line to kindle the fire; the students just served this function. When we were Red Guards, the workers ignored us at first. Why? Why did it become so fierce afterward? No sooner did the workers come out, then we stole . . . PLA guns . . . they [the soldiers] said don't steal our guns, but we paid no heed![8]

As important as the Maoist regime's intent in choosing students to launch the GPCR was the student's interpretation of why they had been chosen. Although they may later have come to feel "used," it was this early interpretation they gave their role that contributed to the purpose, direction and content of their political participation.[9] Virtually echoing Mao on May Fourth and youth in general, Chou Chung-wang felt this way about his role:

> He [the intellectual] has a sort of propelling function with regard to revolution. He has a function of creating theory and preparatory work for the revolution. Thus, in this GPCR, he [Mao Tse-tung] first used us intellectuals to create a mood, destroying the old and erecting the new. It first began with the criticism of the "Three Family Village."[10]

The notion of being potential "revolutionary successors" spurred young people on to an active quest for upward and outward mobility, and encouraged this generation to prove itself at least as fit as its precursors for "carrying the revolution through to the end." And since the targets of the revolution were all those in authority going the wrong way, the new generation was given hope of replacing their misguided elders. If they were the modern counterparts of the May Fourth vanguard, why couldn't they hope to become the post-revolutionary elite of tomorrow?

The youth in the Cultural Revolution were told:

> The world is yours, as well as ours, but in the last
> analysis, it is yours. You young people, full of
> vigor and vitality, are in the bloom of life, like
> the sun at eight or nine in the morning. Our hope
> is placed in you . . . the world belongs to you.
> China's future belongs to you.[11]

And what more encouraging image to give adolescents in China than to depict them as *rising suns*? The untainted youths who grew up since "Liberation" now merely required "steeling" in order to replace those elders who had fallen prey to those pre-revolutionary habits which had permeated the environment of their feudal childhood. The revolutionary purity of this new generation would surely make better raw material for processing in revolutionary practice. Wu states:

> I felt our generation of youth had grown up in a
> period after Liberation. Therefore, we didn't have
> an understanding of former circumstances. Everything our generation was taught was in accordance
> with the new educational system of Mao Tse-tung
> thought. Therefore, they used us to conduct the
> GPCR.[12]

Wang describes a new feeling of restlessness that came over him then:

> We thought then of replacing the older generation.
> Like we wanted to master the world. The atmosphere
> then was one of greatness. I was somewhat motivated
> by this . . . I felt they the leaders were useless.
> I felt they had no get up and go (*kan-ch'i*). They
> were too slow at things.[13]

Thus, Mao was able to draw on the competitive, intergenerational dynamic, the chafing at the bit that adolescents experience the world over.

The "world is yours" call elicited positive reactions and a growing impatience with the subordinate child role. As Shih Chi-t'ang asserted:

> Old people must necessarily leave this world, and
> us! *Additionally, in the unceasing development of
> society, younger people will be more intelligent
> and will all make this world more beautiful* . . .[14]

EARLY STAGES OF THE GPCR IN THE SCHOOLS: EVOLVING LINES OF CLEAVAGE

The Cultural Revolution in the schools began in May 1966, as an ordinary political campaign interrupting the students' preparation for final examinations. Its organizers, activists in the YCL, held meetings and encouraged the writing of wall posters (*ta-tzu-pao*) criticizing remote literary figures in Peking. However, the GPCR soon developed into a characteristically revolutionary experience, challenging, and for awhile replacing, much of the former elite in the schools and society at large. The primary period on which this thesis focuses is from summer 1966 to early 1967. In this time, former authority-controls were weakened and to a large extent eliminated in sporadic intervals. Local and individual spontaneity were at their zenith. Factions developed in the Red Guards, and the "class question" became a central organizing issue. Students could choose between participation and non-participation and the extent to which they would commit themselves on an individual basis.

May 1966

The initial phase of the GPCR in the schools revolved about writing wall posters criticizing the Peking writers (generally called the "three family village," after an essay by one of the writers, Teng T'o). The students in Canton were responding to the oblique cues, months earlier, from the five-man Cultural Revolution group at the center, led by Peking Party boss Peng Chen, whose intent it was to make Mao's first political salvo against his critics in the party apparatus bog down in mere academic criticism.[15] Even as Mao moved directly against the party apparatus in Peking, denounced Peng Chen, and issued the "May 16 Circular" replacing the five-man Cultural Revolution Committee with a radical Central Cultural Revolution Group (CCRG), the impact of inner-party struggle in Peking scarcely had a resounding effect among the masses of Kwangchow. The "May 16 Circular" had called for a mass repudiation of bourgeois, anti-Mao "monsters and freaks" who had allegedly infiltrated all spheres of culture ("Culture" interpreted according to its broadest generic meaning as the German "Kultur" or Communist "superstructure"). Combined with an effort to foment rebellion against entrenched authorities in the schools,[16] the "May 16 Circular" from Peking at first elicited only a moderate campus movement in Kwangchow, characterized by much confusion over what course the movement was to take.

The movement on the campuses of universities and middle schools of Kwangchow was still controlled by conventional activists and authorities, limited to attacking selected teachers in "struggle" meetings. To those Youth Leaguers who identified with the higher authorities, the restriction of the GPCR to attacking this limited group was a safe course, neither jeopardizing their own future nor defying the conventions of previous, ritualistic political campaigns. But others--even those in the "inner circle" of politically "active" students--had broader visions of their role in the GPCR. They began to argue for moving to a higher plane of attack, starting with the principal and school Party Committee and then proceeding beyond the confines of the school. The animating forces behind this upward and outward push varied. Revolutionary principle, personal upward mobility, and reinforcing cues from Peking and other urban centers were involved. But even more subjective factors, sometimes contradictory, seemed to govern the directions these people took. Many individuals in this first radical groundswell derived pleasure from singling out specific teachers and then the principal for vigorous criticism, but had ambivalent feelings about struggling *others* they respected close above them. Thus, on the one hand, the struggle of familiar authorities could elicit the emotional response necessary to kindle a fire under the GPCR in the schools, but on the other hand, a negative *horreur de face-à-face*, engendering severe guilt in attacking a close teacher, seemed to be a factor in inducing the ideologically devoted to look for more remote figures to assail.[17]

June-July 1966

As to be expected, Mao's assault on Peng Chen and the Peking Party Committee prompted officials at all levels and in all institutions to take cover by undertaking the Cultural Revolution in their respective areas and, through top-downward control, manipulating it to protect their own interests--a political posture later referred to as "Waving the red flag to fight the red flag!" In the conventional manner, party work teams were dispatched to schools to mobilize the campaign. In the past, most recently in the *Ssu-Ch'ing Movement*, from 1962 through 1964, mobilization and party control were considered complementary. But since the ultimate purpose now was the shattering of the bureaucracy and party apparatus, the dispatch of work teams from above, coordinated not much later with the encouragement on campus of radical students in their struggle against the higher authorities in the school, seems in hindsight to have been a deliberate attempt to exacerbate the cleavage between authority and student, generation and generation. Although the protests on the part of Nieh Yuan-tzu at Peking University and Kuai Ta-fu at Tsinghua (Peking's technological institute) against control from above were to lead to discreditation of the work teams and serve as an impetus to push the GPCR further ahead on the campuses in Peking,[18] the reaction in Kwangchow was merely to use the struggle against the work teams as a focal point for debate over other issues related in a much more natural and spontaneous way to the social lines of fracture already existing on the local campuses.

The arrival of party-dispatched work teams (*kung-tso-tui*) on the campuses of Kwangchow in June and July struck most people as part of the normal procedure for conducting political campaigns. Since the work teams in Kwangtung seemed to be conspicuously lacking in a general plan of action, they did not have an inordinately stifling effect on the more spontaneous surge to carry the GPCR further. Hence, even when the work team concept was later discredited in Peking and became a focal point for struggle there, it became simply the immediate legitimating nucleus for more emotional debates over other issues--primarily the debate over excluding non-red class children from the Red Guards--in the schools of Kwangchow. The real source of tension among students who chose to involve themselves in the GPCR was between those who, usually of red class background (peasants', workers' and cadres' children), were conservative about moving against people in authority and jeopardizing their own vested interests in the hierarchy and those who strove to deepen the GPCR by more radical action at all levels.

August-November 1966

Between August and November 1966, the aura of spontaneity and radicalism widened. The "Four Olds" Campaign against the families of bourgeoisie allowed the better-class children to express themselves in a more militant fashion while simultaneously feeding the hostility of the victims of this transitory campaign. A definitive decision was made in the early part of this period to exclude all children of non-red background (even former activists) from the organization of Red Guards. This exclusionist act, directed at adolescents who had been politically active, laid the groundwork for the emergence of the question of class background as the key organizing issue for later factional strife when the base of participation in the GPCR would be broadened to include bad class children. In an almost dialectical manner, the forces were massing--or perhaps being manipulated from above--to deepen the GPCR, push it forward, and overturn an old elite.

After their formal creation in August, rampaging Red Guards searched the homes of bad class (or "seven kinds of black") families in search of bourgeois and feudal possessions--clothes, jewelry, books, religious items--to confiscate in promulgation of the "Destroy Four Olds" campaign (*P'o-ssu-chiu*: old culture, old customs, old ideas and old habits). Now the early Red Guards of red class background, anxious to avoid making waves in their own waters, had an opportunity for less restrained action elsewhere. Early Red Guards (of red class background) must have found this campaign exhilarating, while its victims were radicalized in quite a different way. Uncontrolled by specific authorities or guidelines, Red Guard units behaved as they pleased, sometimes finding themselves in the confused situation of competing with other Red Guard units over certain targets, like different gangs coming to rob the same bank at the same time. Similarly, the *Ko-ming ta ch'uan-lien* (revolutionary exchange of experiences) in October-November 1966, involved Red Guards and a lot of non-red classers who passed themselves off as Red Guards in free travel to all parts of China. This experience not only sensitized young people to the nation-wide developments in the GPCR, but also increased their feeling of self-importance as they arrived like visiting dignitaries in the capitals of other provinces. (Ironically, the broadening experience of travel, reducing the provincialism of Chinese youth and opening up new spheres of life to them, was later to prove counter-productive to the regime by serving as an incentive to the disillusioned after the GPCR to pull up their roots and flee to Hong Kong.)[19] It was also during the period from summer to fall that, free from authority controls, many students could withdraw from political activity or approach it in individual ways.

Yet in spite of the frenetic and self-inflating activity for some young people up to this point, the Cultural Revolution still had not fulfilled its revolutionary purpose. The Red Guards represented the backbone of the same student elite as before the GPCR, and were organized according to the pre-existing, hierarchical academic structure. Many of the participants could still treat political activism as a matter of ritual, imposed from above. The one new dimension, the dynamic which was to carry the GPCR to its ultimate depth, was the exclusion of the non-red classes from participation in the early Red Guards or *Chu-yi-ping*. When students first convened in early August 1966, to organize themselves both in response to Mao's recognition of the Red Guards at Tsinghua University and in response to loose Central Committee directives for mass activism, they set about on their own establishing a hierarchical organization. The members of this organization, drawn from the YCL, Student Association and core of "political activists," would have represented neither a change in the student elite nor in the academically oriented (by class level) structures. Through Red Guards, arriving on the Canton scene, Peking quickly made it clear that although the structure was acceptable, only the children of the five red classes (poor and lower-middle peasants, workers, revolutionary martyrs, revolutionary cadres and revolutionary soldiers) were to be included in this "revolutionary vanguard." Students from other social classes presumably were to be left to form their own organizations, and would be expected to submit to the authority of the Red Guard vanguard. Thus, in spite of the formal dissolution of the YCL and Student Association, the only change in the student elite at this stage was the exclusion of still more young people, creating a mass of ostracized youths whose fathers' pre-Liberation occupations now ranged from KMT at one far extreme to "professional" (the latter, comprised of doctors, teachers, etc., often politically active) at the other. The exclusion at this stage of some previously politically active student leaders left a leadership nucleus early in the game around which all other outsiders might cluster, and which could serve as a source of opposition to the original, ordained Red Guards, the *Chu-yi-ping*.

For the GPCR to move forward, the old elite--the one now narrowed down to the children of the post revolutionary social elite--had to be smashed and the organizational structure redefined. Joined by individually dynamic good classers who eventually took the helm, the outsiders did form ad hoc organizations on their own as early as August or September, but ones which eventually pitted themselves against the conservative domain of the "five kinds of red" Red Guards. As the pseudonymous Red Guard activist Dai Shao-ai states, were it not for the support of this alienated, majority constituency of outsiders, he and his mates could not have gained the momentum to "struggle" the Party Committee.[20] Henceforth, all major issues of the GPCR, including the debate over work teams and the growing cleavage between conservatives and "rebels," were to become suffused with the issue of elitism and class discrimination or, as it came to be known by November, the "blood-line debate" (hsüeh-t'ung-lun), and with the resentment it engendered on both sides.

Previous political campaigns in China had "struggled" a minority of targeted individuals as a political lesson and unifying device for the majority. The Cultural Revolution in the schools was different. While not all "non-five-reds" were targeted for "struggle" at school meetings or during the "Destroy Four Olds," they were jeeringly excluded from taking part in the GPCR at schools where they often constituted not a minority but a majority! Perhaps, as much as two-thirds of the student body in the middle schools of Kwangchow were kept out of the Red Guards in August 1966, and as much as eighty percent similarly excluded from participation in the universities because of class background.[21]

Their initial exclusion from the Red Guards and any sort of guided participation in the GPCR served to make of this mass of middle and "class enemy" children a source of uncompromising opposition to the inner circle of "five kinds of red" and to the direction the latter group was taking.

One early Red Guard activist was aware of the problem of allowing such a large pool of people to form organizations, undirected and on their own. He urged his comrades "not to take these students lightly."[22]

His prophecy was correct, and fortunately this particular Red Guard had enough faith in his convictions to defect from the exclusive organization, form his own unit open to middle class membership, and use these disaffected people to advance his assault against the higher authorities.

Other active good class youths also defected early from the ordained body of Red Guards, partly because of personal commitment to certain ideals and their own mobility and partly because of the class cleavage that existed even among the "five kinds of red." It seems that the children of workers and peasants often found themselves at loggerheads politically and socially with the sons and daughters of cadres and PLA officers who considered themselves better than the others and were reluctant to attack the political elite which had given them this personally beneficial birthright. It was such radical good class youths who ultimately assumed command of the gradually amassing dissident faction, the main constituency of which was to be middle and bad class youths.

Almost simultaneously with the formal establishment of Red Guards in August, previous political activists--some from the YCL and Student Association, who had been left out of the Red Guards, and other prestigious individuals (e.g., class cadres) formed small ad hoc units of their own. These groups, sometimes numbering no more than a dozen at the outset, were based not on academic class-level structure but on friendship ties. Intimate friends, having joined together and recruited more friends, then linked up with other ad hoc units, perhaps from other academic classes, a leader of which might be a friend of one of their group. The alienation of those excluded from the first Red Guards and their hostility to those in the inner circle was exacerbated by the treatment many of their families received during the "Destroy the Four Olds," the discrimination they sometimes suffered when they themselves ventured on the *Ch'uan-lien* (individually or as a group) and were turned back because of their class, and the beatings many of them received when they were walking alone on the street at night without proper Red Guard insignia and were accosted by Red Guard patrols.

November 1966

One can not over-emphasize the psychological effect on juveniles and adolescents of a situation characterized by group ostracism and then by a sudden authority-sanctioned invitation to these same excluded people not only to become a part of things but to "seize power." This shift in line at the center occurred in October-November 1966. Whereas ostracism at an early age might have produced an attitude of passive resignation in many of the children plagued with severely negative class backgrounds, it was treated more as a barrier and impediment to progress by so many others who did not experience it until a much later phase in their development. By November, those youths who had been excluded from political activity for two or three years prior to the GPCR, or who were suddenly cast out at the beginning of the GPCR, found an opportunity to overtake the initial Red Guard vanguard. The bearing on their political attitudes of the question of class background--a basic source of peer cleavage from the start--was to be of overwhelming importance.

By late October or early November, the CCRG came out against the exclusionist proponents of the so-called "bloodline theory" for organizing Red Guards. At the Party Center, its defenders, like T'an Li-fu, also linked to the already condemned work team technique of organizing a campaign, were only digging themselves into deeper graves. Chen Po-ta and Chiang Ch'ing had begun to mount attacks against those who would condemn and ostracize the children of bourgeoisie for the ideological errors of their parents. It was inevitable that the cued debate over work teams in the Kwangchow schools would focus on the "blood-line" issue. In the process, a polarization developed between conservatives and radicals: the former reluctant to attack higher authorities or work teams and unwilling to forfeit the advantages of good class background; the latter hostile to the authorities, eager to carry the GPCR to the highest provincial levels, and opposed to the utilization of the class issue to keep people--mostly themselves--suppressed and apart from the political process.

To those who had been excluded from the political process, the class issue seemed to pervade all others. First, it was a source of personal antagonism toward the children of good classers who had ostracized them; hence, it was an inducement to take the opposite side in any debate with these conservative children of "red"background. Second, the class issue, in a very personal sense, seemed to the radicals to reflect the central purpose of the GPCR--a national, society-wide assault against elitism in the cultural and political realms. As Ch'iao says:

> We didn't merely aim at the authorities in school. We aimed at the entire society . . . And the [class, elitist] point of view outside the school was reflected within the school.[23]

For Ch'iao and so many others, class-derived privilege was anathema to them personally and to the organizers of the GPCR. He states:

> The mere fact that whatever the good classers did was all right was itself anti-communist party . . .

They used their privilege as protection . . . Class
status gave then a sort of privilege. And they
wanted to protect their privilege.[24]

Thus, the "rebels," as they came to be called, regarded the
good class organizations as conservative, and attached themselves to the opposite side of every issue in the name of
carrying the GPCR through to the end. Although the good
class organization gradually opened its doors to "non-five-
reds," most of the ordinary and bad class youths were
naturally inclined toward the "rebel" side; only a few
defected to the other side at various points in the months
ahead when the power of their faction seemed to be ebbing.

Late 1966 to Early 1967

When the signals for a "seizure of power" at the provincial level became clearer through graduated references
from Peking to the two party lines (revolutionary, and
bourgeois or Liu-ist) and news of the "rebels" seizure of
Shanghai reached Kwangchow, the "rebels" there began to
organize and consolidate themselves for similar local
action. Between January and April 1967, the "rebels,"
previously ad hoc units, grouped together to form several
Hung Ch'i organizations with central command headquarters.
The center of leadership shifted from the middle schools to
the universities, and the affiliate Red Guard organizations
at the middle schools were no longer organized haphazardly
or given to spontaneous action from below.

The diagram following illustrates the high degree of
organization which developed during this phase of the GPCR
in a middle school *Hung Ch'i* faction. It should be noted,
however, that although specific leaders were now elected at
each level, specialized responsibilities and functions were
still sufficiently fluid to allow each individual to maintain his original sense of initiative and to feel he was
fulfilling his fantasied achievements. In fact, the decision of whom to send to a specific, higher-level meeting
very often revolved about the individual participant's own
desire to volunteer for the task out of personal interest.

In January and February 1967, "rebel" organizations
"seized power" from the provincial party secretary, with
his acquiescence, and then proceeded to attempt to force
the provincial military commander to rally to their side.
Some waverers on the conservative side now withdrew or
defected to the radicals at this point. But since both

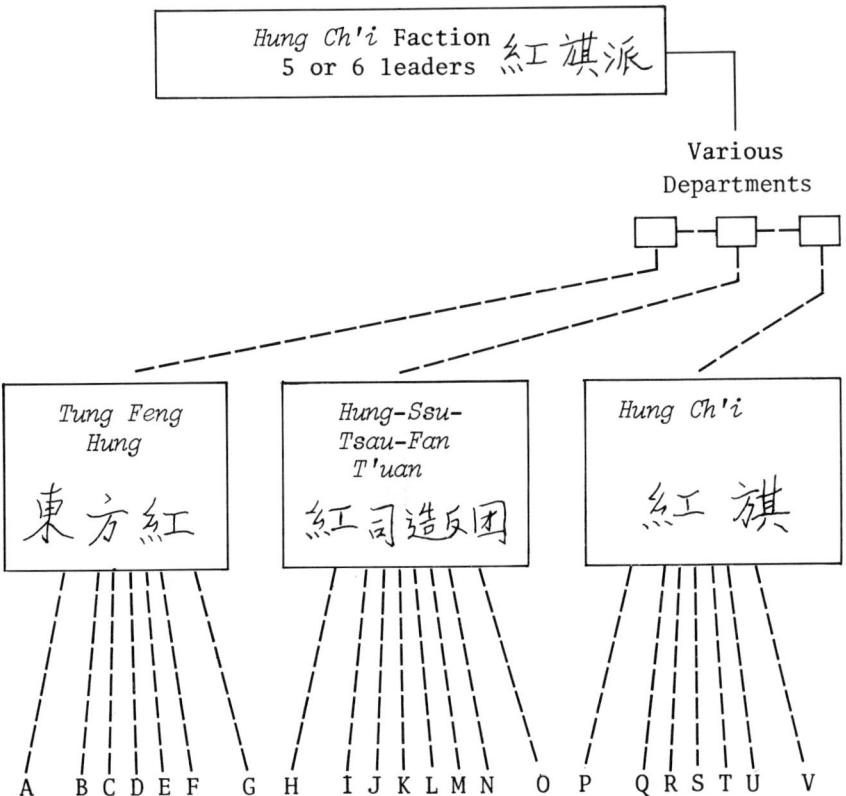

Each of the lettered organizational units at the bottom of the diagram are warrior groups, usually about 12 members each; from the seven or eight groups, three or four representatives were sent to each of the middle level organizations.

sides claimed to be "rebels" now, Kwangtung's military commander Huang Yung-sheng, in an obvious effort to preserve the existing elite, refused to commit himself on the question of which side represented the true "rebels" which the CCRG urged all to support. In March, when military control committees were established at every level and military training platoons sent to the schools, the Peoples' Liberation Army (PLA) asserted itself locally by showing its preference for the conservative Red Guards (*Chu-yi-ping*) and its intent of keeping a lid on the student movement. This effort to suppress the real "rebels" was aborted, however, in April, when Premier Chou En-lai visited Kwangchow and clearly delineated which organizations were regarded by the center as "rebel" and which as conservative. The *Hung Ch'i* groups emerged victorious, and both the military and conservative Red Guards (*Chu-yi-ping*) suffered a temporary defeat.

But Chou's speech only polarized the situation more, the conservatives now forming the *Tung Feng* faction and the "rebels" still operating loosely, grouping under various central *Hung Ch'i* command headquarters. Refusing to acknowledge defeat, the *Tung Feng* conservatives mobilized behind the slogan:

February was yours; March was ours; April is yours; May certainly will be ours.

The months of May passed without any major incidents of violence, but the propaganda of one faction against the other intensified. And in June and throughout the summer, the two major factions took to open warfare, armed with clubs, knives, blades between their teeth for throwing, and commandeered PLA guns. University, middle school, and worker groups alike joined in the fighting. The *Tung Feng* was to gain the upper hand with the call for a "great alliance" (*ta-lien-ho*) and the reassertion of the military's power on campus, but by March the next year, *Hung Ch'i's* banner once again waved high.

EPILOGUE

The rising and falling tides of factional strife continued until spring-summer 1968, when the end seemed to be in sight as new work teams, composed of workers, restored cadres and members of the PLA, descended on the campuses. In this time span, new issues emerged both over tactics and objectives which presented the erstwhile participants of both factions with new choices to make and the opportunity for dropping out. The first and second periods of armed struggle had effected a high attrition among Red Guards. Moreover, despite the surface appearance of anarchy and chaos during the factional strife of 1967-1968, the high tide of individual self-expression really had preceded this period. The armed fighting between factions was only the extension, in *violently* antagonistic contradiction of reform through "struggle." Chiang Ch'ing and later even Mao ("you learn to swim by swimming") had condoned limited violence as a means to an end. But even as the GPCR became more personally hazardous, it allowed less individual freedom. The participating units were part of hierarchical structures of political organization, warrior platoons were coordinated like armies, and the "rebels" in their *excesses* were only responding to encouragement from Peking. Thus, in form, the "rebels" did not evolve into a counter-culture.

These objective circumstances notwithstanding, it is quite possible that *Hung Ch'i* militants who at the outset were resolving psychological conflicts and needs for generational rivalry and succession still travelled in their fantasy worlds as they submitted to the developing hierarchy of a well-organized movement. And the authorities whom many had set out to destroy came to be represented in the persons of their children, the main force of the *Tung Feng* faction.

3. Class Background and Youth Behavior

In order to create this sort of class contradiction to unite the majority behind it, the government has sacrificed another portion of people . . . Sometimes we joked that a few decades later, if government were figuring class, possibly they would not use our generation, but our grandparents' generation.

--the viewpoint of the alienated militant Red Guard Wang (IV-4; III-10-11.)

It is always possible to bind together a considerable number of people . . . so long as there are other people left over to receive the manifestations of their aggressiveness.

--Sigmund Freud, *Civilization and its Discontents*, trans. James Strachey (New York: Norton, 1961), p. 61.

There were some activist elements. It was commonplace for a lot of the students to be unsatisfied with them. After the Red Guards were established, those good class students attacked the others and said their class was bad. Most schoolmates then seized the opportunity to take revenge on them.

--Ch'en Ling-ping (V-9).

    The stigma of bad class background posed a serious obstacle to many youngsters in their attempts to integrate socially with their peers, in their effort to break from parents politically, and in their quest to gain the acceptance of authorities and colleagues for the sincerity of their political activism at school. Even before the intense emphasis on class background in the mid-sixties and the onset of adolescence when many would encounter sudden and unexpected ostracism, some juveniles in this pool of respondents, particularly those of class enemy background,[1] were shoved clear to the margin of society. They were forced to fall back on their father's negative political identity or even to project onto and identify with an unreal political backwardness in their father's behavior. Still others teetered on the brink of such alienation, devising methods to cope with discrepancy between their external environments and their politically backward family backgrounds. These types of individuals, sensitized early to what they believed to be a hostile environment, were unlikely prospects for active political participation by the time of the Great Proletarian Cultural Revolution.

And yet a third group of non-red class children did not perceive any discrimination against themselves until the years prior to the GPCR. A number of these youths, neither socially defensive because of any aggravated concern over bad class background nor deterred psychologically from the pursuit of generational succession through the attempted resolution of conflicts between family and societal roles, were shocked by the class-based ostracism they suddenly encountered in their schools before the outbreak of the Cultural Revolution. For those proceeding at an active pace in adolescence toward father-competitive adult roles, the response to this socio-political red light was not to stop, wait, or turn back; rather, they chose a course of head-on collision with those who sought to block their way.

UNIFORM OR NON-UNIFORM SOCIALIZATION

It is questionable whether, as is sometimes supposed, the ideal continuity between adolescent roles and adult roles and a concomitantly consonant approach to education in the school or productive work at home really existed among youths of bad class background. Seventeen persons out of the thirty-two non-red classers in my group relate that their parents' conversations in the home were clearly ideologically backward, or that they were not obviously out of line but nonetheless seemed to reflect hidden tensions and malaise under the system.[2] The regime itself recognized the persistence of non-uniformity of socialization between home and school in bad class families by citing, as late as the 1960s, a positive example of how a female youth could overcome the backward, intellectual, elitist influences of her family. The model youth in this article refused to sit for the university matriculation examination and instead volunteered for labor in the countryside. The success of her political decision notwithstanding, she testifies that during the difficult period of harassments, pleas, and appeals to filiality by her relatives, a "voice inside" said to her: "You have acted against the wish of your family. In the future you will find it unbearable to stay at home and your neighbors will laugh at you."[3] But "another voice" said: "To be a revolutionary youth, you must not be captured by the old ideology and must turn yourself against the old influence daringly."[4] The struggle in the girl's mind, as between her two ways of life, was resolved in a politically positive way, but the opposite also could have occurred.

Even if parents deliberately tried to teach their children the new ways and encourage political activism, a natural cleavage existed between the two generations. If a child seeking to become part of the new society encountered serious opposition in the social environment simply because of his father's class, he could well either fall back on an imagined or rationalized negative identity with father, just as easily as if the father had been inveighing against the new regime. Consequently, this youth might cynically withdraw into himself and seek to evade and circumvent any deep commitment to the social-political system,[5] or strive to attach himself to a revolutionary sub-culture that might seek to alter or overturn certain institutions in order to facilitate his integration into society.

A revolutionary youth sub-culture was held at bay in the 1950s with the re-institution of a revised form of filialism, but the energies for its recurrence were supplied by subtle environmental cues to youth to assert autonomy in the home, as well as by the changing relations within the family. For the bad classer, the persistence of different role models at home and school--supported by the normative emphasis on the stigma of bad class background--created a confusion leading toward either the eventual formation of an alternative youth sub-culture or the alienated withdrawal of the individual.[6]

Several political mechanisms for either unifying child socialization between home and school or else making the child stand on the side of the school seem to have gone awry because of their inherent imperfections, the overwhelming impact on the child of bad family influences, or the systemic resistances to these children because of a suspicion of bourgeois contamination.

In families of bad class background, some parents were

rather open in their innuendoes about government policy and criticism of the present regime.[7] Uniformity may have been more common, as in the case of Peng, who maintains: "Generally, when we were at school, the head of the house would encourage you to study to be more progressive politically."[8] But the many exceptions seem at least to justify the regime's fear of the older, bad class generation's contaminating the younger. Lo Ping-wen, for example, removed his Pioneer arm band each day before returning home; he was afraid that his "family members would blame him for being too progressive."[9] What is important in this case is not whether Lo's parents in fact were aware of his participation but that he feared showing it off to them. Many parents who had suffered themselves also because of class or KMT affiliation cautioned their children against becoming too involved politically, precisely because of the class stigma hanging over them and the dangers accruing to an unfortunate political choice.[10] Thus, Hsieh, interested as he was in politics, was afraid to cross the line during the GPCR.

Mechanisms which might have served to enforce a uniformity in political socialization between home and school seemed to have proved inadequate for this particular purpose.[11] For instance, self-criticism in political study sessions at school and written self-examination (*Ssu-hsiang chien-t'ao*) are recorded in a personal file (*tang-an*). This dossier is supposed to be shown to the head of the household at the end of a semester. Such a technique, carrying the logical implication that a "backward" father might see his own private complaints against the regime in print as part of his child's political material, perhaps could encourage the father to be more cautious or deliberately positive about the political system. But it could also have the opposite effect of inducing collusion between parent and child in order to resist reform, as in Yüan's case.[12] The child might avail himself of this opportunity to get closer to his father. More important, frankness in adhering to techniques for self-reform could appear more self-destructive than constructive in the long run. Nieh Li-chih describes the disastrous potential of sincere self-criticism:

> When you have said it, they say you're very honest. But when school ends, they add your confessed mistake to a written critique. This critique is entered in your dossier and can be held against you at a later time.[13]

Such a device would not only necessarily bring one's parents into line with one's new way of thinking, but might inadvertantly spur a negative alignment with them.

Of course, an individual would become still more keenly aware of the class stigma as he submitted to this process, and consequently become more resentful of his parents' alleged misdeeds. Indeed, the same procedures which can be cited as an index of attempts at uniformity in socialization and control of value homogeneity conversely might have served to precipitate a break with ideologically backward parents. Theoretically, such a break could lead to a youth's integration into the new society. But even if an individual sought to avail himself of criticism and self-criticism and written self-examinations for the purpose of purging himself before the group and denouncing the "backwardness" of his parents, he could not be certain that he would be taken seriously or allowed to embrace the new ideology and school or political affiliation as an alternate identity to the family. The bad classer was sensitive to an atmosphere of suspicion in which if he were too "positive" he might be dismissed as a hypocrite. Since he had seen others rejected, the risk was apparent to him and often held him back.

Moreover, the necessity for the bad classer to make a total psychological break with his father might have been just too much of a strain on the young individual. Nor was it easy for such a person to endure all the self-criticism and struggle required for entry into the YCL; he would be forced to face his identity with his father and repudiate the fact that he was his father's son. Thus, Lo Ping-kok rationalizes his own reluctance to renounce his father totally and face up to the issue of class which linked him to his father by noting the consequences of such an action:

> If I had reported [my father explicitly and in detail], not only would *he* have been hurt, but moreover I would also have become the child of a struggled rightist element. Although you expose your father's crimes in such a way, the leaders still will not reward or appreciate your action. Later, the discrimination of others against you could even increase.[14]

Hence, if such techniques as *Ssu-hsiang chien-t'ao* were alternatively designed to facilitate a renunciation of parents' backwardness, they failed to protect the individual from the possibly negative consequences--psychological and social--of a well-intended act.

Many individuals apparently decided that the only safe course was to proceed slowly and with caution, hoping they could gradually and reservedly realize in reality the theoretical promise of being able to overcome their original class standpoint, but also unwilling to make so big a jump without the certainty of a place to land. Not only might someone like Lo Ping-kok be incapable psychologically of relinquishing total identity with family, but even if he were able to break away, he was not certain that he would not be caught in the backwash of his own honest admissions. The resistance to the political mobility of bad class youths apparently was commonplace even in the 1950s. A school primer published in 1956 criticized those obstinate and myopic cadres who refused to recognize a YCL candidate's improvement over a length of time and still perceived him as he was at the outset. The primer lambasted such cadres who tend to mutter: "Class background isn't very good; it's better to put him to the test a while longer."[15] Thus, through piecemeal performances of political activism, Lo Ping-kok had to test the water before he could ever immerse himself in a new identity. This was the situation he encountered:

> I always hoped to be able to stand on the side of the school, but this modus operandi was impossible . . . Because at school, they basically did not believe me. Although I expressed loyalty to them this way (i.e., through activist performance), it was still futile.[16]

Ping-kok's turning point did not arrive until the students' struggle (*tou-cheng*) of his father (see pp. 104-105), as a consequence of which he himself was made a proscribed person at school. Other bad class youths, however, much earlier saw the futility of their efforts to gain acceptance and defensively had already assumed a negative sociopolitical identity.

Theoretically, and to a great extent in practice, a parent no longer could control a child's academic career. He neither necessarily paid for any of his child's educational expenses nor generally appeared with his children on middle school and university campuses.[17] Thus, a sort of uniformity of socialization might have been abetted by the mere deflation of the father's educational and career advisory role. But if the separation imposed on a parent from his child's academic life could facilitate the independent political development and social integration of the individual, such discriminatory practices as denial to a good student of the customary waiver of the lower middle school matriculation examination because of his parents' background was a reminder to him of the negative identity he had inherited and of his father's presence as a conflicting, socially stigmatized role model.[18] In the case of Yeh Hen, such practices had the positive effect of making him complain to his brothers and sisters about the fact that his father's faults fell on him; in effect, they exacerbated the generational conflict.[19] Creating a conflict situation forces the individual to choose sides.[20] The seeming injustice of being made to suffer for this unwanted identity could have been as much of an incentive to another individual to embrace that identity defiantly at an early age, rather than go to all the effort later--perhaps in vain--of trying to cast it off.

According to school primers and much broader social literature, the observer might gain the impression of a homogeneity of adult social role models in China, as opposed to the more diffuse role models in American society.[21] But individuals, even the politically active, often erected defenses against the tyranny of this uniformity by secretly joking with their best friends about the "foolishness" of the blind self-sacrifice of many of the idealized heroes.[22] Similarly, many persons resisted attempts to make them conform to the norms mirrored by their peers in the institutionalized criticism--self-criticism sessions at school. The effectiveness of thought reform seemed to vary greatly and was often resisted through ritualized behavior. Chou Chung-wang was relatively submissive in group criticism sessions until he was caught in the Kwangchow railroad station in 1962, toying with the idea of boarding an allegedly safe train to Hong Kong.[23] Then, suddenly, as he was being chastised for this "error," it dawned on him that "previously when [he] spoke, [he] had not stopped to consider first, and therefore every little bit had been recorded by them and was now used against [him].[24] Thereafter, Chou began to suppress his public personality and force [himself] to think something over three times before speaking;"[25] he came to regard it "an impossibility to reveal your inner thoughts."[26] Even criticizing his parents became a procedure for many youths which was more form than content; hence, no guilt was involved, and one tended to become "psychologically numb."[27] As for self-criticism, Hsu Ta-liang says: "It was merely tossing about some terms--there was no real problem; . . .

they were all variations on the same theme."[28] Since small groups normally were divided into "backward," "medium," and "progressive" types, the "mediums" seldom had to do more anyway than echo an abstract line of discussion and focus on small errors; they rarely had to criticize "backward" group members face to face for serious mistakes.[29] If an activist challenged such a person, there was a "formula" for accepting criticism: thank the critic and promise to correct the error, couching the promise in jargonistic slogans.[30] Even the activist had defenses against revealing himself fully. Yang Ying-pu, for instance, recognizing a shortcoming in himself, would project it on another member of the group, and take the offensive by criticizing the other person for what he himself was feeling. Only now, in retrospect, does Yang realize that his seemingly sincere and zealous criticism of others was in many instances a defense against his own unconsciously felt inadequacies.[31]

EARLY ALIENATION

Although mechanisms for unifying the socialization of bad class youth or spurring them to break with their "backward" parents have frequently aborted with varying effects,[32] a more important factor in the actual early alienation of a bad classer seems to have been a basically unfriendly social environment. Of course, the intensity of class discrimination varied both according to the errors or crimes of the father and according to subjective implementation by particular teachers or by certain schools.

In a vertical, authoritarian family, the child of bad class--particularly "class enemy" background--often came to be sandwiched between the hostile pressures from the social environment and his parents' own defensive reactions to these outside pressures. Such an atmosphere created tensions in the home affecting a child's social and political behavior. The child, caught up in such a situation, sometimes ascribed more ideological backwardness to his father's behavior than actually seemed to have existed, thereby making it easier for himself to assume a negative, filial, social identity *defensively* against an unfriendly environment.[33]

Behavior within the family as well in some instances could not be separated from the pressures on the family from the larger social environment. The authoritarian father over time might yield to environmental pressures, but he often also might tighten the reins on his children in order to fight what he perceived to be a hostile outer environment.[34] Indeed, in some cases, it was difficult to determine whether a "class enemy" father, severe with his children, was driven to harsh disciplinary measures solely by his own basic personality and attitudes toward child-rearing or additionally by his defenses against a hostile society.

In the Huang household, all three sons[35] were subjected to the harsh discipline of a father who taught engineering at a well-known university. The father wielded a heavy hand over his children's study habits, social relations and personal behavior. The sons were taught to keep their hands out of their pockets, never to spit on the street and to behave as "gentlemen"; if they did not, they were severely reprimanded. The older Huang was harsh with his sons, but rarely beat them physically; he remained aloof from his sons as they proceeded through school. The children feared and respected their father, and suppressed their hostility toward his nit-picking severity with them. In retrospect, the oldest son Huang Yi analyzes his own suppression of felt hostility as a child and the possible social influences contributing to his father's behavior then:

> At that time in our hearts, we were very happy. I didn't know then why he acted as he did. Only now do I understand . . . It is clear that at that time he could not but act this way because of environmental circumstances. Nevertheless, we didn't understand so well then.[36]

It may be that Huang Yi in part is putting the blame for his father's overly stern personality on social pressures in order to rationalize his own ultimate decision, under the same sort of pressures, to leave China (against his father's wishes); in this manner, Huang Yi may find it easier to reduce the dissonance resulting from his rebellious and unfilial decision to leave father and country.[37] Nevertheless, Huang's retrospective analysis, however clouded by mixed emotions, does not preclude some foundation in truth. Huang now feels that because his father was a prime target in the city during the Anti-Rightist Campaign, the "emphasis on class struggle . . . loomed large," influencing his father's tense behavior with his children.[38]

Huang Yi was "puzzled about why his father should have kept [him] under such strict surveillance then."[39] Huang's father virtually sequestered his children, forbidding them to make friends freely. Now, Huang Yi comments:

> He rarely allowed us to go out and play freely; most of the time we were at home. The important reason was that if we did anything bad on the outside, whereas it wouldn't make any difference in most families--a child played and that was that--in our family, it was not permitted. Because the first thing that would occur to a person was that my father was a "rightist element." We rarely went out to play. But other children could build houses in the sand and play as they pleased. And they could take some things home with them. We weren't permitted to play in this fashion.[40]

Consequently, Huang Yi refrained from normal childhood mischief.

Sheltered as they were from normal childhood peer relations, none of the Huang boys could ever relate to other peers later. They developed a mistrust of compeers in general. Rather than seek the acceptance of others their age, they turned inward, identified with father or leaned on a surrogate figure similar to father in stalwartness. Unencouraged at home in his academic work because he was regarded as the slowest intellectually, the youngest son Huang San got along miserably at school. He did badly in his work and avoided the other children. He describes the situation:

> My grades were bad because I was not conscientious and not compatible with those children of revolutionary cadres and soldiers . . . everyone went out to play, but I didn't get along with them. They liked to make revolution. I didn't.[41]

Thus, the Huang boys, taught to fear the company of others as young children, kept to themselves as they moved from the juvenile period into adolescence. They shunned others and placed themselves outside the scope of the general activities--social and political--of their schoolmates.

Turning away from normal peer integration, the older son Huang Yi and the middle Huang Erh sought to maintain some sort of defensive identity with their father as they moved through the adolescent phase; the youngest son, still a juvenile or pre-adolescent before the GPCR, had not yet begun the search for adult identity.[42] Ironically, however, their father gave no appearance of being ideologically backward, continually stated his loyalty to the Communists and his long-held preference for the Communist regime over the precursor KMT, and urged his sons to be politically active at school.[43]

But the Huang brothers could not accept this identity as valid. Instead, they imagined that their father was actually opposed to the regime and that he felt constrained to say what he did because of his own bad political situation. Despite the lack of any sort of direct evidence, Huang Yi insists:

> When I heard these words, I realized that deep down, he did not want to say this. I realized that due to the environment, he had no alternative but to speak in this manner.[44]

In this rationalization, the sons were encouraged by their mother who, reacting badly to the Anti-Rightist Campaign and apparently somewhat incompatible with their father,[45] had left for Hong Kong with her infant daughter in 1962. On periodic, sneak return visits,[46] their strong-willed mother, in an effort to persuade the boys to flee to Hong Kong, told them that their father really had disliked the Communists ever since the 1957 ordeal.[47]

Consequently, the older boys felt that by overly assuming a backward identity, they were emulating father but one-upping him in their lack of hypocrisy about it.[48] They chose to play out *their* rivalry with father by identifying with his negative side, the government-struggled, effete intellectual and the fantasied anti-communist, rather than the positive side, the devotee of the new regime willing to suffer its flagellations and anxious for his sons to be part of the New China. Huang Yi, for example, delighted in the thought that he was surpassing his father intellectually, and congratulated himself that his own grades were better than his father's as a child. He became an avid reader in upper middle school, finishing a book a day from his father's university's library, to the exclusion of political work and study. In spite of his awareness then that his rivalrous emulation of father was provoking the criticism of peers for his being "expert" and not "red" and that his father's class background would be all the more likely to precipitate these sorts of attacks against him, Huang Yi defiantly thumbed his nose at his peers and kept it in the books.[49] His negative identity was in part his defense against the social ambience he had always perceived to be hostile to himself and family. Huang was able to resign himself to the "destiny of a class enemy," tell himself that "all people who had the same family background were this way," and even forget his hostility toward the government for awhile.[50] He had withdrawn into himself and become politically impassive.

But Huang had a strong father image, at least according to the traditional criteria of social status, with which to identify. What if both parents were weak or discredited models who did not seem to warrant the respect of a child even in the traditional sense? Would the son more easily adapt to the roles of the new society? The question seems to have been decided by society's willingness to fill the void.

Such was the case of Nieh Li-chih whose father had been a capitalist factory owner in the old society and a weak individual in the eyes of his mother.[51] As for Nieh's mother, she effectively abandoned him in 1956, when he was age nine, by emigrating to Hong Kong. Although she later returned on holidays, he recalls with considerable vexation her initial disappearance and his daily expectation of her imminent return home.[52] When Nieh's father also left for Hong Kong during the 1962 exodus, he was left in China with no family role models capable of facilitating his integration into society or his transition into adulthood.

Earlier the obedient and loyal son, Nieh Li-chih, the child, had been caught up in a contradiction between his negative family background and the image of the new socialist man. At school, he was taught about the exploiting classes and had to acknowledge his affiliation by birth with them. He states:

> If I believed what the school said about [exploiters], I would feel my parents were wrong. If I considered my parents to be correct, then my school education would have to be wrong. I was very much trapped in a contradiction. I didn't dare regard what the school said as incorrect. I also felt my parents were right. If I had asked them, an argument would have ensued . . . At that time, I believed the school, but I also believed that my father was not as the school said. For example, the school said all capitalists were bad, but at the same time, I felt Father was not a bad person.[53]

Theoretically, the environment was supposed to encourage the child from a bad class family to face up to his background and to renounce it. And at first, young Nieh seemed to be moving in that direction. When he had to write a composition in school titled, "My Father," he was "embarrassed." The reason was that others could extoll their fathers as workers, but he had to denounce his own father as a capitalist.[54] He reflects now that although he could not think of himself entirely as part of the new generation yet, in primary and lower middle school, he hoped to be able to overcome his background and had already declared formally that he "drew a clear line" *(hua-ch'ing chieh-hsien)* between himself and his father.[55] Although Nieh Li-chih avoided political discussion at home, Nieh's father did feel the need to defend himself as merely a small businessman in the old China, "no real exploiter"; his son did not take him seriously then and regarded him as ideologically out of line.[56]

When Nieh's father, sent to the countryside in 1961, later fled to Hong Kong, Li-chih was forced to choose between severing his bond with his parents and identifying with them. The choice Nieh made was to strengthen his affinity for his family. This decision was affected by the development of such objective circumstances as his failure the next year to qualify for a regular upper middle school despite high academic performance,[57] and a concomitant barrage of letters from his parents in Hong Kong describing the advantages of his eventually joining them there. Already closer to his brothers and sisters than before, and returning home each weekend, Nieh Li-chih assumed a defiantly negative and backward identity in upper middle school.[58] At first, though he already put an earlier dream of joining the PLA completely out of his mind, he still clung to some hope of adjusting to society. He hoped to go on to university by excelling academically, in spite of his inferior middle school placement. But when in physics, a course in which he was at the top of his class, his teacher remarked publicly that Nieh would either end up in the village or in prison, the youth declared open defensive warfare on the system.[59] Perhaps, he now acted partly out of his own unconscious guilt that he might have helped push his parents away by having gone so far in renouncing them in favor of the new political system. "I should have trusted my father more," he says. "What I had done was unfilial."[60] At least it was easier for him to persuade himself that his parents' abandonment was partly his fault and one that could now be corrected than for him to be left without an identity alternative to his family.

In 1965, Nieh attempted to escape from China, only

to be apprehended and expelled from school. With pride in his voice, he proclaims: "I was the first one in Kwangchow to be expelled from school!"[61] Nieh is also as proud that just before that time, he was considered the most backward politically in class, and had refused to admit his mistakes in small group when challenged by the YCL cadre; and when all his peers pledged to go to the village if they failed to qualify for university, he refused to join them.[62]

Small wonder that when the GPCR erupted the next year, Nieh Li-chih, resisting the efforts of his acquaintances to persuade him to participate, abstained for this reason:

> I felt that the Cultural Revolution could have no advantage for our sort of people. Even if I participated, there would be no advantage in it. It would only cause trouble![63]

Nieh Li-chih was still unsure then whether he would try to leave China again, but he was resigned to his alienation from participation. In such a political campaign, he would "stay home."[64] Indeed, he was so alienated that when his physics teacher, Nieh's *bete noir* since he had made that crushing remark, was struggled in *ta-tzu-pao*, Nieh Li-chih was afraid and reluctant to become involved.[65] Nieh's feelings of proscription surpassed his personal vindictiveness. Although he was long beyond the grasp of his bad class parents, when he in turn had grasped for social acceptance, society had turned its back. Now, he was emotionally beyond the purview of the GPCR.

THE OPPORTUNISTIC MIDDLE COURSE

Others, also in most cases the children of "class enemies," had developed mechanisms by adolescence which allowed them to avoid retreating to a negative identity and which enabled them to cope reasonably well with the political system. Despite the apparently deep-seated mistrust bad classers generally encountered in efforts to appear politically positive, these people seemed to succeed in convincing the others that they were at least trying to improve themselves politically. With the advent of the GPCR, such individuals were aware of the dangers of over-commitment politically, inherent in their class background, and hence sought a mazeway that would best serve their long-term interests.

In Wu Kuo-chih's case, bad class background became an excuse for not being overly zealous while maintaining a politically positive appearance. Wu was careful not to antagonize either the authorities or political in-group among his peers by assuming a negative posture. Yet he was aware of the hazards of becoming too politically involved. In primary school he was a Pioneer leader, and until upper middle school, he had always been a *pan-kan* (class cadre) of one sort or another. Moreover, his elders (his father had been executed as a KMT officer) and music teacher, the latter of which had recommended him for further study as a flautist at the Central Music Institute in Peking, urged him to put on an activist appearance (*piao-hsien-ti-hen-hao*). But by 1965, when his friends pressed him to seek entry into the YCL, Wu Kuo-chih demurred because of his fear that if ever there were need for a scapegoat, as a bad classer, he would become a prime target. With humility, he apologized to his friends by saying that he did not feel he measured up to the conditions (*pu-kou t'iao-chien*) for entry.[66] A year later, with the arrival of the GPCR, Wu *did* join his friends at first in the *Chu-yi-ping*, but in name only.[67] As soon as authority collapsed and the GPCR deepened, Wu Kuo-chih judiciously withdrew from any participation. He explains:

> I left the organization. In the beginning, they hadn't organized any Red Guards or at least weren't separated into two factions yet. Afterwards, when they were established, I knew that my family was bad. To participate in the Red Guards, you had to present a dossier . . . they might possibly investigate. I knew the situation, so I withdrew.[68]

To avoid the situation at school, Wu volunteered "to take part in labor in a factory."[69] He states that he had no desire to become involved in attacks on authorities because he feared that in the end "due to your class background, they would seize you."[70]

Shih Chi-t'ang, by his adolescent years, had made an art of deception in order to protect himself against the criticism that might befall a bad classer. The elder Mr. Shih, although a maritime engineer by profession, had been a KMT officer before "Liberation." Young Shih was an extroverted activist and class leader straight through his lower middle school years, but he gradually became aware of the stigma of bad class background by 1964. Before then, he had a "rough idea" of the situation, but deceived himself and others by classifying himself as a "professional" (*chih-yuan*) when he filled out his *ssu-hsiang chien-t'ao;* he told himself, "The scope of this category is rather broad."[71] When he failed to qualify for the YCL at the end of lower middle school, Shih Chi-t'ang, by his own admission, became an opportunist:

> I consider myself an opportunist. In China, because the environment makes you wild . . . So on the surface you must obey them and in reality not obey them.[72]

After his failure to enter the YCL, Shih determined to strive even harder in other ways "to compensate for [his] family's background."[73] But the Cultural Revolution presented him with the dilemma of withdrawing and appearing "backward" or risking an "accounting" which in the end could be detrimental to bad classers. He declares now that if he had been of red class background, he most certainly would have joined the conservative, safe, *Tung Feng* faction at his school.[74] But he was not given the choice. He recalled then that as a child he had witnessed political campaigns and had once seen a targeted individual commit suicide.[75] In 1964, when his father was "struggled," Shih thought not of the ostracism he suffered at school, but of avoiding politics and yet still "finding a future for himself."[76] Feeling that the students in both factions were "tools that were being used," he expediently left the school to participate in his local street Security Brigade (*tiao-ch'a-tui*), thereby hoping to avoid the eventual axe and yet exhibit enough political enthusiasm to warrant his continued study at a university or at least a job in an urban factory.[77]

CLASS BACKGROUND, THE POLITICIZATION OF THE 1960s AND PARTICIPATION IN THE GPCR

Yet, for most bad class children in Kwangchow, even the "class enemies," early alienation or the erection of defenses against social oppression during the first years of primary school were uncommon occurrences. In China, as in American society, the crucial stage for feeling social pressures for group affiliation and relating to adult social roles was during *ch'ing-nien* or adolescence. According to my respondents in general, before that time, although there was a great feeling for collective group behavior (more than has been noted in the West), social aggregates were loosely structured and revolved about interests and talents shared by individuals. In Kwangchow, provided one's father's "crimes" were not too notorious, one's teachers were not fanatical or sadistic, and the contradiction between home and school socialization was not too glaring or made unbearable by an authoritarian father, the school child could enjoy a normal life at primary school in an atmosphere of big city anonymity and there seemed little need on the part of the authorities to dredge up a child's class background for his public humiliation. In the early 1950s, many bad classers in this pool of respondents (including in this category petit-bourgeoisie), played side by side with good class children, sometimes they even visited one another's homes, ignorant and largely unmindful of each other's class background.

Even a child who had been on his guard and on his way to alienation as a young child, growing up in a small homogeneous village where his parents' landlord background was common knowledge and anathema to the villagers, had hope of losing this burdensome baggage in the city. Viciously blamed and scolded by his primary school teachers for the slightest mishap, and afraid to fight with his peers for fear that he would certainly be held to blame, the landlord's son Wei Chau-fan looked to moving to Kwangchow to live with his uncle and attending middle school in the capital as his big opportunity for altering his identity and gaining social acceptance.[78] He felt only the teacher would know his class background.[79] At school in Kwangchow, amid the children of cadres and PLA soldiers, Wei did his utmost to adapt to the social and political environments.[80]

But Wei, like so many others of bad class background, "ran up against a nail" ($p'eng$-$ting$-tzu).[81] As the politicization of the Ssu-$ch'ing$ intensified, a greater emphasis began to be placed on class background, one that was to develop into an animus for political behavior in the GPCR. This pall, affecting not only children of class enemies but those who had considered themselves "ordinary" types (petit-bourgeoisie, intellectuals, professional, etc.), fell on most of my respondents as they were emerging from the juvenile years and entering adolescence.

Just how had class background come to achieve so much importance in the general political environment and in the school milieu by the mid-sixties that it became an overriding issue and behavioral force in the GPCR? The phenomenon represented a swing of the pendulum from an official emphasis on expertise after the failure of the Great Leap to an emphasis on political redness and purity.

With the disappointing failure of the ambitious Great

Leap Forward (*ta-yüeh-chin*) in 1958-59, a movement which had stressed the input into production of quantitative manpower over qualitative expertise, the country had to readjust its priorities. By 1961, when China was going through a period of extreme economic difficulty abetted by natural disaster, admission criteria to secondary and higher educational institutions placed more of a priority on academic performance. The shift in emphasis then from "red" to "expert" necessitated the admission of more children from the enemy classes or middle classes whose intellectual background had affected their socialization and made them generally better students than those with uneducated, proletarian heritages. Life in school then reflected an admiration for expertise, and children with good grades gained the respect of students and teachers alike. At that time, class background seemed unimportant except to those stigmatized by parents who had been "struggled" seriously and relegated to pariah roles. And "redness"-- the other end of the Maoist, dialectical contradiction of "red and expert"--seemed secondary to academic achievement.[82] Respected peer cliques might form as easily around the intellectually astute, as among the athletically skilled; the politically active groups seemed to enjoy less prestige then.

But with each passing year thereafter, class background and political activism criteria gradually assumed more importance for entry into upper middle schools and universities and as standards for measuring a person's behavior.[83] For the really bad classer already suffering in varying degrees, this turn in the general political climate might have become so burdensome as to alienate an individual permanently from the system; for the middle class youth, the sudden development of pressures often induced an attitude of resentment rather than resignation. Unlike his "class enemy" counterpart, he had not been forced to endure from early childhood such harassments as periodic census-taking among "enemy" families.[84] But even many of the "enemy" youths were caught off guard by the sudden intensification of class discrimination. Quite often, the extent to which a child was harassed and ostracized in primary school because of bad class background had varied according to the style of individual teachers.[85]

Now the policy was changing! The turning point in the politicization of the environment was 1964-1965, the zenith of the Socialist Education Campaign (*She-hui-chu-yi chiao-yu yun-tung*) or *Ssu-Ch'ing*. Class came to be emphasized as the first criterion for admission to upper-level schools and to all political organizations; political activism became the second most important criterion. Academic performance was de-emphasized, and sometimes non-red classers who were too successful academically were chastized for placing too much of a premium on "expertise" rather than "redness." Several respondents alleged that matriculation examinations taken by non-red class children for upper middle school and university were "tabbed" *bad class* and either downgraded or not graded at all. Whether this charge is accurate, it is certain that the better students with non-red background were increasingly either being admitted to worse schools than their academic achievement warranted or being denied admission altogether. Those not admitted to upper middle school or university usually were sent down to the countryside to work with the peasantry.[86]

Between 1964 and 1966, the Socialist Education Campaign was manifested in such school-based movements as "Expose self" (*Tzu-wo Pao-lu*), including the "Expose Family" (*Pao-lu chia-t'ing*), "Expose your conduct" (*Pao-lu tzu-chi-ti-hsing-wei*), "Expose your own thought" (*Pao-lu tzu-chi ssu-hsiang*); another movement was one in which a "red" student and an "expert" were to pair off and learn from one another (*yi-tui-hung*). Class struggle in small groups intensified in this atmosphere. Whereas in the past, the major criterion for measuring political activism had been enthusiastic participation in productive labor, now class background seemed to preempt all other criteria.

A normal development of political awareness in the intellectually maturing individual and a concomitantly greater stress on political study in the middle school and university curricula coincided with this extraordinary politicization of the environment and focus on class background. According to one informant, "the emphasis on class struggle in primary school was not as severe as in middle school."[87] He explains the phenomenon in terms of everyone's being "more grown up."[88] The school curriculum itself was designed to meet the challenge of the growing intellectual acuity and receptiveness of adolescents. According to respondents, no special classes in political study had generally ever been instituted at the primary school level, but in the lower middle schools, a course in politics, which met three or four times weekly, was introduced into the curriculum. One respondent, who himself had been mistaken for "red," recalls that the "main subject then was class struggle."[89]

The stress on class and class struggle in middle schools and universities during these years tended to demoralize those bad or middle class youths trying to get ahead and make it in the system. Furthermore, it definitely had a divisive effect on the relations among students. By 1965, the doors were shut to those seeking entry to the YCL. Loose adolescent cliques now became polarized according to class divisions. Some bad class children had suffered ostracism of this sort earlier, but now the children of the middle classes as well found themselves gradually excluded from the prestigious cliques and snubbed by good class children, some of whom previously had been their friends. Even one of the more activist middle class youths, deeply entrenched in the students' political structure at school, sensed that class had become a criterion, though not necessarily the only one, for friendship.[90] Another middle class respondent, later to become a militant Red Guard, had been totally unaware of any pressures on him stemming from his non-red class background *until* he entered middle school in 1963-1964 at age twelve.[91] Some middle class children actually were formally criticized in small group session, though not nearly as severely as the children of "class enemy" parentage.[92] In the eyes of one respondent, a YCL member who linked himself to the "five kinds of red," the difference in social status then between red classers and children of non-red class background was like the difference between "whites and Negroes in the United States."[93]

It should be interesting to the reader just how those victimized by the class issue--particularly those less inured to it in the middle classes--perceived this sudden, intensifying discrimination against them. Pao Kuo-fu, a Youth Leaguer and the son of a party member and hospital director, interprets the phenomenon as a tactic inherent in developing political movements. He says:

> According to my view, every movement conducted by the CCP is educational for the people . . . A movement . . . draws [some people] out for struggle. And this elicits the attention of the mass of other people and educates them.[94]

Another person is less generous about the party's utilitarian motives for making class status a key issue. He states:

> It is because workers and peasants are the great majority and if they [the CCP] can win over this group of people, their political power will be stable. They attack a sector of the people . . . and in this way elevate the position of

the majority, causing them to rally around the CCP.[95]

Perhaps, the latter interpretation, ironically smacking of Arendt on totalitarianism and Freud on the behavior of nation-states in Civilization, was the most commonly voiced among my respondents.[96]

Intellectualized explanations derived from hindsight notwithstanding, the immediate emotional impact of being excluded from political participation and the mainstream of school society because of class background, before and at the start of the GPCR was profound. Blossoming adolescents were at a psychological phase when it was most natural to group into cliques as well as to be receptive to new social and ideological cues. If they just happened to fall into the "red" category, they began to use political and class criteria to ostracize others from their informal groups. Whereas peer groups previously had revolved loosely around many, varied interests, politics now took command, and in-groups, formed on this basis, congealed. The politically correct groups were recognized as the most prestigious by the authorities. Those who felt excluded from the core of political activity, more with each passing year, now felt socially proscribed. Many youths who had never shared common interests in the past now formed one loose outgroup based on political criteria. Ghettoized within the social structure of the middle school or university, these newly ostracized individuals could avail themselves of the GPCR to form a common bond leading to action. Targets of jeering ostracism and sometimes direct struggle during the first months of the GPCR in the schools, they had a foundation for political cohesion among them. They were attracted subsequently by the developing spontaneity of the Cultural Revolution in summer 1966 and the opportunity to rail against the vested authorities and their young activists followers, to turn the inside out! Just as in some American ghettoes, outsider gangs entering adolescence, feeling "against the world," have "implanted this attitude as a reasonable basis for social action,"[97] so the same sort of development took place in the Chinese school during the GPCR. *But in the case of sudden ostracism in the Chinese middle schools, the effects seemed to be most telling among the more overtly father-competitive and upwardly mobile youths.* Ostracism from the political in-group came at a time most crucial to their quest for independence and adult social mobility, and threw an obstacle in their path.

For many bad class youths, ostracism, sudden in its impact, was a phenomenon which developed gradually from the early 1960s, accompanied by their growing resentment of the privileged position and air of superiority (*yu-yüeh-kan*) of the youths of good (red) class background, and reaching its zenith in their exclusion from active participation during the first two months of the GPCR.

One political issue of the GPCR, the debate over "blood line," legitimated and reinforced the bad class outsiders' zeal for revenge, revolutionary change, and personal mobility. Excluded in adolescence from the political process of which they were most eager to be a part, these upwardly mobile adolescents became more radical in their loneness. They were a potentially homogeneous group in the face of ostracism and adversity. With little apparent standing to lose and not consulted at the outset of the GPCR by the red elite *Chu-yi-ping*, they were not predisposed to compromise with their adversaries.[98] They had been left out of and made the butt of the political process. *Chu-yi-ping* Yang, originally part of a small core of fellow Youth League members, politically red students who helped organize the early phase of the Cultural Revolution at his school, was sufficiently far-sighted to recognize the hazards of excluding so large a number of fellow students from the political process of the GPCR. He told a meeting of activists:

> You shouldn't take these students lightly . . . Moreover, we Red Guards are very few in number. If you don't unite with them, they will join together to oppose us.[99]

Both Chu Nan-po and Ch'iao Kuo-hsiung, anxious to get ahead, reacted violently to their exclusion from the first phase of the GPCR at school. Until that time or a bit earlier, they mixed freely with peers of all class backgrounds. They were aware that bad class background might be a career handicap, but they had not yet experienced any discrimination as a result of it. Chu Nan-po perceived the onset of the *Ssu-ch'ing* as the watershed period:

> Before the political cataclysm, making friends was limited by class status. After China's liberation, it did not seem that relations were based on a division between rich and poor. Everyone's standard of living was not too far apart. In making friends,

each person just observed one another's level of knowledge and intelligence . . . [But] after the cataclysm (*ta-pien-tung*), because of the emphasis on "politics takes command" and that whole lot, there gradually came to be a more obvious class division. Because of this, class status affected your own position. So each person's class standpoint had to be stable.[100] With Chinese people, if your friend's class was bad, then you would be held unreliable. Because even though your class was good, people would suspect you if you had landlord friends. They would say you changed.[101]

The onset of the GPCR brought the hatred of red class youths upon the likes of Ch'iao and Chu Nan-po. The families or friends of both youths were hurt by the "Four Olds." A lower middle school student, Ch'iao had just come to realize the seriousness of his class background and the hopelessness of his getting into university later.[102]

Ch'iao's mother was struggled at work, and he himself was jeered at school by his good class peers. In his words: "By the time the Cultural Revolution began, I very much hated those people who attacked me."[103]

For Chu Nan-po, who had just failed in one last try to gain entry into the YCL, resentment over the apparent fact that good classers could join the YCL and perhaps make university in spite of bad grades turned into hatred. He described his evolving attitude toward them:

> I was somewhat jealous of them . . . It began to occur in lower middle school one. By the time of the GPCR (i.e., lower middle three), I hated them still more.[104]

Like Ch'iao, Chu felt the impact of a sudden cramp in his upward mobility. Analyzing the attitude of those in his later-formed *Hung Ch'i* group, he says:

> The class status in our organization wasn't too good. Even before the Cultural Revolution, we had already got it in our heads that we would not make university. *Afterward, when the Cultural Revolution had just begun, I felt that a bad classer had no future anyway. Thereupon I gradually took a side in the split into factions.* Our small friendship clique had discussed class status before the GPCR . . . What should we do?[105]

In fact, both Ch'iao and Chu Nan-po availed themselves of the Cultural Revolution and "blood line" debate to justify ideologically their positions vis-à-vis the *Chu-yi-ping*, their good class peers. Ch'iao says:

> We pretty much hated them for their contempt of us. But we did not reveal it. *We merely used the GPCR framework as a premise for attacking them.*[106]

In Chu Nan-po's testimony:

> Writing big character posters gave me an opportunity to vent my discontent against them. When a *ta-tzu-pao* was written, everyone would read it, and the "blood liners" also would write *ta-tzu-pao* attacking us. Because of this, we schoolmates felt there was even more reason for what we were doing: The blood line theory was counter-revolutionary![107]

Thus, the "blood line" issue became both pretext and reinforcement for vengeance against the insider, red classers. The class issue became the axis about which the later factional feuds at school all seemed to revolve. It was inseparable from the purpose, as the *Hung Ch'i* people perceived it, of smashing a privileged elite. Attacks against good class youths, like the attacks on the authorities, were justified in terms of "their using their privilege as protection."[108] Ch'iao describes the emotional depth of the class issue and, from his standpoint, sums up its impact on the rebels' behavior:

> Later arguments incited began from this class question. Because the so-called *Hung-wu-lei* (five kinds of red) Red Guards, established at the very outset, attacked the "ordinary" and bad classers and concentrated their attacks on bad classers, therefore they created a sort of discrimination . . . This in turn led to the feeling that since you were bad to me before, if you later said something was good, I'd say it was bad, out of prejudice against you. It was this way.[109]

Resentment toward the early exclusive Red Guards, the *Chu-yi-ping*, could be further legitimated by the notion that the youths of red class background were protecting the authorities who had invested them with their privileged status in the student body.[110] Moreover, outsiders could inflate selfish motives for radical political behavior into actions meant to benefit and *serve the people*. Chu Nan-po rationalizes his behavior in terms of a greater social injustice wrought against a larger number of people than himself who suffered at the hands of the good classers. He says:

> It wasn't only because they ostracized me during the GPCR that I felt this hatred. It was a discrimination against the "ordinary" and bad classers! Therefore, we hated them.[111]

Chu Nan-po, Ch'iao and others deluded themselves that, as ordinary classers, they represented the average person and were fighting for an illusory majority, which perhaps seemed a reality in some schools where non-red classers predominated. These youngsters viewed the red class stratum in toto as a privileged elite. They inflated their own efforts to succeed in society into an altruistic endeavor to *serve the people* (one of the key credoes of the PRC).

In a sense, many outsiders seeking to avenge themselves on the politically red in-group were also attempting to compensate for their stigmatized bad class background by proving themselves more politically pure and active than their adversaries. Chou Chung-wang, for instance, who became active in the *Hung Ch'i* propaganda department at his school, notes that he always had made it his business "to perform better to make up for the shortcoming" of not being affiliated with a formal political organization.[112] In the *Hung Ch'i* Red Guard faction, he hoped to show that the stance of bad classers could be truer to Mao than the behavior of his good class correspondents.

As they formed ad hoc "red class" groups to challenge the Party work teams, established Red Guards, and the authorities, these outsiders organized on the basis of informal peer relations, and managed to convince themselves that they were now the prestigious group on the road to real power and in-group status. At Ch'iao's school where the bad class and "ordinary" class students constituted the overwhelming majority and the original *Chu-yi-ping* numbered only slightly more than thirty, his friendship clique of approximately ten youths formed one Red Guard unit, combined with mutual acquaintances in another class to form a larger group, and joined the fully-constituted, centralized *Hung Ch'i* faction during the Great Unity (*ta lien-ho*). Ch'iao was a key leader and organizer at first among good friends,[113] and only withdrew later during the armed struggle (*wu-tou*). Speaking of his original Red Guard unit, Ch'iao boasts: "Our power was very great."[114] Similarly, Chu Nan-po, who, eager to get ahead, remained active in the GPCR to the finish, recruited his early ad hoc unit (twelve members) from his friendship group. He says:

> We were just about the same Red Guard group as friendship group. *Hung Ch'i* faction members, we formed the XX war brigade. Afterward, some others entered our group, while others leaned toward the *Chu-yi-ping*.[115]

A larger group which eventually developed at Chu's school in a snowballing pattern was organized by these few.[116]

Both Ch'iao and Chu, leaders in challenging the in-group, made an aggressively proud defense of their group as being a better lot of people than their adversaries. Ch'iao rationalized his own early exclusion from the YCL and good classer groups by impugning the character and behavior of their members:

> Had they been a very good organization . . . , then I would have felt pitiful [for having been excluded]. But just not measuring up to *their* conditions for joining, I wasn't at all sorry over not being part of their style of behavior . . . After the Cultural Revolution began, they had special privileges with which I was displeased. What they said was Gospel. They forced their thought on others.[117]

In other words, Ch'iao was a better person in his estimation for not having been one of their ilk. Sour grapes! And Chu also elevated his Cultural Revolution status by denigrating the earlier good class, in-group members:

> We felt they were useless . . . they were bad in athletics and not strong physically and also got sick. Their grades were also the worst. They just relied on their fathers being workers, peasants or current military officers to smell sweet. We were very contemptuous of them.[118]

Chu Nan-po's epithets against his good class peers are reminiscent of a revolutionary party challenging a decaying, thin-blooded aristocracy. Alienated from the social and political order, he and others strove for the power they felt had been unjustly denied, and rationalized both their previous proscription and their quest for status in terms of the corruption of an existing elite and their own good intention of democratizing society.

WANG LOK-CH'AO: A CASE STUDY OF THE INTERACTION BETWEEN PRE-GPCR CLASS OSTRACISM AND INTRA-FAMILY DYNAMICS

Why should some non-red class children have become so radicalized by their sudden ostracism before the Cultural Revolution, while others responded by either withdrawing from participation or just following the tide? The answer seems to lie in the extent to which social and political ostracism was perceived to frustrate psychologically motivated drives to rivalry with father, and inter-generational succession through upward mobility in society. Indeed, every one of the pool of respondents who indicated an extreme sensitivity to being excluded from political participation and social acceptance just prior to, or at the start of the GPCR, had also been most openly striving to prove himself the better of his father in the assumption of an adult role in society. The case of Wang Lok-ch'ao serves to illustrate this point.

Respondent Wang's irritation over class discrimination against him from the authorities and those good class peers to whom he sweepingly liked to refer to as "their children" began in his first year of lower middle school and culminated in his leading an assault, then not yet officially sanctioned, against the Party work team sent to his upper middle school in the early phase of the GPCR, June 1966. As Wang neatly explains his behavior:

> If politics had no oppression on me, I would not have taken an interest in politics. I preferred mathematics and sports.[119]

Although he perceived no prejudice against himself in primary school where many of his friends were sons of workers, cadres and soldiers, this inter-class intercourse gradually deteriorated as he proceeded through school. When Wang reached lower middle school, students became more aware of one another's class background. In the case of his relationship with one "rather good school chum" of proletarian background, both parties "discovered that the gulf between [their] families was very large"; although they never severed relations completely, they grew less intimate and "had a little prejudice toward one another."[120] The reader will observe that as Wang took notice of his friend's malaise over being associated with him because of class differences, he also reacted in kind. "In front of him [my friend]," Wang says, "I did my utmost to avoid cursing the children of higher class cadres, and he did his best to avoid cursing us 'sons of bitches'."[121] Wang rationalizes his own status by telling himself that although "at first [he] admired them," he later "came to feel that they [red classers] were crude and unintelligent."[122] As the pressure was brought in formal small group sessions to own up to one's class background during several small political campaigns like the "Self-Expose Movement" (*Tzu-wo pao-lu yun-tung*) held during the pre-GPCR years, Wang felt uncomfortable in the presence of his good class peers at the elite school he attended.[123] Theoretically, a bad classer could reform himself through such self-criticism, but Wang found it difficult to bear this newly highlighted stigma outside the classroom, and began to react paranoically to those about him. He overreacted to their attitude, and developed a deep-seated resentment of their claim to superiority:

> When I heard them brag about their fathers, I got very incensed. There was nothing remarkable about them. Apart from their fathers' being rather good, they, the children, did not necessarily measure up.[124]

Outside class, his fellow students began to pick on him because of his class background. In the dormitory, some students taunted him for being against the collective, and broke his things. The organizers of the activity against him were sons of revolutionary cadres, and one was a member of the YCL. Making a generalization to himself about the rottenness of all good class children, Wang perceived himself on the other side, and joined forces with a few schoolmates who were in a similar position. He chose those friends in response to a growing feeling of "isolation" emanating from the succession of small political campaigns at school.[125] In Wang's words: "The more they [the others] criticized, the more I acted up. It was like resisting them."[126]

Wang began to "lean to one side."[127] He might eventually have renounced his class and joined the YCL if his peers had not been so hostile to him in lower middle school form three, both inside and outside school.[128] Wang describes his assessment of the situation for himself then:

> On the one hand, I was concerned that my class was not good enough for the YCL. On the other hand, my papa told me not to join a political organization . . . My papa said that dynasties often change.[129]

Ironically, Wang had been competitive with his father all along and earlier had regarded him as backward and irrelevant.[130]

The openness of his relationship with his father from the third year of primary school onward encouraged him to compete more freely with his father with the intent of replacing him on the "pecking order." Commenting on his relationship with his father as early as when he was in primary school, Wang says:

> In his thought he possibly regarded me as a child. Nevertheless, he gave the appearance of having a discussion with me on an equal plane.[131]

If Wang's father treated him as an equal but still considered him a child, it was Wang's design in his adolescence to resolve this contradiction. Given the democratic atmosphere in his home, Wang felt sufficiently autonomous to choose both the academic and political tracks for proving himself to his father.[132] But because society would not facilitate his adopting an alternate identity and permit his upward mobility *even academically*, he was driven to assume his father's political stance defensively. The stigma of bad class background might have encouraged competition and mobility vis-à-vis the older generation in his family, but it also in the end forced him to accept that identity because of the futility of trying to change it.[133]

The key turning point for Wang was his failure to qualify for a regular middle school despite his outstanding academic performance. As he puts it:

> At that time, I couldn't get into the cadres' sons' elitist school (i.e., the upper forms of the one he was already attending--his first choice). I just made a *min-pan*[134] school . . . It was the worst school. *Like falling from heaven to earth.*[135]

In this "fall," Wang found himself in the company of students with a similarly bad class background. Whereas Wang of necessity had been thrown into friendship with a few bad class peers who also had a difficult time toward the end of lower middle school,[136] "now just about everyone in the school was [his] friend."[137] They were all "ordinary" or "class enemy" children.

With the onslaught of the GPCR, eventually "just about the whole student body became *Hung Ch'i* (rebel) faction members."[138] Previously isolated and restricted in movement as one of only a few outsiders, Wang was now part of one mass of outsiders crammed into one school. He states:

> Everyone's class was the same. Our standpoint was also the same. Everyone leaned toward *Hung Ch'i* and wanted to gain freedom.[139]

Simultaneously, more attentive and receptive to his parents' backward talk, his "vision widened gradually."[140] Seeing his family oppressed by *Chu-yi-ping* during the "Four Olds" *(P'o-ssu-chiu)*, Wang was all the angrier.[141] Wang experienced the agony then of witnessing his father, capped and labelled, being hauled through the street.[142]

Like the spontaneous group leader in a prison seizing upon a cause for which to demonstrate, Wang was in pouncing position as the Cultural Revolution deepened. Earlier in the semester, against the recommendation submitted by the YCL cadre for another candidate, he was popularly elected class leader *(pan-chang)*. He found himself in the position of being a natural spokesman for his fellows, quite the antithesis of his earlier personality and role at middle school.[143] When the GPCR work team arrived on the scene, Wang exploited his "prestige in class" to head a small group of Red Guards specifically formed to counter-attack the work team because of the latter's anti-bad-classer activities and government affiliation.[144] For him, the class prejudice had just become too "obvious" in the "blood line theory" the work team attempted to implement.[145] He became an activist Red Guard, later zealously engaged in armed struggle, but ironically never remained the top leader he was at the outset. The reason for his decline was that all the higher leaders were of good class, the "blood line" debate notwithstanding. What was Wang's aim in participating in the GPCR?

> I merely hoped society would get more chaotic and a new generation would emerge from this chaos.[146]

An increasingly alienated individual in the previous order, Wang's avowed purpose was now to overturn it.[147] Wang never considered himself political until the opportunity came along.

> I became very interested in politics from the time of the GPCR to the present . . . First, politics paid attention to me, and I was a victim of its oppression. I began to get acquainted with politics.[148]

In spite of the fact that he was forced back on a negative class identification with his father, Wang was now bent on a course of social action which would still fulfill his aspirations toward generational succession, if not academically then politically. Now he was acting in the interest of his father's ilk, when his father per se would not have dared to engage in such action himself.[149] In spite of, or really perhaps because of, his father's fears, he fought in the hazardous armed struggle. And although he knew his father was opposed to his participation, Wang almost deliberately, on an unconscious level, placed his hand gun in his father's desk with the outcome of provoking his anger.[150]

BACKGROUND AND BEHAVIOR: A SUMMATION

The institutional devices created in "post-Liberation" China to facilitate a logical transition in socialization from home to school, based perhaps less on insuring uniformity than on the notion that a latent contradiction between family and society is best exposed in order that it be resolved positively in the interest of society, sometimes went awry among children of bad class families. Children who became sensitive at an early age to a hostile environment because of their unfavorable class background often fell back on a safe, negative, political identity with their "objectively backward" families; or if intra-family restraints were minimal, they developed opportunistic techniques for coping with social pressures. For the most part, such socially non-integrative trends among young children were restricted either to those of "class enemy" background or to those who experienced arbitrary and subjective discrimination from "red" teachers with a special grudge against non-proletarians.

Probably the majority of the petit-bourgeois or middle

range children were not subjected to any remarkable class discrimination until the height of the *Ssu-ch'ing* Movement in the mid-sixties. Increasing social and political ostracism in those years affected different people in different ways. The more politically and socially upwardly mobile adolescents were the most frustrated and susceptible to political radicalization.

The key point to which the reader's attention should be drawn in this chapter is that the social or political behavior of youths was a function of the interaction between the external and internal environments. In the Huang case, even the father's authoritarian treatment of his sons could be attributed in part to the pressures of a hostile outer environment. In turn, the sons' mistrust of others and rigid identification with their father as a prime target in the Anti-Rightist Campaign was influenced both by intra-family dynamics and a threatening society. Hence, any adolescent rivalry with the father had to be played out on a politically safe plane. In spite of the fact that the father was overtly sympathetic to the goals and ideals of the communists, competition along a political line of cleavage (e.g., active participation in the GPCR) was obstructed by the anti-social personalities of the Huang boys, the objectively hostile political situation in which they found themselves as young children, and the subjective opportunity for the older Huang sons to compete with the "intellectual" side of their father's identity.

The antipode of the Huangs, the Wang family was not subjected to class-antagonistic social pressures in the years following "Liberation." The father's personality was open; he was tolerant and encouraged the autonomous behavior of his son. In a friendly society, young Wang could play out his rivalry with his father in a manner that would give him maximum Ego satisfaction and social integration. He could strive to be a better scholar than his father, without excluding the option of political activism. When both his social and academic upward mobility suddenly were impeded at the peak of his adolescence, Wang's behavior reflected a reaction to social change, but in terms of the same psychological dynamics which had already become salient for him. Sudden social ostracism and blockage in upward mobility amplified earlier motivational patterns and created a new context in which they could be fulfilled.

As we shall see in the next chapter, personality and intra-family dynamics often could provide the basic energy and direction for political behavior in adolescence. In this chapter, we have seen that they could also be molded themselves by society over a long period and/or redirected by the exigencies of the immediate social context.

4. The Competitive Dynamic Between Parent and Child: The Projection of Inter-Generational Rivalry in the Family on to Political Behavior in the Great Proletarian Cultural Revolution

> *These men, not all of whom were in fact fathers themselves, became our substitute fathers . . . We transferred to them the respect and expectations attaching to the omniscient father of our childhood, and we then began to treat them as we treated our fathers at home. We confronted them with the ambivalence that we had acquired in our families and with its help we struggled with them as we had been in the habit of struggling with our own fathers in the flesh.*
>
> --Sigmund Freud, "Some Reflections on Schoolboy Psychology" (1914).

We have seen that the Cultural Revolution resonated with the political and social alienation of a large number of non-red students in the middle schools and universities of China. It also tapped a dynamic of inter-generational competition between adolescents and their superordinates, already manifest in varying degrees in intra-familial behavior. The repressed individual, completely submissive to his father, now seems to be a rarity in the People's Republic of China. Even if one could deduce on the basis of sparse evidence that the Confucian family system in the past produced universally authority-submissive children, one can no longer argue that the internalization of the norm of filial piety, badly battered in the process of social revolution, prevents father-son competition in childhood or suppresses it.[1] Nor does the sudden delegitimation of authorities in society necessarily unleash in all directions the hostility supposedly seething within a severely suppressed person; rather, it permits the individual to channel normal adolescent hostility into constructive adult-oriented behavior.

We will see in this chapter that varying forms of family interaction produced differing types of competition, some generally more successful than others in gaining satisfaction through politically channelled behavior. Competition expressed politically in a vertical father-son relationship was often tantamount to complete defiance of the rigid and politically intransigent father; it necessitated a total break, often very difficult psychologically, and the filling of a subsequent identity vacuum by gaining clear-cut political acceptance from society. If such an effort to gain political acceptance were thwarted among those psychologically capable of breaking with family, the son was apt to fall back on an identification with father. In the more horizontal father-son relationship, rivalry was paradoxically more acute because of the proximity in status between two generations,[2] but mutual respect either induced a greater area of shared values or militated against the father's imposing himself on the son's area of independent behavior. The latter form of inter-generational competition usually was realized successfully in politically active behavior.

Inviting attacks on the authorities, the organizers of the GPCR, perhaps inadvertently, induced the adolescent to project childhood impulses to compete with his father on to the authorities in school and in society. The emphasis on the theme of "revolutionary successors" fired the individual into making the leap into adulthood. The path to succession was not a sure one, nor was it clearly charted, nor necessarily a distance short to travel. As Mao had clearly stated, the "revolutionary successors" would be tested in combat and the failures eliminated. For the ambitious Red Guard militant, the act of zealous participation often meant *proving oneself* better than father within the parameters of the new social value system. In order to qualify for adult status, the socially integrative adolescent had to trace a continuity between acquired communist values and the limits of tolerance of parental values which had been learned in the home.

PROVING SELF TO FATHER RE-CHANNELLED

One should understand that this act of proving oneself was not to signify a simple identification with the father or father-surrogate in the immediate environment. Father-surrogates in the school and political hierarchies had for the most part been delegitimated, albeit only temporarily in some cases. Those beneath them had been invited to brand them as elitists, revisionists and "monsters and freaks." The father in the family, whether proletarian or of questionable class background, was perceived by his children as backward, obsolete, and irrelevant to the rebirth of revolution.[3] The young person was not supposed to adopt his father's role values or aim to play father to the subordinate masses. He was supposed to test himself and the values of the practical ideology he had acquired in school in the concrete experience of revolution. In the process, the youth was to evolve a new revolutionary identity for himself which would reflect itself in the *renewal* of revolution in society. He was not to be like his father. According to the Maoist vision, he would not simply be rebelling against a father only to adopt his father's values in an adult role. As "revolutionary successor," he should not succumb to intellectual elitism or arrogance of power but learn to coordinate self-initiative with the act of serving the masses.

The traditional, filial proving oneself to a parent was naturally supposed to undergo a metamorphosis. Traditionally, proving oneself to a father or bringing glory on family, in effect as a form of emulation insuring a self-replicating elite, seems to have been motivated by a dynamic of inter-generational rivalry. Although no overt rebellion necessarily was involved, why else was the desire to be as good as father or carry on the good name of the family such a compulsive one?[4] Of course, in the old China, generational succession could be resolved through self-evaluation based on identification with the father or father's heritage. In the new China, the individual was now to prove himself primarily to himself and society and simultaneously attempt to gain acceptance for his actions from his parents. Yao Yuan-fang's article in 1956 on the new version of filial piety explained the problem this way:

> Some parents hope that their children will make more money and rise to higher ranks in officialdom. This is naturally the reflection of the old ideology on family fame and riches to bring credit on the family, *and we should not support it* . . . In dealing with such a situation, we must be cool and patient, and be adept in making use of the personal experience of the old people, the facts easily understood by them, *to assist them to rid themselves of the old ideology and to establish a new ideological outlook.*[5]

The child was essentially presented with the dual task of maintaining the *form* of emulating parents, while educating parents to accept the new social values reflected in his own behavior.

Apparently the hope was that through the new values permeating the social environment, the competitive dynamic of proving oneself to parent(s) could be remolded into glory-seeking for nation and people instead of just for family or self, and rechannelled into positive, socially conscious participation. Since the communist revolution, youngsters had been taught to be politically active and to give priority to serving the people. As a child in Primary three or four, Wang had "thought this way."[6] At that time, as a health supervisor on the street, he "forbade people to spit in the street . . . and felt everyone must maintain the national welfare."[7] First recruited into the Pioneers (*shao-nien-hsien-feng-tui*, or in abbreviated form, *shao-nien-tui*) in primary school where children met in groups to criticize their social behavior, and later exposed to more concrete political indoctrination, many still unalienated young people naturally set their sights on entry into the YCL as they approached their second year of lower middle school. As Lan Weiying explains:

> The most important thing is that having gone through so many years of what amounts to political education or study, my awareness in that area was heightened. It was natural to proceed along that path. I proceeded gradually from the Pioneers toward the YCL.[8]

Furthermore, within the school milieu, peers sometimes exerted an influence which served to reinforce the impact of all the self-sacrificing, revolutionary heroes held up to the children as embodiments of the new ideals and values. In the early years of primary school, Wang, like many other post-revolutionary children his age, dreamed of becoming a PLA officer. But this fantasy, a common product of child socialization, was given additional impetus because "many of his classmates had fathers who were army officers."[9] These influences notwithstanding, in the vertical father-son relationship, which continued to persist in substance in many families,[10] proving oneself still meant conforming to father's values and his expectations of his son. We will see this more clearly in the later discussion of Mr. Yüan, the most traditional child on a continuum of change reflected in my pool of respondents. It will also be apparent that what is in one aspect emulation of the father is motivated by an underlying generational rivalry.

But even the traditional syndrome of proving oneself to father and bringing glory on family did not necessarily preclude political ambitions. Hsu Ta-liang, whose father encouraged him to study in lower middle school to become a scientist because it was most "glorious," later would have liked to become a cadre because "at that time (i.e., upper middle school) . . . it was rather good and comparatively glorious."[11] This was the "official" mentality of the old society. During the Cultural Revolution, Hsu became an active Red Guard. Mr. Chai speculates that he would have been a Red Guard leader if his parents had not been such intellectual snobs. Chai's mother taught Chinese in middle school and encouraged him to be literary, and his father, a three-generation skilled worker, prided himself in being self-taught in several branches of mechanics and engineering, and read constantly. As Chai explains the peculiar situation:

> If my parents had a low level education, they would have been much more innocent and uncomprehending. Nor would they have taught me not to quarrel or fight people. Of course, they would have hoped that I'd make more of a name for myself. Possibly, I would have been a Red Guard commander.[12]

Proving himself to his parents, Chai effectively abstained from the GPCR and buried himself in his books.

Parental value priorities concerning political participation were an important variable in determining whether a child from a vertical relationship would enter the political arena. But even if a father was opposed to political activism, a youth might still be able to rationalize political participation by choosing to emphasize that in the new social context such behavior fulfilled father's demand for glory, while choosing virtually to ignore any of his father's personal predilections against politics. Although more often than not bad class parents seemed to prefer that their children choose a path to success other than politics, in some instances the son could justify his own political behavior in terms of the father's oblique stress on success. Although Lo Ping-kok's father stressed the importance of education to achieve success and was clearly ideologically backward, the thrust of his exhortation to his sons was "that in the future [they] become useful persons in society."[13] Lo Ping-kok recalls that his family taught him to do some earth-shaking enterprise by making contributions to society.[14] Reviewing his militant Red Guard experience, he says:

During the GPCR, I felt that I was making a big
contribution of this sort, but later on, it most
certainly did not turn out to be that way.[15]

Asking what his *life view* (*jen-sheng-kuan*) is now, Lo Ping-kok, after hazarding the long swim to Hong Kong and struggling to survive in a foreign economic system, ironically spouts these words:

To truly serve the nation and the majority of
people. No matter what enterprise is involved,
I can do it.[16]

What was his world view on the Mainland? "I very much hoped to serve the nation."[17]

Some adolescent youths seemed to come close to resolving the contradiction between the need to "prove oneself" to meet father's expectations and proving oneself fit for serving society. Among my bad class sample, the virtual resolution of this conflict often appeared to stem from a rebellion against father which did not surpass the limits of tolerance of the father's occupational value orientation. In other words, if the father encouraged fame or glory in the context of old intellectual or bourgeois values, he also accepted or even psychologically rewarded political accomplishments. This sort of compromise between father and son was contingent on the extent to which the relationship between them was horizontal or relatively egalitarian. It was left to the son to attempt to transcend the Ego dynamic of glory for family or self, gained through the pursuit of "official" status, in order to serve society to the extreme limits of self-sacrifice. Chu Nan-po's father primarily hoped his favorite son would become an engineer because, according to young Chu's perception, "his [father's] prestige would be high and to have produced a famous son, he would also be very happy."[18] Chu Nan-po's father reminded his son from time to time that his ancestors had been Ch'ing officials, and encouraged him by saying: "We want our forbears to respect us."[19] But while encouraging his son academically, Chu senior also rewarded Chu Nan-po's political achievements at school. Young Chu recalls one very happy event:

When I became *chung-tui-chang* in the Pioneers
. . .[20] my father felt very glorious. Because
his own child had put forth effort and gained
glory for the family. Thus, he was very
happy.[21]

Therefore, when Chu Nan-po sought entry into the YCL and later actively joined in the GPCR, one of his thoughts continued to be that these pursuits would bring honor on his family and ancestors.[22] Of course, he was more concerned with serving society. The question was to what extent he would be willing to surrender his autonomy and fully submerge self in the masses. Just how one participated in political struggle, rather than participation itself, was determined by the individual's real objective. The persistence of the vertical relationship between father and son in modern Chinese society as well as the residual concern for reflecting success on the family in such a way as to accommodate the occupational and status priorities of the elders inexorably fostered the self-replication of existing and past elites. These residues were counter-productive to the fulfillment of the Maoist vision. Hence, here is a reason for the Cultural Revolution, and yet again for the transport of proud, self-important youths to the countryside for a lifetime of studying the thought and feelings (*ssu-hsiang kan-ch'ing*) of the peasantry. One activist Red Guard leader, who at a very early stage in the movement had led his Red Guard contingent to the City Committee headquarters to complain about the protection of authorities at his school, now pinpoints the difficulty of being a "revolutionary successor" without becoming arrogant over the prospect of success and the opportunity to laud it over the others:

> I had been enthusiastic about life and about the Communist Party's leadership. Because of this I decided to contribute myself to this society. I wanted to be a cadre and serve the masses. Of course, I wanted to become a cadre, and also hoped to put on an air of superiority (*yu-yüeh-kan*) for others to see; I had something of the thought of "officialdom" from the old society. Another coexistent thought was to serve the masses, derived from the Communist Party . . . I had been displeased with the principal of the school, but I did admire his official prestige . . .[23]

THE VERTICAL FATHER-SON RELATIONSHIP:
TWO BROTHERS

Even if the dynamic of proving self to father has not yet been rechanneled into proving self to the masses (and certainly a sample of refugees is hardly a measurement of

the success among those who remain in China), the form it
has taken to express itself does reflect the developing
openness in the family and the acquisition of values, in
the broader environment, favoring political involvement.

The seepage of new norms into the early socialization
process is a slow one, dependent upon the parent's willingness to bend to the times as well as on the responsiveness
of the son's personality to environmental cues. One should
expect greater change over several generations, given a
fairly constant social environment. But the case of two
brothers, Lo Ping-wen and Lo Ping-kok, is an excellent contemporary microcosm of this very metamorphosis as well as
the resistances to it.

Lo Ping-wen was the next to the youngest of twenty
children.[24] Born in 1947, his formative years were also
the first years of post-revolutionary adjustment. Lo's
father was "traditional" and beat him severely for "important things," such as brawls with his playmates "whether
he was right or wrong."[25] Old and strict, his father in-
timidated him "spiritually" all the time.[26] As a child,
Ping-wen was happiest when his father was away from
home.[27]

Conforming to the model of the traditional father, the
older Mr. Lo, apart from being arbitrarily strict and demanding, gradually withdrew from Ping-wen as Ping-wen moved
on through primary to middle school.[28] Lo Ping-wen recalls:
"When I was a toddler, he loved me more than the others
. . . When I got big, he no longer loved me."[29] In his
aloofness, which was characteristic of the traditional
Chinese father, the older Mr. Lo to a great extent abdi-
cated disciplinary and supervisory responsibilities to
Ping-wen's next older brother, and directed him to examine
Ping-wen's homework and watch over the boy regularly.[30]

Although he identified with his father in personality
because he was a male and regarded his mother as "socially
useless,"[31] Ping-wen found himself generationally alienated
in part from his father. His father attempted to compel
him to study *Ku-wen* (classical Chinese writing), which
Ping-wen considered boring and irrelevant, and sometimes
offered material incentives for committing classical texts
to memory. Father also annoyed his son with ideologically
"backward" remarks contrasting present times with Kuomintang
rule.[32] Basically, Lo Ping-wen viewed his father as ideologically irrelevant:

> My philosophy was different . . . My viewpoint and
> attitude were different from his . . . The studies

with which he was concerned were different from ours. We studied how to do a thing well. [ed. political study or *cheng-chih hsueh-hsi*] What he studied was not this, but in the area of so-called thought reform (*ssu-hsiang kai-tsau*).[33]

Nevertheless, Ping-wen never found it in himself to break away from his father. His childhood reactions to his father's punishments were restrained. His rage reactions, limited in number, were confined to running away from home for a day or so.[34] He never spoke up to his father. Even when he perceived his father to be unjust in treating him harshly for a playful scrap with a friend, perhaps over an argument he did not provoke, Ping-wen stood in silence as his father beat him, "only refusing to capitulate (*pu-fu-ch'i*) internally."[35] Although Ping-wen's response to the Mao story about disobeying father[36] is that "in feudal society the son obeyed the father but now should look at reality and discuss his thoughts,"[37] he avers that were he in the same situation, he would bow his head and simply not capitulate internally to this blow to his self-respect.[38] Moreover, Ping-wen indicates disapproval of the modern trend toward equality between father and son and regards it as a usurpation of the prerogatives of the father. Lamentingly, he states:

> Unfortunately, the educational responsibility of Chinese parents now is not very large. They feel that when they [sons] grow up, they are not their own. They are the nation's.[39]

In bemoaning this trend toward the depletion of the father's authority in the home, could he not be excusing his own incapacity to fill such a vacuum? Could not this attitude be a rationalization for his own inability to confront a father who did not sense that the environment was undercutting his power and who would have found little environmental sanction in opposing a legitimately, self-assertive son? Ping-wen recalls:

> Sometimes I would say to my older brother: "I don't necessarily fear father. But I wouldn't dare say it when he was there.[40]

In other words, he had to protest his fearlessness toward father before his older brother in order to try to convince himself, but he could not confront father directly and thereby really get out from under him. Instead, he coped psychologically with the problem by telling himself that "father did things the way they should be done." He was "afraid of him, but at times could not help but admire him."[41] Does Lo Ping-wen consider himself a filial son? "Correct, it could not be that Chinese people since ancient times would extirpate it entirely."[42]

Lo Ping-wen's failure to get himself either to express his hostility toward father overtly and directly or to break through the vertical stratification in his family was manifested in his political behavior as well. As a pre-adolescent aware of his father's ideological backwardness and the comparative purity and political acuity of his own generation, he gloated over his perception that "they [father and elder brother] studied articles for the sake of *thought reform*, while what [he] read was not for that . . . but out of an interest in current events, just as in the case of his peers."[43] To a small degree, he was competing continuously with father and elder brother, reassuring himself that he was the NOW generation politically when in fact he was performing the same motions as his father and brother.[44]

At first, he did want to integrate himself politically into society. But even as a young schoolboy, when he became a squad leader (*hsiao-tui-chang*) in the Pioneers in Primary form three, he was afraid to make his situation known to his father.[45] It is important that he could not muster enough courage in the new environment to assert his value autonomy from father. He tried to exist on two levels at first by hiding his political activism from his family. He describes the circumstances:

> I didn't wear my red arm band at home or on the street, only at school . . . I didn't let my family know my situation at school . . . I was afraid they would say something. My school gave me a criticism to show to the head of the family . . . I didn't want to let my parents see it in order to keep them in the dark about my [activist] performance.[46]

His misgivings revolved about this question: "Would my parents blame me for being too progressive?"[47]

Lo's father had encouraged his sons to strive for personal success through a remarkable achievement of some sort. But in lower middle school, Ping-wen shied away from trying to enter the YCL, not because he did not envy

their prestige or regard the League as a good path for
personal upward mobility, but because he could not make
the break from his family. Midway through upper middle
school, in 1963-1964, as class politicization began to
pervade the atmosphere, he told himself that he could no
longer meet the standards for entry into the YCL.[48] He
had already begun to retreat to a psychologically safe
identification with family. Instead of attempting political integration, he spent his days during the next summer
at Chung Shan Library reading stories about Mao and other
communist leaders to learn the key to their success. Lo
Ping-wen fantasied then becoming a leader, even though the
realistic conditions precluded such a possibility. Still,
he tried to convince himself that in spite of his class
background, he had hope of realizing himself. He recalls
that he thought to himself:

> I had no opportunity to use the usual method (i.e.,
> entry into the YCL and Party). If I personally had
> talent, I could still rise high.[49]

Driven back on the strictly "bourgeois" vision of individual success because of the stigma of bad class background in the social environment and the fault of his own
early socialization and personality, Ping-wen became severely alienated when he failed to qualify for university.
His failure stemmed not from his performance on the university matriculation examination, but from his bad "class
enemy" background.[50] Thus, Ping-wen was denied the opportunity to develop his individual talents within the normal
realm of socialist society.

Forced to accept the harsh reality of his class background and the fact that he was to a large extent proscribed from an active role within the present social system
he decided to enter the Foreign Language Institute in Kwangchow, but his family footed the expenses itself.[51] Although
he seemed no less interested in politics, his behavior at
the Institute was markedly reactionary in orientation. He
and a few friends listened to BBC English language broadcasts in secret, ostensibly to improve their English;
however, he found it amusing and illuminating to match BBC
news reports against local accounts of the same events.[52]
Ping-wen began to pride himself on his sophistication and
political cynicism, and even debated news items with
trusted friends.[53]

When the GPCR burst on the scene in his first year at
the Institute, Ping-wen abstained from any sort of

participation, including travel on the *Ch'uan-lien*. He recalls his state of mind then:

> At that time, I was very clear about the fact that because of my bad class, it was inappropriate to participate in this movement. If I had participated, I would have taken part in the *tsao-fan* faction.[54]

Ping-wen resisted the constant pressures to join from his four or five good Institute friends, all of whom were participants and all but one of whom were in the rebel faction.[55] He moved home as the tumultuous fighting erupted between factions, and excused himself by feigning mental depression.[56] But his friends visited him at home and continued to try to persuade him to join their respective factions.[57] Ping-wen unrelentingly refused to join in the movement:

> My personality was lively, but owing to my own contact with various factors and influences in society, I was frightened . . . Although when I was small I could kick up a storm as I pleased, now things were serious and not so simple as that. Because I was more mature in my thinking.[58]

In point of fact, Lo Ping-wen's testimony does not bear out his claim that as a child, he ever really would have "kicked up a storm" at home or at school. Unlike other young children, including his younger brother Ping-kok, he remained relatively impassive in the face of harsh disciplinary treatment from father. As a "class enemy" whose father did just the opposite of offering emotional support for politically oriented behavior, and as an authority-submissive personality, young Ping-wen could not maintain a dual existence--politically active at school and backward and submissive at home; nor could he break away psychologically from his family identity by denouncing father and actively seeking entry into the YCL during the open years of the early 1960s.[59] He chose instead to go it alone, or rather pursue a bourgeois individualist path of seeking to develop his talents for the sake of personal success and achievement. On his own, he studied about Mao's success, but not Mao Thought. By the time of the advent of the GPCR, group participation did not seem to him to be the appropriate path to success because of the politically cynical defense he had long before erected

against class ostracism.60 Nor was group affiliation
likely to fulfill his emotional need to stand out as an
individual in order to compensate for the long-denied
Ego autonomy vis-à-vis father; all along he had dreamed
of being a hero and leader.

Four or five years younger than his next older brother
Ping-wen, Lo Ping-kok was a different sort of person. He
was born in 1951 and was the youngest and most favored child
in a very large family. As children, both he and his next
older brother shared a common awareness of generational
cleavage and their father's obsolescent recidivism, but
Ping-kok's personality permitted a more vigorous response
in his earlier years to their authoritarian and ideologically backward father.

Whereas Ping-wen's anger at father was limited to conscious suppression and rare temporary flights from home,
Ping-kok quarreled directly with the old man. In 1962, his
father punished him for doing some small business together
with some of his friends in transporting produce from
countryside to city and selling it privately. According
to his father, a child's place was in the home or school.
Feeling his father was unnecessarily holding him back,
Ping-kok, then age eleven, protested his father's interference directly, causing his authoritarian father to beat
him still more. Thereupon, young Ping-kok ran away from
home and slept the night in a vacant building on the bank
of the Pearl River.61

Ping-kok was happiest when he was at primary school.
During his hours spent at home, he resented his being
watched over too closely.62 In fact, this early desire to
feel free of authority and mix with peers is related to his
attitude toward the GPCR in his later adolescent years.
"The GPCR," he says, was his happiest adult experience,
"because our faction occupied a good position and I was
not restricted by my family."63

Although Lo Ping-kok feels that for the most part as
a small child, "there was no other way" than running away
from home to express his anger because of his "limited
power," he was unwilling to tolerate the same sort of
restriction on his autonomy when he got older.64 He states
unequivocally:

> When I was rather grown up and was scolded by him
> [father], I would reason with him with the intent
> of persuading him.65

Thus, by the time of his adolescence, unlike his next older brother, Ping-kok was at least trying to forge a more horizontal relationship with his father. As the youngest son and most favored in the household by both parents, perhaps Ping-kok could get away with more and was more manipulative. Another explanation for his autonomous behavior in a family patterned on traditional filial submissiveness was that Lo Ping-kok, more than his older siblings, was and perceived himself to be a child of the post-revolutionary epoch.

Born in 1951 and entering primary school during the Great Leap, Ping-kok not only was aware of his father's ideological "backwardness" but deeply ashamed of his background and sensitive to any reference to it, direct or indirect.[66] He explains:

> At that time, I was discontent with my papa's many opinions and often felt ashamed of my family's class background and resented my papa for it. Previously, he shouldn't have been a capitalist. From the time I was in Primary three or four, I began to think in that way.[67]

Ping-kok was an activist in primary school, and by Primary three or four, had become a *chung-tui* leader in the Pioneers; although he did not hide his political role from his father, neither was he patted on the back for it. Ping-kok regarded his father as backward and was contemptuous of him:

> His view of politics was always to regard what the Communist Party said as no good . . .[I knew] this from daily remarks, from his daily routine talk and activity.[68]

How did young Ping-kok deal with his father?

> I didn't debate [his opinions] with him. Sometimes, I merely returned to school and, in receiving theoretical education, wrote a document exposing my papa. It said that before Liberation how he exploited the workers and how bad he was.[69]

We shall see that traditional Yüan Ching-po, in preparing a required critique (self examination or *ssu-hsiang chien-t'ao*) at home, wrote it in collaboration with his parents. Ping-kok had clearly gone much further than either Yüan or his own next older brother in the direction of renouncing his father. Ping-kok truly had attempted formally to "draw the line" (*hua-ch'ing-chieh-hsien*) as best he could. Additionally, he volunteered to represent his class in addressing school meetings and engaged freely in launching criticism against others in his small group meetings; he felt no guilt afterward.[70]

Lo Ping-kok tried to "stand on the side of the school,"[71] but in his pursuit of social and political integration, he was plagued by the guilt of running away from something. The father from whom he was attempting to extricate himself came to be symbolized by the spectre of bad class background he felt was pursuing him. Even in primary school, which he recalls as his happiest years and relatively free of the class discrimination to come later with the onset of the *Ssu-ching* movement, he was haunted by his class background.[72] He paranoically perceived every reference to class exploitation in small group sessions as a personal slur and sign of "disrespect to himself and the others."[73] Instead of making a clean breast of his class and seeking to change his class standpoint through repeated self-criticism and practice rather than through a one-time declaration, he was still identifying unconsciously with his class or father's class. When he should have joined in the attacks on class exploitation, he felt personally offended by them. Of course, this ambivalence toward father had been manifested earlier in his unwillingness to cite specific examples of his father's backwardness in written criticisms of the man; he was afraid of getting his father in trouble at work and branding him as a person who "disseminated counter-revolutionary opinions."[74] Moreover, when he submitted these critiques to the school, he "never let papa know afterward"; in retrospect, he regards this restraint as a redeeming feature of his political ambition.[75] He feels that he at least avoided hurting his father's feelings. He was only able to go so far.

Lo Ping-kok's rebelliousness against father was ambivalent, and perhaps the increasingly politicized environment demanded too much of the young person in a traditional and bad class family; he could not make the necessary psychological break in time. In 1963-1964, at the zenith of the *Ssu-ch'ing*, his earlier dreams of becoming a cadre were shattered.[76] He was brought face to face with the external objectification of his ambivalence--the class background about which he avoided thinking. Ping-kok's experience then is best stated in his own words:

At that time, the entire nation waged the class education movement . . . Everyone had to reveal how the capitalists and landlords exploited the workers and peasants, how the counter-revolutionary elements had oppressed the people. At school, it was conducted with ardor. It was often this way. Our school at that time often asked those workers and poor peasants to come to discuss their hardships during the Kuomintang period. Once our school organized us to go to a factory to hear the workers there talk about how the capitalists exploited workers. But the thing was just right--that factory was precisely my father's factory. The workers talked about the so-called things to expose. All of it was directed at my papa.[78]

Previously an activist element in school who wrote articles for public posting and spoke at meetings,[79] Lo Ping-kok was ostracized by his schoolmates, and fell back completely on a reactionary identification with his father. As a young child, Ping-kok had regarded his father as an exploiter and had been contemptuous of his father's early protestations that his behavior before "Liberation" had "coincided with social morality" at that time.[80] Now he began to think in terms of his father's innocence and was furious at his peers at school for what he regarded as their hypocritical condemnation of his father and ostracism of himself. He recalls: "The main thing was that at school I received a blow to my spirit; I felt then that what my father said made sense."[81] He began to think to himself that some of his peers, while still unclear about his father's capitalist background, had even approved of his father when the elder Lo earlier visited the school.[82]

Class was central to Ping-kok as the outward aspect of father to which he had clung psychologically. He deliberately had avoided absolving himself of that identity because to do so would have meant a total denial of a linkage with his father and the worth of his father's existence. Now in early adolescence, when peer reinforcement and in-cliques and out-cliques were usually most important to the individual and pervaded his social milieu, "class background" also became a source of acute social and political ostracism for him.[83]

During his ostracism at school, Ping-kok began to link his own fate to his father's, his own identity to his father's.[84] Ping-kok recalls his brazenly open, "reactionary" behavior then:

> There were several times at school when we were taught how the capitalists ate people and exploited people . . . But in the afternoon after school let out and I returned home, I would discuss these things with a few schoolmates and say: "The capitalists are not this way; some people depend on their two hands to make a living." Afterward, this affair came to be known to my teacher, and he criticized me. Also on one occasion, the newspaper said the Chinese army had defeated a band of KMT guerrillas. After I heard the news, I said to my schoolmates that this was a mere rumor.[85]

In the few months after the verbal assault on his father, Ping-kok drew closer to the old man who had always indulged him as the youngest and favorite child. According to Ping-kok:

> [My relations with my father] were much closer. I felt that my papa in reality was not that sort of person. He should not have received such an explosive attack . . . .[86]

On an open and relatively one-to-one basis with one another, father and son "spent a lot of time chatting."[87] Ping-kok reminisces, holding back tears:

> The contents of our conversations--Because at that time I began studying traditional Chinese literature, what we discussed had to do with life, humanity and the philosophy of man. I felt his views on many world questions were correct.[88]

Thus, for a short while, Ping-kok was treated as a man, but he had to conform to his father's expectations of him to get this satisfaction. And this newfound relationship could be no more than a Pyrrhic victory for either party. Six months after the incident at the factory, as father and youngest son were first learning to relate to one another, the seventy-two year-old man died. Ping-kok was plagued with guilt.

Just after his father's death, Lo Ping-kok had recurring nightmares in which his father appeared as a ghost. His emotional reaction was as follows:

There were two points. One was that I wanted to
approach [get closer to] him because he was my
papa--father-son emotion. Second, I was extra-
ordinarily afraid because I often heard ghost
stories. [If I had been able to talk to him],
I would have said this--that I am a loyal son.[89]

This dream reflects the guilt Ping-kok still felt for
having been disloyal in his rebellion against father. It
is significant that although Ping-kok would like to tell
his father he is loyal, he bristles at the thought of
defying convention by approaching him on this basis. The
emotion involved here is fear, but Ping-kok does not attempt to drive the ghost away. If there is an ambivalence
of love and hate impulses reflected in this dream, there
is also one of action to draw close and inaction in the
face of a frightening, threatening father. Ping-kok tells
the interviewer that he was both unwilling and unable to
drive the ghost from his room. The reason for this incapacity appears to be the same reason he was ambivalent
earlier about renouncing his father and his own identity
with him--a residual filial submissiveness.

In the year following his father's death and preceding the onset of the GPCR in the schools, Lo Ping-kok did
his best to make it known publicly that he identified with
his father. He acknowledges that he was *guilt-ridden*,[90]
and recalls:

After he [father] passed away, I felt and often said
that I was the son of a capitalist.[91]

The GPCR provided Lo Ping-kok with an opportunity to
resolve his inner conflict over whether to assert himself
in an independent adult social identity or to identify with
father. First, he attempted to prove himself by volunteer-
ing for production; he was eager to play a role in
society.[92] Second, the prospect of joining the radical
faction at school allowed him to use the "class issue"
("blood line debate": *hsueh-t'ung-lun*) to change society.
He could engage in real revolution against the social
order and rationalize simultaneously that he was doing
battle with the class which had been his and his father's
oppressors. At last, Ping-kok could play a politically
active role in society, not because he was no longer opposing father, but because he was representing his cause, his
right to rehabilitation. As he remarks:

> At that time, class was 100% clear in my thought
> . . . I was the son of a bourgeoise and should
> participate in the armed struggle (*wu-tou*) to
> overturn the society of the ruling class.[93]

and:

> I merely thought that if our faction could gain
> the upper hand from May to August 1967, the
> victory of our faction would be beneficial to
> many, many people . . . [especially with regard
> to] class and change in the social system.[94]

Ideologically, he sought to democratize society and make it less discriminatory. Ping-kok reasons that he was attacking not only abstract authorities but "all those who were on the stage" whom he had resented since 1964, and who had "waved the red flag to oppose the red flag."[95] But only political activity with his father as his *cause célèbre* could satisfy Ping-kok psychologically and ameliorate his guilt over his basic competitiveness with father. Asked if he still believes in ghosts now, Ping-kok significantly, I think, replies: "I stopped being afraid of ghosts when the Cultural Revolution began."[96] He had become his father.

Already his father's proxy in his zealous participation in the GPCR and the form it took in his effort to correct the class situation, Ping-kok also fantasied replacing authority figures or father-surrogates in society:

> One could stand out even to the extent of many
> people [including myself] thinking that the author-
> ities, after these existing authorities were des-
> troyed, would be themselves. There were many of us
> students who thought this way . . . Nevertheless,
> later consequences all caused us to lose hope.[97]

Ping-kok further asserts that at the outset of the GPCR, he wanted to be a hero:

> At the very beginning my brain was completely
> filled with those thoughts (i.e., of being a
> hero and heroics)--some thoughts like overthrow-
> ing the capitalist-roader authorities and later
> everything would be better! I was completely
> full of those sorts of thoughts.[98]

Ping-kok never made a connection in his mind between the term "capitalist-roader" and his father's "objective" classification as a capitalist before 1949.

Young, and lacking any previous deep political experience, Lo Ping-kok reflects that his decision to throw himself into the movement when it was later only to prove counter-productive to his own interests was also the result of his naivete. He says:

> At that time, I still didn't understand society. I was merely concerned about my studies and what work I would eventually do. But I didn't predict in the least how the GPCR would develop. In reality, when the Cultural Revolution had been on a few months, it was not clearly revealed yet.[99]

For his older brother Ping-wen, class background had grown more of a nuisance to which he resigned himself as he got older, rather than a barrier suddenly placed in his way just when he was making the most "progress" and when peer acceptance was most important to him. Immobile, but never entirely excluded (i.e., he had old good-class friends even during the GPCR, which did not erupt until his late adolescence), Ping-wen had become cynical. On the other hand, Ping-kok, psychologically predisposed to actively contesting father and more attuned to the cues and pressures from the environment for political activity, met the sudden opposition to his mobility in the question of class background. The impact of this blockage was all the more profound for his having deliberately begged the question all along; divesting himself earlier of his class identity would have meant to him the complete renunciation of father and a total change of identity (adoption of the proletarian standpoint) he could not afford psychologically. Falling back at first on the precarious identification with father which could not satisfy his impulse to rebel, Ping-kok ultimately strove to resolve the conflict between proving himself in society by actively participating in the GPCR. In the end, he was beaten, and many of the people he had challenged were restored to power.

Lo Ping-kok had never broken the unconscious bond of his father's bourgeois values. The Cultural Revolution had been a personal fight for his own success, and certainly he could never qualify ideologically as a "revolutionary successor" because of his subjective interpretation of the Cultural Revolution and the fact that the restoration of former authorities "caused [him] to lose hope" about his place in the system.[100] When he did join the political struggle, he was replacing and representing his own father, and would never play son again. After the Cultural Revolution, when he was sent to the village and thrown into circumstances he found humiliating, he continued to strive for success in attaining an adult role. Ping-kok convinced himself that escape to Hong Kong was still a bolder form of self-assertion than militant participation in the GPCR. He says:

> I felt to escape to Hong Kong was a much more courageous action than waging the Cultural Revolution.[101]

SIGNIFICANCE OF LO BROTHERS

What is significant about the Lo brothers in demonstrating the variance in behavior in a vertical relationship between sons and father is both the resistance of the primary group to environmental change and its increasing susceptibility to such change. Both brothers were aware of the new environmental political norms; one moved to identify with them rather than with his "backward" father, but the other made scarcely a move at all. Although the two brothers at different intervals were forced to identify with father, the older brother's identification was induced by his own personality and the youngest son's was the product of both negative environmental re-enforcement for his attempt to be a part of the new society and declare himself separate from his father and by the residual emotional bond between father and son objectified in the class issue. Were it not for the class issue or the intransigence of an ideologically backward and dogmatic father, there would have been no need for young Ping-kok to be forced back on an identification with his father. If it was Ping-kok's weakness to be unable emotionally to sever completely the ties between father and son in sacrifice to society, perhaps the regime was demanding too much too soon in asking a Chinese son to make such a total psychological break from his family.

As a product of a bad class vertical father-son relationship, Ping-kok could only partly resolve the conflict between being what his father wanted and serving society. As often seemed to be the case, the vertical relationship

here demanded a total break in order to escape the imposing
figure of the father, and such a break would have engendered intolerable guilt.

FATHER-SON COMPETITION IN THE HORIZONTAL RELATIONSHIP AND POLITICAL PARTICIPATION: PAO KUO-FU

Generational rivalry seems to be more effective as a dynamic for political participation when it is predicated on a more horizontal interpersonal relationship between parent and child.[102] A youth can successfully compete with father within the relationship, without jeopardizing the continuance of the family relationship or being forced back on a complete identification with the father.

Even if the values of father and son are diametrically opposed in the more horizontal relationship, given a mutual respect for each other's autonomy, the son can maintain a dual-faceted existence without the need for secrecy or concealment.[103] For awhile until dissonance-causing circumstances push him to one side or the other, he can play a political role at school and remain relatively reticent about his activities in the presence of his father, if neither father nor son care to make politics a basis for relating to one another in conversation.[104]

Nevertheless, I think it can be safely assumed that a close, open, and relatively egalitarian relationship between father and son, as in the case of Pao Kuo-fu, can be conducive to shared values or value compromise. Such mutual respect, as we shall see below not only does not preclude generational rivalry but encourages it.

Pao Kuo-fu's father was technically of "petit-bourgeois" classification (*ch'eng-fen*), but his subjective background nonetheless was compatible with communist norms. He came from a peasant family (perhaps with a small plot of land of their own to till) and worked his own way through medical school as a part-time nurse, leading a very spartan life as a student. A doctor, he eventually, after "Liberation," became medical director of his hospital and Party branch secretary. In Pao Kuo-fu's own testimony:

> I feel my father was completely devoted to curing the illness to save the patient. Morally, he was upright. He was completely for the sick people.[105]

The elder Dr. Pao and his children were quite close. They respected one another. When Father could grab some free time away from his occupation with medical research and hospital work, he would take his children on outings. Pao Kuo-fu perceived him as a "protective."[106] Moreover, Father invited Kuo-fu to express his own opinions in family discussion and generally assert himself as an independent person:

> My family very much liked to listen to my opinion. They asked me what I wanted to do in the future, Whether I would be a doctor . . . I was not interested in politics then, so I rarely discussed it.[107]

Pao Kuo-fu cannot recall his father's ever beating him; his father preferred to reason with his children instead. Nevertheless, Kuo-fu's response to the story of the thirteen-year old Mao reflects his own disposition to assert his autonomy in the face of even mild scolding. Kuo-fu recalls this incident with mother:

> As you told this story, it caused me to recall a consequence that is worth reflecting on. Once I wanted something--it seems it was a book--but my older sister wouldn't let me read it . . . I was very angry. I picked up a shoe to throw it at her, but missed and hit the window behind, breaking it. When mama found out, she got angry . . . at that time, my mother scolded me and said: *"If you run out now, don't come back!"* "You don't want me--Do you mean to say I cannot live?" I replied. *Such a bold Chinese, I went out and ran off to school* . . . I thought that I wouldn't return . . . Mama and older sister came to fetch me. They came to school and saw my teacher. They all searched for me, so I hid. Very obstinate, they continued to look for me. I thought then: "They've looked so long; it's already 2:00 A.M. Although I'm angry inside, since mama was so good to come for me, I should not treat her with this attitude." I knew I was mistaken . . .[108]

Enjoying an open relationship with his parents in his childhood, Pao Kuo-fu listened intently as his mother spoke of his father's accomplishments. Not only did his mother tell him about how his father served the people medically and had worked his way through school,[109] but she also described an occasion, when an activist element in the Party, "papa had gone to Peking to meet Chairman Mao as a representative of the people of Kwangchow."[110]

At first, young Kuo-fu wanted to become a doctor like his father. His older brothers were scientists, but Kuo-fu felt that his father "needed an assistant for his research work."[111] Consequently, he showed only ritualistic interest in politics at school. He joined the YCL, as his father had joined the Party, but he "did not care much about politics; [his] father's influence was the main thing, and that was to exert [himself] in his studies."[112] This was Pao Kuo-fu's attitude when he began upper middle school:

> I could take or leave being a cadre. If you (impersonal) want me to serve as one, I will. If you don't, I won't.[113]

But with the onset of the Cultural Revolution Pao Kuo-fu suddenly took a radically different turn. His father had not placed himself so far above his son that he could not be effectively challenged from below. Putting aside his books which no longer seemed to him a feasible vehicle for success, Kuo-fu threw himself wholeheartedly into the movement by late August and became an activist "rebel" (*tsao-fan*) Red Guard, the leader of a small unit at first, outside the perimeters of the legitimate Red Guards. Asked how his father would have reacted to his participation, Kuo-fu became very indignant. Sitting on the edge of his chair, as if a nerve had been pinched, he declared in a voice a few decibals higher than usual:

> My father didn't discuss the question of my participation. *He did things his way, and I did things my way.* Nevertheless, I feel that everyone ought to make his own individual contribution to society.[114]

Had Pao Kuo-fu parted ways with his father? After all, his father was a Party cadre in addition to a medical expert. The answer to this question seems to be affirmative in the sense that Kuo-fu intended to strike out on his own in society, even if it meant--or perhaps because it meant--treading on his father's toes. Although Dr. Pao could not but accept the legitimacy of a political role in serving society, he also happened to be the butt of the very movement his son was helping to wage. The workers in his hospital had made Dr. Pao the No. 1 "capitalist-roader" in the hospital and the prime target of attack. And Pao Kuo-fu not only knew this fact but callously advised his father to take his medicine.

> When I went to Peking (on the *Ch'uan-lien*), I talked with him first. He said: "I didn't make any mistakes; my merits are 70% and my mistakes are 30%. I feel this way now and I will feel this way in the future until the day I die!" I said: "People have spoken excessively. Nevertheless, you ought to be more enlightened" . . . In reality, it was by no means as simple as I made it then.[115]

Circumstances insured that Pao Kuo-fu's decision to play an active role in the GPCR could not possibly reflect affective neutrality toward father. Kuo-fu notes that his father had come to him for sympathy and indirectly had sought an ally in him.[116] Yet, his decision to take his father's plight lightly at the moment and turn his back on him was not one which ideologically violated the long-range political standpoint of his father.

Pao Kuo-fu set off with his group to see Chairman Mao in Peking. If his father could serve society one way, he felt entitled to do it another--through waging revolution. But while he was in Peking, Kuo-fu received a cable that his father had died suddenly of a heart attack. Pao interpreted his death this way: "He got a serious illness from his anger; the government paid no attention to him, so he died."[117] As Pao perceived the situation, his father simply could not understand why, after the contributions he had made, he was being treated in such a manner.[118] In Pao's view, his father had been victimized by those like himself. Pao Kuo-fu's immediate reaction to his father's death was to make the defense of his father and those like him his *cause célèbre* thenceforth in the GPCR. Prior to the official formation per se of the *Hung Ch'i* (rebel) faction at his school, Pao Kuo-fu's militancy increased. He actually took the lead in a mass debate over struggling teachers:

> I got into one public debate just before the establishment of my faction. *At that time, my father had just died. Why he died and how he died--I analyzed in my own mind. Because of this, I spoke on the question of teachers. I offered my viewpoint, based*

> *on my father's situation.* Teachers were all good
> . . . Their purposely wanting to teach us to be
> bad--this situation was very rare . . . I didn't
> agree with making teachers crawl like dogs. I
> also quoted Mao Tse-tung: "As long as a person is
> not anti-party or anti-society, he is part of the
> people."[119] . . . A lot of people agreed with my
> opinion and there were those who opposed it. Be-
> cause of this, there was a debate and division
> into two large factions (i.e., *Hung Ch'i* and *Tung
> Feng*).[120]

Father's death provided Pao Kuo-fu with the opportunity to focus on the issue which he considered responsible for the attacks on his father; it was those attacks to which he ascribed the old man's heart failure. Through this action, young Pao was absolving himself of guilt and replacing his father at the same time. Circumstances changed, Pao Kuo-fu's motivation no longer was to involve father displacement; he had become his father but still fighting for an appropriate role in the new society. He further describes his subjectively motivated behavior then:

> I organized 300 students . . . the time of the
> division into factions--January [1967]--two months
> after my father died. This development of circum-
> stances could not but change my point of view . . .
> A lot of people hoped to take part in the Red
> Guards; their purposes were different. Some hoped
> to change society and thus founded an organization
> with one point of view . . . They wanted me to go
> along with them in founding a larger organization
> (i.e., out of the smaller units of fifteen or
> twenty persons in existence then, and of which he
> was one leader) . . . I summoned the small groups
> to come into our organization . . .[121]

And during the anarchic armed struggle between factions which ensued shortly, he "tried to make a contribution to society, cause the Red Guards to treat . . . the intellectuals, who had made a contribution to society, correctly."[122] He attributes this effort to the fact that his father's "misfortune had weighed heavily on him."[123]

However, with the failure of the *Hung Ch'i* faction to achieve ultimate success in the GPCR, Pao Kuo-fu lost interest in everything. He considered the "worst aspect of the GPCR" to be:

> The matter of my father's passing away and my
> failure to do anything about it. Then I lost
> interest in everything![124]

Pao Kuo-fu lost interest in his studies, in political activity, in all activity in the People's Republic of China.

Thus, we see in Pao Kuo-fu a touch of rebelliousness against father in his initial pursuit of an activity he knew to be inimical to his father's immediate dilemma then, consequent guilt when his father was fatally victimized by this sort of activity, an anxiety to change the direction of that activity and thereby assuage guilt and represent his father too, and his utter despair when he failed to accomplish his purpose. The father-son relationship had a definite bearing on Pao Kuo-fu's decision to engage zealously in the Cultural Revolution, and the death of the father shaped the content of his participation. But Pao Kuo-fu's essential choice of active political participation, at bottom, was not a breach of his father's values; it was an assertion of personal autonomy and mobility in adolescence with the aim of becoming his father's co-equal.

Not just a matter of defiance as in the vertical relationship, rivalry in the horizontal relationship is more intense and more salient because the son feels he stands a greater chance of success in being recognized by his father as an adult. Quite often, the proximity in status of father and son also will be accompanied or even abetted by a sharing of values. In this sort of situation, the son may find it easier to move up in the political system and embrace its values, as well as to assert himself against father, without having to move too far in either direction. Pao Kuo-fu was proceeding in this direction, but his father's death made of his participation in the GPCR an opportunity, indeed an emotional necessity, to represent what he perceived to be his father's cause and to identify too closely with it. Only the chance circumstance of his father's death seemed to make the competitive dynamic of generational rivalry here counterproductive in the end to Kuo-fu's fulfillment of the ideal of proving himself to father and to the ideological demands of the new society.

FEELING BIG

Participation in the Cultural Revolution meant a lot of things to many different people--keeping faith in the polity, response to a strong ideological appeal (concretized in the person of Chairman Mao), a path for upward mobility, the maintenance of position of in-group status and the quest for this status by "outsiders," an opportunity for "outsiders" to take revenge on the former in-group who had ostracized them, a temporary escape from routine schoolwork or perhaps just following the current. But all the active participants and many of the passives shared a common surge of adolescent self-importance as they assumed adult roles during the GPCR.

The GPCR was an opportunity to grow. Among Lan Wei-ying's reasons for his Red Guard activism was ideological commitment. He says: "To strengthen my nation . . . ; to write *ta-tzu-pao* or take part in an organization was just a manifestation of loyalty to Chairman Mao."[125] But he adds:

> I wanted to cut a smart figure. It's also possible that most youths wanted to feel important.[126]

Using his own experience as a frame of reference, Chou Chung-wang reminisces:

> It was as if he were a big hero. At the outset the Red Guard could wear an arm band and could speak as he pleased.[127]

And Yeh Hen, whose father had been classified as a class enemy, describes the fantasies of personal upward mobility pervading the atmosphere then:

> Everyone [at first] had this dream. Everyone felt that after the fighting, he might be Major or City Committeeman.[128]

For those who engaged in armed struggles, the Cultural Revolution became a real fight-to-the-death revolution. Wei Chao-fan says:

> At that time, I wasn't afraid. Only now am I afraid. I didn't know then that death was valueless. Then I felt self-righteous inside. Later, I was overthrown.[129]

But to some extent as well, playing at being an adult, as in modern Western society, could also describe the behavior of youths in the relatively free atmosphere existing at school during the GPCR. Reflecting intellectually now on the Cultural Revolution, Yang Ying-pu and Pao Kuo-fu each comment that perhaps factional warfare was to some extent an extension of childhood games; this time, however, they were dealing with "real enemies" and wielding real guns. The factional struggles even remind Pao Kuo-fu of how he imitated war heroes as a child. But both respondents assert that at the time, it did not seem like a game!

Trivial manifestations of adult role-playing were also characteristic of the freedom of the GPCR. Both Ch'iao and Wang mention that they began to smoke then. At his first interview, Ch'iao flaunted his cigarettes and remarked self-consciously that he began to smoke during the GPCR. Later, I explored the reasons. After expatiating on everything from tension to taste, Ch'iao states:

> There is also a rather laughable reason why I began smoking. It was as if when you took a drag on a cigarette, you might possibly appear more mature and grown up.[131]

As for Wang's smoking:

> There was this sort of inducement from the GPCR. For example, a Red Guard wanted to be master (*chu-jen*) . . . we did hope to become somewhat older and experienced, *like an adult*.[132]

Perhaps Chou Chung-wang's evaluation of his feeling during that period best reflects the emotional effects of personal autonomy and the illusion of mobility. Like so many others, Chou delighted in being able to assume a role in society, beyond the confines of school. "From the time I was born until I left China," he declares, "I felt that chapter in my life was the freest, freest in atmosphere."[133] He states:

> When we were struggling the provincial party committee, we detained, at our school, Chao Tzu-yang[134] and others who were the biggest authorities, and carried out struggle and criticism of them. At that time, we were very happy inside because these people were big figures before the GPCR. Who would have dared to shake them?! But now they knelt before us. If they said something, it was a pathetic response. I felt I was very great![135]

"Whose contribution to society was greater, yours or your father's, Mr. Chou?" He replies:

If I compare in that context [my father's] sphere
of service was rather narrow. He was merely
limited to a circle.[136] But my sphere was rather
broad and embraced the masses.[137]

This answer is no clear indicator of competitiveness in
Chou's case, but it is far from filial!

Militant participants in the GPCR as well as many of
the less militant participants, if not "tempered and
steeled" as proper revolutionaries, at least perceived
themselves as aged and made sophisticated in the process.
Lan Wei-ying's interpretation of his mother's reaction to
his telling her he was about to leave China is interesting:

Based on her weakness, if she was excited, normally
she would begin to cry. But possibly when she saw
that her own son had really grown up now, she was
not necessarily stimulated to cry.[138]

Thus, he and others had traced out an adult identity through
the GPCR, even if the nature of that identity precluded
staying in a Chinese village.

TWO EXTREME CASES ALONG A CONTINUUM OF CHANGE

No longer submissive as children, most persons I interviewed concerning their childhood, adolescence, and the GPCR
can be placed somewhere along a continuum of rebellious
self-expression. In today's society in the PRC, the adolescent cannot completely suppress his natural desire to replace his father. On the contrary, the environment encourages him to improve upon the older generation, and indirectly admonishes the father to learn from his son. Very
gradually, a horizontal relationship seems to be developing
between father and son.

The seepage of environmental change into the family
socialization process is slow. Since no one can predict
unilinear environmental change in Chinese society, one cannot be certain that integration between family and society
will proceed a certain way. However, indications now point
to a seemingly unalterable expansion of individual craving
for autonomy and rebellious self-expression, a dynamic for
political participation if properly chaneled and controlled.

Let us look at two extremes along the continuum of
change reflected in the sample--an example of identification with father in a conservative father-son relationship

and one of horizontal generational rivalry--and their relation to political participation in the GPCR.

A. Yüan Ching-po

Graduated from upper middle school in 1964, Yüan Ching-po had been unemployed for awhile and then only partly employed in a street factory before the outbreak of the Cultural Revolution. Yüan so identified with his father and his father's "class" that he perceived the GPCR from the outset as an attempt to undercut his own negative social identity and as an obstacle to his achieving success in a "proper" career, his supporting the family financially, and completing the filial circle.

From the time Yüan was a small boy, his father had been very strict with him and encroached on his autonomy. He examined Ching-po's homework weekly and ruled on which schoolmates could be his friends. Thus, even Yüan's peers were decided by father.[139] Despite Yüan's generally high academic standing, his father helped him prepare for the lower middle school matriculation examination, and even "guessed the questions."[140] In upper middle school Yüan sometimes had to come to his father's room to study and do his homework.[141] Later, when it became obvious that Yüan could not qualify for university because of his "class enemy" background, his father "was very worried and thus *thought of ways to help [him] find work.*"[142]

Yüan Ching-po never expressed an opinion in the household until after his father died in April 1966, when he suddenly came to play an advisory role in the home.[143] But until his father's death, Yüan was diffident and thoroughly obedient to his elders. His response to the Mao story:

> He should have taken his scolding. And after he was finished being scolded, the affair would have been settled.[144]

Yüan identified with his father politically. He sympathized with his father when he paced the floor at night anxious and guilt-ridden over his having informed to cadres on former KMT colleagues who had fled China. Yüan heeded his father's advice to be politically cautious and "never speak freely," lest one become a sacrifice to the new system.[145] Much later, when his co-workers questioned him about his apparent unfriendliness at the factory, Yüan apologized for his "personality."[146] He so identified with father that his own identity and father's seemed intertwined. Asked in interview whether his father was afraid of life, he replies: "He was born into a bad class (*ch'u-sheng-ti-pu-hao*); he was always afraid that political movements would cause trouble for him."[147] It is significant that the expression *ch'u-sheng-ti-pu-hao* (literally, born badly) is an idiom applying only to those of this generation whose class background is unavoidable because of birth, and should not be used to refer to someone of the last generation who voluntarily became a KMT and an historically determined "class enemy." Moreover, from the outset, Yüan Ching-po himself perceived the GPCR as causing trouble for him, when he could have joined in the movement as it developed. Father and son were united in their alienation from the system.

Yüan never even considered breaking away from his father's influence. In fact, in preparing his political autobiography for school, he made sure to show the text, only ritualistically critical of his parents' class, to his mother and father first. "It was I myself who wanted them to see it!" Yüan says.[148] Not only did Yüan never dream of becoming a cadre, but at a very early age he decided that to be a "progressive" was an "impossibility" for him.[149]

To the extent that Yüan could ever consciously feel anger toward his father, that hostility revolved about his own difficulty in finding an adequate job. Yüan wanted badly to prove himself to his family by becoming its source of financial support. Primarily, in accordance with his father's values, the path to career success started with attending a university. However, Yüan found that in 1964, when he sat for the university matriculation examinations, a record of redness in political behavior and class background took precedence over academic performance. Yüan was unable to qualify, and only then momentarily questioned his identity. He recalls his father's efforts to console him at that time:

> He felt that it was not something a person had control over. It was political . . . He just said that you don't have to go to university to learn; one could teach himself . . . At that time, I was emotionally confused, extraordinarily mixed up. I couldn't bear listening to this consolation at that time . . . I said: "You speak just to speak. But reality does not accord with what you are saying"

> . . . I told him he could teach himself . . .
> I was angry.[150]

Yüan was angry and frustrated because the father he wished to serve was depriving him, though through no choice of his own but as a consequence of his political classification, of a chance to succeed. In the new socio-political system, Yüan's dependency on father and identification with him constituted an obstacle to success and the completion of the filial circle.

In effect, Yüan was angry again when his father died in 1966, just a short while before the outbreak of the GPCR in the schools and factories, denying him the opportunity to prove himself to his father in the latter's lifetime. Yüan's understanding of his own emotional reaction then was that he felt guilty. He says:

> I was in real agony because I felt that he had taken care of and supported us far too long. Possibly I myself didn't give my parents advantages and was unable to support them . . . It has already been a few years since my father died, and I am still very guilty . . . He supported me so much, but I made no achievements in the area of enterprise or economically.[151]

In point of fact, Yüan's father did not support his family. Since "Liberation," he had been unemployed, and lay about the house, except for undertaking some odd jobs like tutoring in English.[152] The family depended largely on help from overseas relatives in Canada. Did Yüan really perceive his father as the family's supporter? He was the only person in my pool of respondents who, when asked what he would do if his father, as in the Mao story, unjustly accused him of laziness, responded: "I would see whether or not he was lazy himself."[153] Nor did Yüan's father ever so much as suggest that his only son was remiss in not finding a good job. Yüan acknowledges that his father realized it was not because "[Ching-po] did not want to work, but because of "class" that he could not find employment."[154]

Yüan had an emotional need himself to be a successful adult and complete the filial circle. His guilt over his father's death really seemed to be engendered not by his neglecting to fulfill genuine obligation to his father while the latter was alive, but by the anger Ching-po felt over his father's death's robbing him of the opportunity to prove himself and complete the filial circle in his

father's time. Rationalizing his later decision during the
GPCR to leave China--a decision he feels his father would
have disapproved were he alive--Yüan says: "I felt that
although my father had died, he had *died very conveniently*," i.e., before the suffering wrought by the GPCR.[155]

Yüan's purpose in life was to make a success of himself according to traditional "bourgeois" and intellectual
standards, with the end of materially aiding his family.
As a child, his heroes were those who led upright, smooth
lives and were still successful. He thoroughly identified
with his father. And when the GPCR came along, he regarded
it as an effort to undermine all that was of value to him
and his father. He empathized with the so-called "bourgeois" teachers targeted for struggle at school. He says:

> Of course, they were influenced by the bourgeois
> class, but I also was this way . . . I share
> something in common with my teachers.[156]

Most traumatic for Yüan at the outset of the GPCR was
the "Destroy Four Olds" (*Po-ssu-chiu*). Red Guards came to
his home and ransacked it in search of feudal and bourgeois
cultural objects. They destroyed books as well as objets
d'art. But what bothered Yüan most was that they burned
his father's Christian Bible, a book to which his father
had turned for solace and daily prayer.[157] These actions
were a threat to the status quo of Yüan Ching-po's psychological identity. Like the person seeking to explain his
own horror at rapid social change, Yüan exclaims, in recalling the "Four Olds":

> We Chinese ought to have our own extant traditions
> . . . Chinese tradition in the area of morality
> and culture was conservative. If we consistently
> followed China's old traditions in our actions, it
> would seem that the present wave of criminal activ-
> ity in our society would be reduced.[158]

But was *traditional* Chinese morality and culture represented
by a Christian Bible? No, but his father's was!

Apart from perceiving the GPCR as a threat to his identity, Yüan considered participation in such a political
movement to be a waste of the energy he was saving for his
own version of personal success. Yüan resented political
activists at school and managerial cadres at work for being
"opportunists" who acted for personal advancement.[159] But
Yüan himself would have "seized the hour" if he had

possessed the confidence that in the end he would accomplish his own ideal. He explains his attitude toward participation in the Cultural Revolution:

> If I wasted my emotional energy, then I wouldn't be able to obtain the things I wanted. This is very unworthwhile. Because you must pay the price for a certain sort of thing--in time or some other commodity--in order to strive for a certain goal. But if in the end you can not obtain it, this is a very unfortunate thing for you . . . . If you put your body and soul into the GPCR, it would have no advantage for you. One must not waste emotional energy.[160]

Yüan's difficulty had been in making a place for himself, consistent with his own career values, in an adult world. He feels that part of himself, like his father's personality, is "hesitant and irresolute."[161] He believes he only overcame this aspect of his personality once--"in coming to Hong Kong and completing a matter."[162] Yüan says:

> This is a thing which I carried off rather successfully. In order to come to Hong Kong, I spent a lot of years and emotional energy and thought of a lot of methods in order to be able to succeed in the end . . . Now that I got here, isn't it an enterprise representing great success![163]

To this end, he rationalized that his father, who would have disapproved his leaving China, had died "conveniently" and escaped the bitterness of the Cultural Revolution and the post-GPCR *hsia-hsiang*.[164] As he prepared to leave, his dreams at night were filled with images of his father supporting his wish to leave China; after failing the first time and turning back, he dreamed of his father saying to him, "All right, go ahead!"[165] While he had to rationalize his guilt over acting independently of his father, in reality he could not extricate himself from that psychological dependency. He often dreamed also of his father standing silently at his side as he worked or as he conversed with peers.[166] And although he made it successfully to Hong Kong, he now finds himself "plagued once again" by that part of his personality which is "slow-moving [like father's]."[167] His inertia is his father's.

B. Chu Nan-po

Chu Nan-po became a Red Guard leader in the *Hung Ch'i* faction at his upper middle school during the Cultural Revolution. He organized a Red Guard unit of fourteen students in August 1966, and later represented the unit at higher level meetings. Eventually, he became one of the three leaders in a group of three hundred members, and was responsible for organizational and propaganda tasks.

From his early childhood onward, Chu Nan-po enjoyed an open relationship with his father. His father punished him rationally, and seldom found it necessary to resort to beatings.[168] Chu feels that if ever his father did beat him unjustly, he "would have had the guts" to reason with him. Nan-po says:

> I would not oppose his beating me. I would oppose the fact that what he said was unreasonable.[169]

If his father had been the type to punish arbitrarily at frequent intervals, Chu says: "It is very possible I would have left home."[170] But the elder Mr. Chu was tolerant of Nan-po even when angry at him, and would encourage him to "speak out" and defend himself. If young Nan-po's excuse happened to be "just so much mumbo-jumbo, then he would blow up . . . [but] if it made sense, then he would not lose his temper."[171]

Always identifying with his father's personality and expressing greater affection for him than for his mother,[172] Chu Nan-po felt close to his father. Although Nan-po recalls that his father was frequently irritated with him for disturbances in bed when the boy slept together with his parents as a toddler,[173] he feels that he and his father developed a much greater affinity for one another emotionally in later years.[174] Indeed, Chu Nan-po's happiest period was in late primary and lower middle school when he had no anxieties and his "father took care of [him]."[175] Chu Nan-po recalls their relationship during his pre-adolescence:

> We were equal! I had some of these feelings. When I was small, he was rather upset with me; after I got older and had a mature personality, it was easier to be compatible . . . But it was still a father-son relationship; there was still a taste of taking orders.[176]

It was the growing, but not complete, horizontality of their relationship that served as the groundwork for Chu Nan-po's rivalry and adolescent push for increased autonomy. Chu Nan-po feels that his father's closeness to him when he reached pre-adolescence was based on the elder Chu's interest in serving as a teacher and guide to a maturing son.[177] Moreover, Nan-po's father liked to listen, and by the time of his entry into upper middle school, the two men were even more intimate.[178] The proximity of father and son fed the autonomy of the maturing Chu Nan-po and stirred him to greater mobility vis-à-vis authority figures at school as well.

In lower middle school and upper middle school, Chu Nan-po's drive to assert himself in the short run almost impaired his long-run quest for mobility. Politically active and conscientious in productive labor all along, he was eager to join the YCL and later even to join the Communist Party in order to gain personal prestige and "bring glory on his ancestors."[179] Desire for personal achievement and proving self to family was confused with an ideological wish to serve the socialist society. However, socialized for upward mobility in the home, Chu would not tolerate those teachers who were still less permissive than his father. Thus, Chu's effort to qualify for the YCL was frustrated by his repeated outbursts against his teachers.[180] By the time he got to upper middle school, Chu Nan-po had a flagrant confrontation with one teacher who had awarded a higher grade in penmanship to a female student, rather than to Chu who prided himself in his calligraphy. According to Chu:

> I cursed this teacher behind his back and wrote on the blackboard: "Teacher is unjust in his grading." Afterward, when the teacher found out, he had the school admonish me--hold a meeting to admonish me.[181]

Although these struggles for individual recognition through self-assertion vis-à-vis authorities at school prevented Chu from getting into the YCL, they were an important dynamic in his zealous participation in the Cultural Revolution and in his targeting of certain teachers. He resented their infringement on his individual autonomy and their denial to him of the prerogative of questioning them. His defiance of teachers during the GPCR seemed to fulfill the same adolescent emotional need as his defiance of his father who opposed his participation in the Cultural Revolution.

Questioned about his frequent mischief in class before the GPCR, Chu Nan-po explains:

> What he [teacher] said I had accepted and obeyed. When I was small my personality was more placid . . . As the years went on, I felt that what the teacher said was not necessarily correct (*pu-yi-ting-tui*). Therefore, I didn't much obey what he said.[182]

And questioned about his defiance of his father who, on the basis of *Po-ssu-chiu*, opposed his youngest son's active participation in the GPCR, Chu Nan-po says:

> [I nevertheless participated] *because what parents say is not completely correct (pu-shih-wan-ch'uan-tui)*. If you are completely obedient to him, you have no autonomy yourself. Then to be a person has no meaning. If you obey the directions of others, you yourself will have no independent point of view. The measure of filiality should be respect for parents and whether your relations with parents are intimate. He told me not to get involved in the GPCR. I felt it was a good thing . . . Therefore, I didn't obey him.[183]

Chu Nan-po explains the motivation behind his composing numerous *ta-tzu-pao* himself, emotionally criticizing teachers and cadres:

> The authorities at school had no ability. Moreover, the binds upon the student in the system were too fierce . . . Because I made a very tiny mistake, they recorded it as a big error. In 1963-1964, my mistake was having a run-in with the Chinese language teacher. I said he gave me a low grade. If there had been no GPCR, I wouldn't have had any way to express my discontent and opinion toward them.[184]

And Chu Nan-po explains his defiance, unfilial by traditional standards, of his father's adamant request that he abstain from the GPCR because of the personal risk to himself and others:

> We Chinese of the current era cast off the feudal customs of the past few decades and feel there is no such thing as "filial" or "unfilial" . . . I

generally rather respect parents, but this point doesn't figure as [traditional] filialism . . . Not to obey is not unfilial.[185]

Thus, Chu Nan-po felt that, as a child of the post-revolutionary epoch, it was his right to rebel, to express himself as an individual, and to "be a person." He did not feel an obligation to obey unreservedly either his teachers at school or his own father, or to accept their judgment as final. Chu Nan-po's eagerness for self-expression at school made him appear too undisciplined for YCL membership, but it found an ideal channel for release in the GPCR. In the Cultural Revolution, Chu Nan-po could assert his personality as he strove to realize his earlier ambitions of upward mobility in society. Did Nan-po feel that his father's advice against participation in the Cultural Revolution even as early as August 1966 was ideologically backward, and hence not deserving of any consideration? He answers:

I always feel older people's thoughts are backward and not with the current of the times.[186]

Quite the opposite of Yüan, who remained submissive to authority and rationalized that he was saving his energies for a non-political achievement that would have pleased his father, Chu Nan-po leaped at the chance to assert himself against the authorities, increase his stature, and advance himself in the "revolutionary" cause of serving the nation politically, a long-range occupational direction to which his father earlier had given his approval. Although Chu Nan-po resisted his father's opposition to his participation in the GPCR and to his risking his life in armed factional struggles (he proudly asserts: "I don't think father would have ever participated in the *wu-tou* if he had the opportunity"[187]), his behavior was not really inconsistent with the political values he had learned in the home. The elder Chu had always told him that what the teacher "taught was the standard" and that he should be politically activist at school; father's historical anecdotes were consonant with the dialectic interpretation of history which he had learned in school.[188] Chu Nan-po's father was openly pleased with all his sons' political accomplishments at school. Although a pall seemed to set over the home when he tried to discuss political questions directly, Chu Nan-po always attributed this phenomenon to the parents' lack of confidence in their own ideological adequacy.[189] Thus, when Chu Nan-po joined in the GPCR, although defying his father's authority to deter him at the moment and challenging the teachers who like his father also thought that what they taught was the "standard" and their decisions beyond question, he still really was staying within the limits of the essential behavioral norms his father approved. Chu Nan-po perceived the Cultural Revolution as his opportunity to make it. He would not let his father stand in the way. This was Chu Nan-po's end objective in participating in the GPCR:

> Our nation's reform depended on us youths. Therefore, during the GPCR, we had this ideal. Second, through the Red Guard activity of a self-made organization, I would evaluate my own ability to work.[190]

Through the Cultural Revolution, Chu Nan-po could strive for an adult identity in personal stature and work role. Moreover, he was able to link his own self-aggrandizement to the legitimate ideal of serving society. He says:

> At that time, I felt participating in the Red Guards was like being a big man. As a Red Guard, I dared to say anything.[191]

and:

> I felt that to be a man after one's talent is developed, one should make a contribution to the people and country.[192]

This was an ideal he had discussed earlier in small political study groups at school and which he now could attempt to realize through his own initiative in the GPCR.[193] Chu Nan-po at the outset might have seemed like the closest embodiment of the ideal blend between the individual's psychological quest for autonomy and the political goal learned at school of "serving the masses." But the question was whether his autonomy, which in the company of political values had governed his participation in the GPCR and grown in the course of that activity, could be submerged once again in the authorities' version of what constituted service to society?

Like the intellectuals of the May Fourth, Chu Nan-po projected his own perceived growth in personal autonomy and freedom on a *subjective* ideological hope. This was his personal goal, not the official one, for the GPCR:

The main thing was consideration of the whole nation. Through the students', workers' and peasants' movement, to make the country even better and let the people be freer.[194]

Also, Nan-po's self had become too inflated to accept the submissive humiliation in store for him as the GPCR subsided. He states:

I particularly liked the Cultural Revolution because it was this way then. Mao Tse-tung produced the Red Guards to conduct a political revolution, a cultural revolution and an economic revolution. He used the Red Guards for all aspects. I thought . . . that by means of the GPCR, we would reform the political system . . . But the outcome was the reverse! The outcome of the GPCR was that we toilers for the GPCR were sent to the villages to till the fields. They wanted *us* to till the field. That was just too hard to take! Ha![195]

NON-POLITICAL COMPETITION IN A PROLETARIAN FAMILY

We have examined the child of non-red class background whose avenue for generational rivalry was in political activity, who responded to the call for "generational successors," and who participated in the GPCR. Would it be possible for a child of red background to remain more unresponsive to the Maoist call for revolutionary successors and to compete with his father along non-political lines? After all, unlike the youth of "questionable" background, he could hide behind his "class" to engage in what might otherwise be conceived of as politically passive behavior. Moreover, since his father was already adjudged relatively pure politically, could the youth perhaps derive as much psychological satisfaction from non-political competition as from surpassing his father in the political arena? The case of Chai Cheng-li, from a family of workers going back three generations, should make these questions salient for future research.

Chai's father was a skilled worker who "revered Mao Tse-tung" and said "Chiang Kai-shek was a useless tool (*hsiang-huo*), a corrupt man."[196] In the perception of his son, the older man "truly looked up to the Communist Party, not falsely."[197] And yet Chai's father, a man of intellectual curiosity, who gained his middle school diploma after work and who read engineering manuals in his spare time, allowed free debate in his household and would even tolerate his son's occasional anti-orthodox political beliefs. "He believed in the Communist Party," says Chai, "so he didn't care what you believed in."[198] Nevertheless, Chai's father was a severe disciplinarian in all other areas, particularly his son's performance in school. If young Chai's grades fell, the older man would often beat him with a stick.[199] According to Cheng-li:

> To outsiders, [father] was very warm. But to family members, he was very dictatorial . . . Papa's words were the law and we had to follow it.[200]

Thus, except in the area of political debate which the father seemed to enjoy and even encourage, he was an authoritarian parent. Chai believed that a typical father in China could hit his son as much as he liked with impunity.[201] Nor would Chai dare to oppose his father.[202] Chai can recall vividly an instance of arbitrary and unjust punishment at the hand of his father:

> Once a schoolmate left his work report in my briefcase. When I came home after school, my father asked me to go out on the street and buy some things. When I came back, my father had seen my schoolmate's work report, had mistaken it for mine, and noticed that it was bad. And so he gave me a beating. Once he realized later on that it wasn't my work report, he still didn't apologize to me.[203]

Chai was hurt because it was his father's overt lack of remorse that really stuck in his memory, but he was able to tell himself that "for a father to apologize to his son is a loss of face."[204]

Chai's father was traditionally authoritarian, and in passively submitting to his father's sometimes unfair punishments, Cheng-li was a traditional son. The vertical relationship between father and son was further highlighted by the father's failure, conspicuous to his son, ever to praise him for his achievements either in the presence of others or in conversation between them.[205] Chai rationalized again that his father "privately was proud of his intelligence."[206] Thus, this proletarian family was characterized by a vertical inter-generational relationship, but with two distinct features:

1) The father tolerated and enjoyed political debate in the household.
2) In spite of his proletarian background, the father respected book learning and made academic excellence the sternest of demands on his offspring.

Chai reacted to his father's strong commitment to communism and political activism with contempt. Chai says he always felt that if his father so strongly favored the system, he should have risen to the position of cadre or even factory manager.[207] The elder Chai had even attended university for awhile to be trained specifically as a cadre, but according to his son, had balked at the responsibility of overseeing and informing on others.[208] Cheng-li feels his father was too "righteous" for his own good.[209]

Because his class background protected him to a great extent from harsh political indictment at school, Chai Cheng-li never assumed a leadership position in the Pioneers or aspired to be an activist or YCL member. "We [good classers]," he remarks, "were still better off than activists with bad class background."[210] To Chai Cheng-li, Father's expatiations at home about communist ideals were just so much braying. Young Chai devoted himself instead to intellectual pursuits. When a YCL member deliberately sought him out as a friend and urged him to take a greater interest in political organization, Chai used various ruses to avoid his company.[211] Chai's primary concern then was getting into university, and he comments that "only if [his] class background had been bad would [he] have used political progressiveness to get by."[212]

Even if one can accept Chai's choice of intellectual pursuits as his primary concern without any keen sense that he was necessarily competing with his father, both the role of Chai's mother and his choice of major concentration at university point to the motivation of rivalry with father. Chai's mother was an upper middle school graduate by the time of "Liberation." During the Anti-Japanese war, she had joined a unit of the KMT for a few months as a telegraph operator and then, "feeling the KMT was corrupt," withdrew.[213] Chai notes that although she spoke of her disenchantment with the KMT, she openly expressed her dissatisfaction with the communists. The following quotation is especially interesting not only because it reflects his mother's open contempt for his father's politics but because of the contrast between being an intellectual and being a communist. He states:

After Liberation, *because she was an intellectual*, she was very unsatisfied with the communist set of values. She hated them . . . At home she publicly expressed her dissatisfaction with the Communist Party and frequently instructed my papa, saying he was ignorant.[214]

Asked how his father would respond to an anti-communist remark from his mother, Chai replies:

He didn't make a sound or engage in dialogue. So my education from the time I was small was both red and black.[215]

Was his father perhaps afraid of being humiliated further before his children?

In effect, driving a greater wedge between son and father, Chai's mother, herself a frustrated author and now a middle school teacher, "consistently expressed the hope that [Chai Cheng-li] would follow through in [her] ambition (i.e., to be an author)."[216] His father, on the other hand, felt that he should learn a skill like electronics, in order that Cheng-li might "succeed him at work." According to Chai Cheng-li, his father argued that in the new society, practical study of this sort "would guarantee that [he] never would have a problem with regard to livelihood."[217]

For Chai, the chasm between intellectual and proletarian grew wider: his father was a proletarian, his mother an intellectual.[218] Even his mother's favorable words to her son when he was younger about his father had been backhanded compliments which served to deprecate the father's proletarian identity. Chai states:

When she disciplined me as a child she would say: *"Although your father is a worker*, he never spoke coarsely or crudely or scolded people. He is very courteous. *You're a student. Why do you speak so coarsely?"*

Question: How did your mother feel generally about workers?

She had no prejudice. Well, anyway, she felt a worker was one rung lower than an intellectual.[219]

Indeed, in the word association test administered at a different time, Chai, responding all along in opposites (e.g., masses--leader; father--son), concludes with intellectuals--proletariat.[220]

In the end, Chai Cheng-li chose to major in Chinese literature at the university. To please his mother, he had pitted himself against his father's better judgment and the man it represented. Chai could read a mechanical manual cover-to-cover several times (and he was to experiment with this alternative when the GPCR interrupted his education), but he could not retain one axiom or fact.[221] He had a mental set against learning manual skills.

A *Chu-yi-ping* in name for only a few weeks, Chai abstained from participation in the GPCR by the time of the "Four Olds" (*Po-ssu-chiu*). At first, the prospect of participating in the *Chu-yi-ping* was a sort of privilege, but he could not sustain any interest in it at all.[222] The GPCR had interrupted Chai Cheng-li's education, and yet when asked what disturbed him most about the movement, he replies that it was the restoration of normality on campus and the return to classes. Why? Chai reflects:

> When the propaganda work team (*hsüan-ch'uan-tui*) entered my school (ed. the respondent refers to the people's propaganda teams in late summer 1968),[223] they didn't understand anything at all and were our teachers.
>
> Question: How did you handle this?
>
> There was nothing I could do. My father was also on the work team.[224]

Chai did not protest openly, but curiously lost interest in school, volunteered to *hsia-hsiang*, and determined to leave the PRC. He is now studying literature at a private KMT-sponsored college in Hong Kong, writing articles in semi-classical style for local newspapers, and thinking of applying to Taiwan University to resume serious study of the Chinese Classics.

SOME FURTHER COMMENTS ON THE COMPETITIVE DYNAMIC

Competition with father or father-surrogates[225] seems to have been one key variable in influencing the active political participation of adolescents in the GPCR or shaping its content and giving it direction. The Chinese child now is openly sensitive to and resents parental encroachment on his autonomy. One might hypothesize that the earlier cultural need to suppress one's self made the developing pattern of self-assertion and open rivalry with parents more obvious and flamboyant.[226] Although it is more difficult in a vertical relationship than in a horizontal one for the child to assert himself successfully against his father's influence, the competitive dynamic can still be operative. The difficulty in a vertical relationship is that rebellion of a political and social type tends to be more tenuous and susceptible to being aborted by the guilt engendered in defying father and by a greater need on the part of the young individual to have his behavior reinforced and supported by the outer social environment. In a horizontal relationship between father and son, generational rivalry can be more intense because a son's proximity to his father on the social ladder makes the idea of replacing him more realistic. Moreover, generational rivalry through political channels is likely to be more salient because the closeness of the father to his son is more conducive to value compromise and to the father's willingness to identify vicariously with his son's achievements.

Although the pool of respondents on which this study is based is small and can at best only be impressionistic on the quantitative basis, I think it still would be illuminating to comment briefly on the responses of my total group of informants in reference to the discussion of the paradigm cases above. All but two of the militant activists in the whole group indicated generational cleavage and rivalry with father; all those who actually led Red Guard units were openly competitive with their fathers.[227] Of the fourteen "horizontals" in the group, all were overtly competitive with father; eleven of these were Red Guard Participants, and nine militantly so; the other three "horizontals" who abstained were of "class enemy" background and indicated acute social alienation from early childhood.[228] Of the twelve clearly-indicated "verticals," only six were overtly competitive with father, though most indicated awareness of hostility toward their fathers in anger-provoking situations; all six "competitives" in this category were Red Guards.

A parent's political values could be important but were not the key factor in a child's course of competitive behavior. Some children of politically active fathers, like the worker Chai or peasant Tseng, abstained or assumed only passive roles in the GPCR, perhaps even because their fathers were so politically involved.

Others, like the Huangs, who could choose between the father's bad class label and his subjectively activist political stance, were compelled by both personality and environment to compete on the basis of the former identity. And some offspring of blatantly ideologically backward parents, like Lo Ping-kok, became active political participants.

In the political participation of youths during the Cultural Revolution, when variables other than generational rivalry were also clearly indicated, the competitive dynamic still seems to have lurked in the background as a complementary force for directed rebellion (Lan Wei-ying in Chapter 6, for example).

Father-son competition was not only an inducement to participation, but it could also shape the content of participation. In the two cases where competition was interrupted by the death of father and concomitant feelings of strong guilt, the son continued to utilize the political forum as an arena for his self-expression. He made his father, in essence, a *cause celèbre* and in so doing not only ameliorated his guilt but moved from the level of competing with father to replacing father.

All instances of classic adolescent competition with father and/or father-surrogates will inexorably be followed by guilt feelings. Not one of the Red Guard militants in the whole pool of respondents escaped this emotion. Interestingly, even those like Yüan and Lo Ping-wen who abstained from the GPCR felt tremendous guilt in their decision to leave China. The very act of abandoning home and country was an unfilial, unloyal assertion of individual autonomy, cutting against the grain of culture, past and present.[229]

When generational rivalry and the assertion of individual autonomy affected the political behavior of adolescents, the rivalry was always within the threshold of tolerance of the father's own body of values. Thus, the choice of political involvement as an arena for playing out generational rivalry was predicated always on the father's acceptance of that activity as a legitimate form of achievement, as a bonafide pathway for his son to *prove himself*.[230] Pao Kuo-fu's mother described his father as politically active and proudly told her son of Dr. Pao's official visit to meet Chairman Mao; Chu Nan-po received parental accolades for his achievement in the Pioneers; and even Lo Ping-kok could make the "class issue" in the GPCR a *cause celèbre* through which he could represent his deceased father and rationalize that through his GPCR activity, he was actually conforming to his father's emphasis on personal success in society.

Of course, the regime still faces the problem of whether proving oneself to family can be made consonant with proving oneself to nation and the revolutionary tide of history. This contradiction is perhaps one that can be resolved over time as intra-family relationships become more enlightened, horizontal in form, and potentially progressive in content. Present trends seem to indicate a growing responsiveness on the part of not only the son but the father as well to the new behavioral norms cast into relief since "Liberation." If a father can learn to encourage autonomy just as the son is encouraged to seek that autonomy from him, then both father and son alike should develop a sensitivity as well to the new political values and ideals. But would a youth whose father is "politically positive" rebel by deliberately abstaining from political participation? Unless, in the future, politically positive values are not shared by both parents in the home or are perceived as irrelevant to real adult roles and values, as among many rebellious American youths today, there would be no reason for youth rebellion and self-assertion to be politically "reactionary."

5. Peer Relations and Political Participation in the GPCR

As the Cultural Revolution proceeded in the schools, the formation of Red Guard groups and the recruitment of new members were heavily influenced by peer relations and the pressures exerted by peers. To a certain extent, a student's decision to participate in the GPCR, whether as a mere follower or in a more active way, partly could have been affected by his susceptibility to being influenced by the behavior of his friends. Among the more passive participants, peer pressure often was the predominant motivation for participation. The decision to abstain altogether also could have been influenced by affiliation with an anti-social, "backward" element or with friends who, out of an understanding perhaps that the individual in question had a severely bad class background and might thereby jeopardize himself by becoming involved in the movement, advised him to remain aloof from the activity.

Since the Cultural Revolution was relatively free institutionally and left a considerable authority vacuum, adolescent youths were cast adrift together in a fluid milieu. At the juncture of pre-adolescence and adolescence, it is not unusual for peer relations to play a key role in an individual's psychological growth. In searching for an adult identity, he sees himself in the mirror of peer behavior, and often is heavily dependent on the acceptance of his peers. The Chinese youth during the GPCR was separated from the institutionalized group activities, including the small political study groups for awhile, but he was not removed from the currents and counter-currents of informal peer group activity.

Some youths, however, were more receptive to peer group activities than others. Ability to relate to one's peers seemed to depend in part on the degree of one's self-esteem and the extent to which trust in others had been inculcated in the home and reinforced at school. In the childhood home environment, it appears that the more

horizontal the relationship between parent(s) and son and
the greater the element of mutual trust between them, the
more likely a youth was to place faith in his peers and
relate easily to them. Quantitatively, thirteen out of
fourteen "horizontals" made friends easily at school and
demonstrated a high degree of trust in others. Ch'en, for
instance, had a facility for making friends, and often introduced himself to unfamiliar schoolmates.[1] Ch'en's
household was very egalitarian. His mother deceased, he
lived together with his brother and father, and decisions
were reached "democratically." In fact, at one point in
the interview, he slips and refers to his father, brother
and himself as "we three brothers."[2] The following is an
excerpt from his word association test:

Q. Son
A. Friend
Q. Friend
A. Father[3]

Except for several cases where ease in relating to others
was observable to the interviewer, the measure of trust
depended on the respondent's direct self-evaluation, as
well as on responses to questions concerning degree of
willingness to confide in close friends and speak easily
with casual friends; questions concerning willingness to
share valued possessions as a child and adolescent; questions concerning willingness to join in informal discussion among unintimate peers or to introduce oneself to an
unknown schoolmate. Although there was nearly a one
hundred percent correlation of high trust with horizontal
family socialization, only four persons from the vertical
category (total N. = 12) exhibited a *fair* level of trust
with others. All those who stated that no one outside the
family could ever be trusted were from vertical background.[4]

Nevertheless, even among the "verticals," ability to
relate in some way to peers was far more varied (indeed
most belonged to peer groups and only a few really isolated
themselves). This phenomenon appears to suggest that a
number of other factors intervene in affecting the course
of peer relations. The Chinese adolescent or pre-adolescent in my sample who had no friends was a departure from
the norm. Many respondents state that if one were to have
no friends, one would either "wither" or become emotionally
ill.

For most respondents, serious friendship and peer
group association began after Primary five at about age

thirteen.[5] The GPCR caught most of my respondents in the last year of lower middle school or early years of upper middle school. Friends drew one another into their small Red Guard units.[6] The peer pressure on the individual to participate in some fashion--even tokenly--was intense. To resist at the outset, as many did, was all the more remarkable.[7]

The atmosphere of fresh camaraderie which the GPCR created had a strong appeal to many adolescents. According to Chu Nan-po, it was a time for losing some old friends and gaining many new ones.[8] For those with relatively extroverted personalities, the GPCR provided greater breadth for self-expression and forming new peer relations. Lan Wei-ying, who often liked to have long conversations with friends and associates before the Cultural Revolution, now found himself debating total strangers in the street about newly-posted *ta-tzu-pao*, and enjoying every minute of the spontaneous, public conversation.[9] Even the rather shy Chou Chung-wang was drawn out of his shell and discovered that friendship came easier during this period. He describes the effect of the changed atmosphere:

> I made rather numerous friends . . . On the one hand, it was due to the relations between comrades; everyone had common thoughts and common points of view. On the other hand, it was because the period of the GPCR was freer than any other time before. I already told you how free I felt during this brief period. We could carry out rather frank conversations among ourselves and honestly declare our opinions in public and exchange thoughts.[10]

The *Ch'uan-lien* itself was a further opportunity for the individual to strengthen bonds between friends and meet new comrades, sometimes culturally and geographically quite removed from oneself. Pao Kuo-fu had sexual relations for the first time with a female companion on the road. Lan Wei-ying and Yü Ming-li particularly like to reminisce about the new friends they made in Peking, Shanghai, Tientsin and far-away places, and how they continued to correspond with them after returning home.[11] Yü fondly recalls striking up a relationship in Ninghsia with a *Hung Ch'i*, a member of the *Hui* ethno-cultural minority group.

> We were compatible in thought . . . we went to Inner Mongolia, Peking, Shanghai together, and he also stayed at my house for a week before going

back to Ninghsia . . . We met in this fashion: I went to XX City. I wanted to buy a map. I asked a person, "Comrade, where is there a local map for sale?" He asked me where I was from. I said, "Kwangchow." He said, "So far!" and he asked me where I was staying. I said that I had nowhere to live, so he told me to billet at his factory. Thus, I got to know him and we gradually became close.[12]

THE PASSIVE RED GUARDS

More than one third (N. = 13), a plurality of the respondents, fall into the passive category. They attended meetings and struggle sessions during summer 1966, but never assumed a position of responsibility and seldom stayed on for the first armed struggle between factions. One passive, Red Guard follower described the way he was drawn into early Cultural Revolution activity.

On the one hand, I joined because my schoolmates participated. On the other hand, it was because I had nothing to do at home. When they asked me to take part, I participated. It was they who wanted me to take part.[13]

Simply to explain passive participation as a natural phenomenon of the whirlwind effect of a political movement or in terms of ritualistic genuflections to the polity is not wholly adequate. With the collapse of authority, disintegration of normal organizations and the eventual danger of joining the "wrong" faction, the lure to abstain was at least as much of a counter-pressure.

During the early phase of the GPCR, from May 1966 through the beginning of the next year, peer pull seemed to serve positively as either a prime inducement to joining a Red Guard faction or at least as an important factor in reinforcing basic responses to ideological positions and subjective needs for self-expression. Because of his uneasiness over "class"[14] and sympathies with strategic and ideological positions of the "rebels," Yü was predisposed to joining the *Hung Ch'i* faction. In his words:

My thoughts inclined toward the *Hung Ch'i* faction . . . Even if the *Tung Feng* people had tried to pull me into their organization, I would not have joined. Because I basically had nothing in common with them.[15]

Questions of political stance and personal friendship ties were difficult to separate in Yü's case. As an upper middle school student before the Cultural Revolution, he had become part of a closely knit clique.[16] When the GPCR materialized, Yü found that all his good friends had attached themselves to the *Hung Ch'i* faction. Apparently, this consideration took precedence over others, even the chance of his faction's failure. He states:

> Even if I had known in advance that the organization I participated in would fall from power, I would still not have taken part in the *Tung Feng* faction . . . If some had participated in the *Tung Feng*, then possibly I would have participated. Because if I were together with intimate friends, then I wouldn't feel isolated . . . In my case, the influence of friends was rather large.[17]

But neither ideological inclination, hatred of the good class children, nor friendship ties were sufficient to impel Yü into active participation. He returned home not long after the first armed factional struggle was getting underway.

Widespread among the passive participants in the GPCR were young people who, prior to the movement, had constituted an aggregate of bourgeois-types, still somewhat maladjusted to the new system. These people were on the outside but lacked any desire to get inside. Nevertheless, by virtue of their politically negative cohesion, they could constitute a reservoir of potential GPCR recruits which, once tapped, would pour into participation. If one or two informal group leaders of such a clique could be persuaded to join the Red Guards, the others, wary of losing the few friends they had, might follow suit.

As a young child, Yeh Hen was unable to resolve successfully the conflict between his father's "pre-Liberation" status as a capitalist and his own position in the new society. Young Yeh was eager enough to be accepted at school, but he actually thought it reflected well on himself to admit, even in study group, that his father was a capitalist, "not a bureaucratic capitalist who used official position to oppress the people . . . [but] an ordinary person who did business . . . and earned money."[18] Yeh Hen, in fact, was proud of his father's personal success ("I liked to say my father was a bourgeoisie"),[19] and says he was shocked that the others in his primary school group not only would not agree with him but criticized him for "supporting the interests of the bourgeoisie."[20] Perhaps, Yeh Hen, the child, was then only trying to gain some attention and distinction for himself. But the criticism he received had a strong effect on him. Doing nothing to correct his peers' evaluation of him, young Yeh thereafter never spoke up at all about his family. He did accept the notion that bourgeois status and contamination might have influenced his slow work in productive labor, but this belief did not cause him to strive to reform himself. Rather he adapted by choosing friends carefully, being very circumspect and hanging about with those who also shirked labor.[21]

By lower middle school, Yeh Hen became part of a group of three or four mischief-makers, perhaps a counterpart of juvenile delinquents in our own society. Yeh felt his group enjoyed prestige simply because they were able to intimidate the others at school.[22] In this group, he was not a leader but a "regular member." But when he became a matriculant at a five-year veterinary medicine middle school, Yeh found himself completely out of his element. Most others at the school were good classers and politically red. He only made a pretense of being compatible with the lot and was very "hypocritical" about his comradeship with his fellow students.[23] Forming a close bond with only two other students of similar background and political disposition, Yeh found himself, together with his new friends, flaunting his "bourgeois" clothes, sent from relatives in Hong Kong, in the school dormitory. He resisted conforming to the uniform style of dress, a simple deviation but with considerable significance in an adolescent phenomenology.[24] Why did Yeh Hen wear different clothes?

> Because my mama wouldn't let me imitate their dress. I couldn't do this. At home, I received a bourgeois education; at school, I received a proletarian education. So this was a subtle class struggle.[25]

Clearly, the bourgeois line was victorious in this struggle in Yeh Hen's socialization. If Lo Ping-wen as a child could remove his Pioneer armband before returning home in an effort not to disturb his parents, Yeh Hen, a maturing adolescent, could have thought of a way to adhere to standard apparel to blend with the majority at school. However, in reality, Yeh had no desire to conform to

official norms, but was satisfied with the approval of his
few friends, bourgeois like himself. The question arises
whether Yeh Hen would have gained anything socially from
an attempt to mesh with the larger body of his peers, and
he essentially answers this question for himself by saying:

> My ideology was smashed when I entered veterinary
> school because I was born badly. But no matter how
> you perform politically, no one will believe you.
> No matter how you act, I felt there was no way to
> force your way in . . . I neither belonged to the
> "left" nor to the "right." I was in the middle.
> But Mao Tse-tung says there is no middle group. I
> was an outsider.[26]

The fault, however, for his being an outsider apparently was as much attributable to Yeh's own early identity with his parents and reluctance to resist pressure from his politically negative social group from lower middle school onward, as it was to the unwillingness of good classers to trust his sincerity.[27] Yeh Hen was clearly afraid of losing the respect of his friends, even if they did not enjoy the respect of the authorities. He was dependent on his group. He replies negatively to a question about whether he ever dreamed about becoming a cadre or joining the YCL, and reasons: "They [i.e., my friends] would have cursed me for whitewashing my own bad class background."[28]

It was because of the same desire to maintain a salient group bond that, when his fellow bad classers opted to join the *Hung Ch'i* Red Guards, he followed. Yeh Hen was lumped together with all the bad classers at his school in the course of early Cultural Revolution "struggle."

> They ostracized us. They said that people must be
> divided according to categories of masses, and animals have to be divided according to species. They
> said we people were to be separated from the
> masses.[29]

Now, in addition to his two initial friends at school, Yeh Hen found himself in the company of the whole lot of bad or "ordinary" class students. Since both his closer friends and most of the others became Red Guards, Yeh did as well. In the face of "struggle," he joined with his fellow sufferers and followed them into the Red Guards. Once in the *Hung Ch'i* organization, he assumed a follower's role. As Yeh explains his position:

I wanted a comfortable role in the Cultural Revolution. If I didn't join, the others in the group would have had no respect for me.[30]

Yeh Hen was also offended by his having been treated as a pariah and by the early Red Guards' units rampaging through his family home, but his decision to join the Red Guards was based less on revenge than on his friendship with people who really sought this revenge. Asked how he would respond to being without friends, Yeh Hen replies: "I would have a nervous breakdown for sure."[31]

THE ACTIVE PARTICIPANT AND MILITANT

For the potentially militant Red Guard, existing peer group ties and the development of new friendships through the network of the GPCR could reinforce other more dominant motivations for behavior. It is important to note first, that all the militants had been very social and had actively pursued friendship with their peers all along; second, that the majority had been class cadres (*pan-kan*) at various times (though not necessarily just prior to the GPCR); third, nearly all perceived themselves as popular and some actually stated that they commanded the respect of others, usually because of academic or athletic prowess and the willingness to help others in these areas.

Among the militants whose own personal motives and ambitions could sustain long-term participation in the GPCR, the atmosphere of camaraderie, which developed further as the movement deepened, buttressed their sense of purpose and involvement.

For those like Pao Kuo-fu, Chu Nan-po, or Lan Wei-ying who had made a significant break from the protective family in a further adult-oriented assertion of autonomy, peer acceptance became of prime importance in bolstering their push for autonomy. Chu Nan-po revelled in the opportunities for group life provided by the GPCR. Ecstatically, he proclaims: "You could go everywhere and there was something of an organizational life!"[32] But Lan Wei-ying, who also treated the GPCR as an extension of earlier peer activity, makes it a point to add that friends were not a central factor in his decision to take an active part in the Red Guards. He says:

Even if you [a friend] did not participate and also wanted me to abstain, I possibly wouldn't have gone along with you then . . . To participate or not is something for each person to decide for himself.[33]

Because the break he attempted to make from his father before 1964 through political activism was more radical, Lo Ping-kok's need for a new identity and peer acceptance was much more acute. When he was denied these because of the shame and ostracism following the incident at the factory,[34] he completely fell back on a negative identity with his father. After his father died and the GPCR presented itself as an appropriate medium for realizing his earlier wishes to assert himself politically, Ping-kok thrilled at his integration into peer group life. Now, because he was a Red Guard leader, those of his peers who had eschewed his company and criticized him earlier "realized their ideological mistake" and sought him as their friend.[35] They filled a vacuum in his life.

Armed struggle and the general "organizational life" of the Cultural Revolution lent to the affinity among peers. Many of them, "warrior friends" (*chan-you*),[36] seemed to have had a deep sense of affiliation and acceptance. As Chu Nan-po depicts the circumstances: "Some during the GPCR became as one during difficulty, ate together and slept together."[37] Moreover, a youth from one school, through the medium of common organizational work, now could make friends with youths studying in different schools or working in factories. Why was this so?

> Because when they established an organization, it was not simply in one particular school, one particular factory or cell of an organ. But many cells joined together. And often a central department was set up in the city, and through it, the people one came to know were rather numerous.[38]

A *Hung Ch'i* or *Tung Feng* Red Guard at a certain school was able to link up with his correspondent in another school or work place by presenting "a document of introduction"; "in an instant, they could be familiar friends."[39] Chou Chung-Wang discovered that, as a worker in the propaganda department of his faction, he came into contact with people from various organizations, and the opportunities for making friends proliferated.[40] Even when subjective, personal interests differed, the "common" causes and points of view for which they were fighting seemed to serve as a strong friendship bond.[41]

In any movement, social pressures play an important role.[42] In the GPCR, recruitment procedures came to be well organized under the Red Guard organizational network.[43] Pao Kuo-fu, Chu Nan-po, Yang Ying-pu and others were specifically assigned recruitment tasks. Activist leader Yang used *ta-tzu-pao* and personal persuasion to influence compeers to join his faction. He describes his activity in this area.

> I wrote calls to action, using political emotions; they had an inciteful character. Second, in conversations with friends, I spoke publicly and called on some friends to participate, put on a good appearance. I called on those schoolmates who had not been in the YCL to strive to gain the confidence of the Communist Party.[44]

And even earlier in the summer, ad hoc groups were still in the process of forming, a group from one *pan* (class) would combine with a group from another *pan*, perhaps at a much more advanced grade level. The merging of such groups was induced by the informal friendships already existing between their memberships.[45] Moreover, by combining and broadening their base, they widened the field of peer relations from which they could draw new members.[46] Some of these groups appear to have been segregated sexually, not because there were no girls in a particular class, but because before the Cultural Revolution these boys and girls did not "play" (*wan*) together.[47]

Committed primarily to the ideals of the "rebel" conglomerate and the medium it provided for self-assertion, Lan Wei-ying drew on his friends to create his own small ad hoc unit in August 1966. Here is a case of informal peer affiliation influencing the configuration of Red Guard organization. Three or four of the twelve members of the unit were Lan's close friends before the GPCR. Alike in their political views, they helped him recruit the other members, and ultimately called their small organization "*Hung Ch'i wei-ping*."[48] Lan Wei-ying had this feeling about the phenomenon: "Sometimes, because you participated, I also unconsciously participated."[49] In August, together with his small group of "rebels," he went to Peking on the *Ch'uan-lien*. Upon returning to his school from Peking, Wei-ying found that all his friends, close and casual, were part of the new *Hung Ch'i* faction. Moreover, as he entered the school grounds again, Wei-ying, out of touch with local developments since he left, crossed the turf (in this case, the basketball court area) occupied by the *Tung Feng* people. Aware that he was not one of their own, several *Tung Feng* members surrounded Wei-ying and began to give him a thrashing. In the midst of this melee, some *Hung Ch'i* warriors, who knew Lan Wei-ying and had been his friends before the Cultural Revolution, came to his assistance. This incident further influenced Lan Wei-ying to integrate his originally ad hoc group into the broad, formalized *Hung Ch'i* faction, to become an activist, and to engage in armed struggle.[50] Apart from the urge for revenge generated by this affair, Wei-ying had learned a lesson in the value of friends.

The course one's friends took also could affect the form of one's own activity. In the early phase of the Cultural Revolution, Lo Ping-kok was not really very enthusiastic about traveling on the *Ch'uan-lien*. And because friends volunteered instead to do productive labor in response to a call for volunteers rather than to join a Red Guard unit at school, he also chose to go with them.[51]

Nevertheless, though an individual might have found it to his liking to go the way of his friends, he might not have had this option open to him and might have been restricted by his immediate environment. One of Pao Kuo-fu's recently graduated school friends had become a factory worker. Although he was of Pao Kuo-fu's ilk, socially and ideologically, he joined *Tung Feng*. Pao explains the situation:

> Our point of view about participating in one faction was rather consistent. Why did my worker friend participate in a faction hostile to us? Because the environment forced him to participate in that faction. He could not escape taking part in it.[52]

Pao Kuo-fu's friend was faced with a situation in which everyone at his factory--his fellow workers--had joined *Tung Feng*. Thus, individual choices were modified by circumstances of the environment and cross-pressures from alternate peer groups as well as by pressures from friends and close companions.

THE NON-PARTICIPANT IN THE GPCR

Just as the nature of the peer group relationship could help draw an individual into the Cultural Revolution activities and further perhaps satisfy his need to belong and have a sense of purpose, it could also persuade him to proceed in the opposite direction. Most respondents were not entirely alienated from the mainstream of society despite the high degree of ostracism they might have had to endure before the GPCR. But sometimes, activists were aware that a certain friend had severely bad class background or a history of father's previously being struggled, and might deliberately refrain from pressing their friend to join the Red Guards or take part in armed struggle, out of intelligent compassion for him. As Ch'en Ling-ping says: "It was my friends who urged me not to participate. They said, 'For someone of your class background ["enemy"], participating has no advantage.'"[53]

Still other interviewees already had a strongly negative, "outsider" identity well before either the *Ssu-Ch'ing* or GPCR, which manifested itself at the adolescent phase in peer affiliation with an alienated outgroup. Not necessarily "class enemies" (a few, like Fei, were of petit-bourgeois background), these individuals sought the company of others with similarly alienated personalities and common points of view. Fei's group only participated ritualistically at the very outset of the GPCR in May and then withdrew hastily long before factions formed.[54] "In essence," he says, "none of my good friends participated."[55] No one attempted to persuade him to participate after he returned home.[56] In fact, Fei's three best friends, whom he knew since nursery school, all encouraged him and one another to run off to Hong Kong.[57]

Although never personally the victim of discrimination in his childhood because of his bad class background, Yüan, whom we have seen earlier so closely identified with his father, sought out only bad classers like himself as friends.[58] Inhibited and rather insecure about other people's attitudes toward him even in Hong Kong, Yüan's personality made him a natural "outsider." In upper middle school, three years or so before the GPCR, Yüan began to form serious friendships. He discusses his outgroup affiliation.[59]

In practice, this type of informal peer affiliation reinforced backward political behavior. Yüan's group deliberately set out to thwart the reform objectives of small group meetings for political study at school. Yüan recalls:

> Sometimes we would take the teacher's topic [for group meeting] and mutually decide how we would discuss it, in order not to let him spot our mistakes.[60]

When he went to work in a factory, Yüan Ching-po studiously avoided associating with his comrades there, whom he identified as "activists." He made certain to arrive at the factory only five minutes before work time in order to avoid informal conversation.[61] When the GPCR broke loose in his factory, since he was already "very isolated" from his fellow workers, he stayed home.[62] As for the influence of the middle school friends with whom he still associated regularly, it was reactionary. None of them participated in the GPCR either, and they were all "alienated" like himself.[63]

In assessing the influences of peer group identities, we should never forget the extent to which types of friendship formations, or even their absence in certain cases, may have been influenced by family socialization and the relationship between father and son in the first place. Sometimes, the vertical family socialization of a bad classer interacted with a hostile social environment in such a way as to abet the early alienation of the individual growing up in the PRC and force him either into isolation from close bonds with peers or into choosing his friends most cautiously for their similarly "backward" political perspectives. Whereas a child from a relatively open family relationship was apt to have high self-esteem and a natural proclivity to trust others and relate well to them, the child from a vertical parent-son relationship was less disposed to trust his peers easily. He was less likely to fall into the trap of Pao Kuo-fu who, emerging from a relatively horizontal family matrix and expecting to enjoy at least as good relations with his own peers as with his parents, was rudely awakened midway through primary school by a few bad experiences resulting precisely from his openness; in one instance, someone was denounced publicly for something he had uttered in confidence.[64]

While one's growing alienation could be attributed to negative environmental reinforcement, the "vertical" child's basic mistrust received positive environmental reinforcement.[65] From the outset, he was wary of politically active peers and careful either to keep to himself or to shelter himself among peers of similar class background or commensurately "backward" thinking. Huang Yi, whose father had been a key "struggle" object in the Anti-Rightist Campaign of 1957, found it most convenient to form friendships--all nevertheless reserved--with those who, like himself, "were dissatisfied with society."[66] And before he even casually befriended a schoolmate, he "had to check what his class background was like."[67] Of course, this approach to peer friendships, extremely common to bad class children, was a politically negative influence on the individual, and the authorities at least tried to discourage such early outgroup formations. As Huang Yi says:

> If it is a case of two people with bad class status being together, people will also have criticism: "You're always together. Doing what? What bad things are you engaged in?"[68]

Such peer formations occurred nevertheless, in part perhaps because the authorities seemed to take even more concern in preventing good and bad class children from becoming friends, the assumption being that the latter could have a pernicious influence on the former.[69]

Another defense of the mistrustful against the possibility of betrayal in peer relations was to wear several faces in the presence of most people, but be truly friendly with only a few or none at all. A youth alert to the problem could learn at an early age how to sense the political hue of any person in whose company he happened to find himself, to know what sort of things to say in different situations, and to appear friendly on a superficial level.[70] But such guarded individuals would rarely allow themselves to fall into deep relationships which could hurt them or sway them politically, and were in essence socially alienated. In Nieh Li-chih's view: "Everyone was . . . , as the Chinese say, one person with two minds who could not be counted for much."[71] In fact, an extreme example, Nieh Li-Chih, alienated at a very early age, virtually isolated himself and took pride in his negative identity and ideological backwardness. He boasts now about how he managed to withstand the pressures to participate in the Cultural Revolution. Nieh Li-chih's words:

> It was an achievement because when you returned to school, they would say, "Now it's a time of revolution!" If you didn't participate in either faction, well ----[72]

Of course, as we have seen in our discussion of sudden class alienation and ostracism in adolescence and political participation in Chapter 3, identification with certain outgroups before the Cultural Revolution did not preclude political participation, but, quite the contrary, often was the matrix fomenting militancy during the GPCR. When the alienation occurred under certain circumstances and the anti-social outgroup was predisposed to link itself to a revolutionary social cause, the "outs" seemed more militant than the "ins." The more revolutionary social objectives and style of behavior could only have taken root in the context of peer groups composed of people alienated by a similar phenomenon (e.g., class discrimination and ostracism) and responding *as groups* in a similar and naturally coordinated fashion.

PEER RELATIONS: A SUMMATION

Peer formations were as much a product of individual personalities and types of family socialization as of environmental circumstances. The peer relationship was predicated first on the individual's ability to relate to his fellows and then on the quest for friends with common personality traits, interests, and points of view. Although severely bad class background undeniably was a strong influence on some childrens' degree of isolation and circumspection in choosing friends, the evidence indicates that the question of how much trust was instilled in the family environment was of primary importance. Regardless of class background, youths from authoritarian homes seemed more disposed to mistrust others and approach peer involvement with a great deal of reserve; they would be more resistant to general peer involvement in a political movement and more likely to cling to a narrow circle of proven friends.

In adolescence, individuals generally are more responsive to peer pressures. For the adolescent sucked into the Cultural Revolution as a follower, the behavior of his comrades seemed to be a dominant motivation. Such a person just wanted to be regarded as one of the boys. The active participant, on the other hand, was more often interested in advancing himself and accustomed to assuming the lead over his fellows. In this pool of respondents, the activist Red Guards usually took the lead either as individuals or with close friends in forming ad hoc Red Guard groups, recruiting others and linking up with casual friends in other groups. These persons were very social, very popular, and usually would command a following rather than just follow the lead of others.

Once informal peer groups and patterns of relating to peers were formed in adolescence, they played an independent role as well in helping to determine an individual's choice of options during the Cultural Revolution. And the lure of new and more widespread friends fighting for a common cause in the GPCR also seemed to appeal to the adolescent in his search for further group acceptance and ideological purpose.

6. Youth and Authority

Although no deliberate efforts in this study were made to test general attitudes toward authority in terms of measurable criteria,[1] the self-generative impressionistic data of free flowing and sometimes free-associative interviews indicated that among the more rebellious youth, patterns of behavior in the home were projected on the environment. In more permissive, horizontal family relationships, rebelliousness against teachers at school could be characteristic of behavior even before circumstances of the GPCR permitted.[2] In this way, any authority figure who blocked a youth's upward mobility was subject to challenge from below. Even a good class youth would defy authority at the appropriate time if he felt it stood in his pathway to success. In more vertical home environments in which the son was rebellious, the youth could transfer rivalrous antagonism toward father on the authorities in general under the more liberating conditions of the GPCR.

On the other hand, the child who was authority-submissive in the home was not likely to direct an open volley against his superordinates in the outer environment. When the GPCR developed, he passively followed the general trend if it was not at counterpoint with his parents' values; or, alternatively, he was so resentful of the authorities, on whom he had long ago projected the antagonistic feelings he could not consciously admit he even felt for his father, that he abstained.

THE UNALIENATED ACTIVIST: REBEL WITH A CAUSE

Lan Wei-ying was inclined to a political, adult role choice both because of his father's admiration of achievements along those lines and because of his own ideological commitment to the system. Although somewhat ambivalent about how to treat a child in the new environment, his father indulged him in his political activities and fantasies, and then suddenly infringed on his autonomy just as he was most anxious to assert himself as a responsible person in adolescence. It was not surprising then that Lan Wei-ying either would balk at those authorities who blocked his way during the same period as he strove for individual autonomy outside the home, or would welcome the opportunity to release this hostility politically.

The son of a low-level, street office administrative cadre with a petit-bourgeois classification, Lan Wei-ying at an early age received parental approval for political achievements in school. His father had been classified as petit-bourgeois, but was politically active in his work and even enthusiastic when he was sent to a "May 7th Cadre School"[3] during the latter phase of the GPCR. Thus, in contradistinction to a type like Lo Ping-wen, not only did he not have to hide his status in the Pioneers from his father, but he was celebrated for his accomplishment. Indeed, he recalls that the happiest day in his life was his initiation into the Pioneers at age nine or ten. He reminisces:

> I still remember that in primary school on April 28, 1960, I participated in the Pioneers. That was my happiest day because I wore a red handkerchief . . . a glorious thing when we were in primary school . . . My parents were very happy for me. I thought I forgot that day long ago, but how is it that I've still not forgotten it?! . . . They, my parents, were very happy. I went to a park for the announcement that I'd joined the Pioneers. My Mama specially prepared two red eggs for me to eat.[4]

This recollection is significant for two reasons: first, that his political activity, no matter how limited (he was yet to become a squad leader--*hsiao-tui-chang*--in the Pioneers), was welcomed by his parents; second, that his parents praised and actually rewarded him for an accomplishment, in contrast to the traditional pattern of ignoring or deprecating a child's achievements and pushing a child compliantly to do better.[5] Lan Wei-ying's family clearly represented a departure from the traditional model. They encouraged his autonomous development and applauded politics as an avenue for this self-expression.

Lan Wei-ying became a political animal. In lower middle school, he was the second highest-ranking student in his politics class.[6] He fiercely engaged in criticism and self-criticism at group meetings, and diligently picked out faults in group members which did not conform to the communist ideal.[7] Eager to take his place beside his older brother and sisters who had become Youth Leaguers, Lan Wei-ying faithfully attended YCL preparatory classes. But at that time, because of the politicization of the environment and emphasis on class during the *Ssu-Ch'ing* and afterward, he found it difficult as a non-red to enter the YCL.[8] In 1964, when his father himself was "struggled" at his place of work, Lan Wei-ying knew his political career was at a standstill. Moreover, the YCL stopped recruiting in the lower middle schools and it became too late to apply.[9] But Lan was still keenly interested in political mobility.

When the GPCR began, Lan could take up where he left off. Lan Wei-ying regarded the Red Guards as a functional extension of the YCL:

> When the GPCR began, it seemed that the Red Guards had replaced the YCL organization. Therefore, there were many people at that time who wanted to enter the Red Guard organization. But its conditions were very strict. Afterward, the conditions for participating in the Red Guards were easier. Like if you didn't let me participate in your organization, we few people could organize a Red Guard unit together . . . So we also set up Red Guards . . . We wore red arm bands. It had the appearance of being very prestigious.[10]

To this day, Lan Wei-ying maintains that if he were to return home, he could think of no more glorious career than to wear the uniform of the People's Liberation Army.[11] And he feels that if he had been successful in his effort to become a Youth Leaguer before the Cultural Revolution, "he would possibly have become a member of the *Tung Feng* or conservative faction."[12] "In most people's minds, a YCL member is already a cadre, *a cadre*!" he exclaims.[13]

Thus, on one level, with the sanction of his parents, Lan Wei-ying had charted a political course of upward mobility in which political status was of prime importance. Participation in the Cultural Revolution could be predicted. Yet on a deeper level, one can examine the roots of his hard push for mobility and the reasons for his adolescent proclivity, Cultural Revolution or not, *to defy authority in a directed way*. It was this dynamic that supplied the energy he put into political participation.

Lan Wei-ying's relations with his father were abrasive

and complex. As a small child, he felt it encumbent upon himself to obey his father and resist only "internally."[14] In an effort to inculcate filiality, his father would tell him stories about how a daughter would sell herself in Old China to pay for the funeral of a deceased mother."[15] But as he grew older approaching adolescence, Wei-ying and his father faced each other as equals. In Lan's case, as in many others in my pool of respondents, the maturing child got into frequent debates with his father which were couched in political language. Transitionally horizontal in their relationship, father and son found it difficult to "relate" (*hsiang-ch'u*) to one another; Lan Wei-ying still is in a quandary as to why his father could not trust him.[16] Wei-ying demanded autonomy in accordance with the new communist environmental norms, and his father was sufficiently sensitive to these outside pressures against his natural proclivity to authoritarian behavior to react awkwardly in his son's presence and strive to avoid confrontations. Young Lan Wei-ying could no longer allow his father to discipline him in an authoritarian fashion. He asserts:

> When I was young, if I didn't obey my father, that was unsatisfactory. Because he would beat me. But later (age 12 or 13) when I grew up, he wouldn't dare act up with me.[17]

A further issue complicated the father-son relationship. Paternal Grandmother lived with the family and often taunted Lan Wei-ying's mother. In the absence of his father, who was more sympathetic anyway to his own mother, Lan Wei-ying frequently interceded in their altercations and defended his timid mother. On one occasion, when Lan was about sixteen years old, the situation got out of hand. Wei-ying screamed at his grandmother, "Although you are the last generation, you yourself have acted and spoken badly"; he threatened to report her to the local police station.[18] When Grandmother told Wei-ying's father, the older Lan flew into a rage. Lan Wei-ying describes the scene:

> I still have a scar now . . . I ran, and he chased me and beat me with a great big stick . . . He hit me until the blood flowed. Of course, I was very angry. I left then and only returned after spending two days at a schoolmate's house. He asked me to return.[19]

Lan Wei-ying's mother "remained neutral after the incident." "But from that time on, [Lan Wei-ying] very rarely spoke with [his father]," and his father avoided situations in which he would have to play the superordinate role to his son.[20]

As he recalls this incident in depth, Lan Wei-ying's speech becomes more rapid, and he free-associatively places it in the context of the GPCR experience:

> *I was so old* and he still beat me. So I was very angry. Two days later, my older brother came to my schoolmate's house. He wanted me to go home with him. *That was just about the time the GPCR was beginning. Lower middle school three. There was only a year before the GPCR was upon us!*[21]

What bearing did his father's infringement on his individual autonomy in this instance have on Lan Wei-ying's sudden recollection--on the surface, strikingly out of context with his previously pure narrative about family relations--of the imminence of the GPCR?

The answer lies in the way Lan Wei-ying utilized the GPCR to vent his anger on authorities. He picked on only those teachers who had forced him in the past to suppress himself and/or appear small before his peers. His anti-authority behavior in the GPCR had definite direction provided by the psychological need to assert himself as an independent individual and by the specific blocks to this self-assertion. For instance, he recalls that his *pan-chu-jen* (home class director) then had severely embarrassed him in front of the class for not handing in the required number of compositions. Concerning his motivation for harshly criticizing this teacher during the GPCR, he remarks:

> Imagine his proclaiming it before the whole class! I was old then. I had my self-respect. So I wrote that he had used examinations and his teaching work to oppress us classmates, to oppress students.[22]

Lan Wei-ying further notes:

> It was this way. Most teachers were rather strict . . . We were frequently singled out, faulted by those teachers or given a bad critique of our work. When we had the opportunity, we all wrote, saying that the teacher had taught us such and such revisionist things.[23]

Previously compelled to respect authority and denied the opportunity to defy a harsh teacher "because of the many restrictions on [us],"[24] Lan Wei-ying and others availed themselves of the GPCR to strike out at the teachers who had been severe with them. "Sometimes a teacher was rather strict and would often scold schoolmates in class," he says. "We took this opportunity to write *ta-tzu-pao* (big character posters) about him."[25]

If Lan Wei-ying used the GPCR to lash out at school authorities who had put him down, he also flaunted his participation in the Red Guards in the face of a father who was reluctant to have his son so involved. On the basis of his own experience with past political movements, Lan Wei-ying's father urged his son not to become involved in what seemed to be more than an ordinary campaign, and he cautioned his son that there would be no advantage to him in participating.[26] But Wei-ying only resented his father's attempt to restrain him. He states:

> My father wanted to ask me to go to the countryside. Afterward, I established an organization. At that time, I was filled with revolutionary thoughts . . . During the GPCR, I completely disobeyed father. I was already a big boy then![27]

In fact, at the time of the first factional armed struggle, passing his father on the street, Wei-ying brandished a hand gun he had on his person. He told his father then that he "was going back to sleep, not to fight."[28] His father had already seen the gun in the house sometime earlier, and had argued over it with Wei-ying.[29] He deliberately ignored his son this time.[30] Lan Wei-ying's father had taken his son aside frequently enough "to explain the fierce bearing [the GPCR] had on life and death."[31] This is how Wei-ying responded:

> He wanted me to refrain from participation, but I was very impulsive then. I couldn't be saved . . . Because I was his son, he spoke to me this way. But he would merely incite my opposition still more.[32]

I find this an ironic role reversal of the traditional ideal-type situation in which a father, whose son dares to protest this action, beats him all the harder.[33]

Other reasons for engaging in the Cultural Revolution notwithstanding, Lan Wei-ying clearly derived satisfaction from defying or attacking the father or father-surrogates who tried to infringe on what he considered his broadened prerogatives as a mature individual. His continual references to being "too old" or "a big boy" attest to his adolescent growing pains.

ONE RED PEASANT'S DEFIANCE OF AUTHORITY: UNALIENATED BUT UNPOLITICAL

As we observed in Chapter 4, a youth of good class background could operate within a protective shield. Of course, the extreme deviant would come under fire, but the person who subtly defied conventional authority or resisted total conformity in the political arena seemed to feel secure enough that even if he were subjected to criticism, it would be in the form of "gentle drizzle."

Such was the case of Tseng K'ai-lao who always felt a part of the new society, naively accepted the need for ideological study, revered Mao Tse-tung, and yet never really was interested in conventional political activity. He wanted to be different!

Tseng came from a village where he was one of only a few his age to attend lower middle school in the market town. His father (the leader of a Production Brigade other than the one in which his family resided) and he were very close and demonstratively affectionate to one another. Tseng states:

> Papa loved me more than Mama . . . because throughout he cared for me . . . [When he returned from his periods with the Brigade], he consistently asked me how I was doing in school. It was this way between us.[34]

And even when Tseng eventually got into serious political trouble for seeing off some city friends as they were about to flee to Hong Kong rather than fulfill their *hsia-hsiang* obligations, his father only scolded and reproached him. Tseng observes that in this instance his father was at his angriest with him.[35] Psychologically, the two generations were quite close.

Because of his family background and his own good grades, Tseng was selected as a class leader (*pan-kan*) straight through primary school. He accepted this position, which he regarded as obligatory.[36] He submitted to criticism and self-criticism because he accepted the notion that "in this way relations between people are made better."[37] By the outbreak of the GPCR, he admits he truly believed in and admired "revolutionary heroes" like Lei Feng and took for granted without any questioning the dictum that all targeted teachers were "capitalist roaders."[38]

Yet his passive acceptance of the system in general and the GPCR in specific did not obviate rebellious tendencies which had begun in his juvenile years. As early as primary school, his ambitions had surpassed reality. He dreamed of being a "hero," not even like Lei Feng but "as great as Mao Tse-tung."[39] Moreover, these fantasies, rechanneled, became the thrust of his concrete behavior in middle school. He resisted the demands of his superordinates to assume a politically active organizational role:

> The teacher asked me to apply to the YCL, but I refused to participate . . . So did others, but I didn't participate. I don't know why either.[40]

The justification, at first unclear to him, for defying the authorities and the conventional expectations of him at this juncture in his life began to materialize in his mind. Tseng was in the process of concretizing his adult goals, not in the pursuit of a political career like his father's, but in the desire to become an intellectual. In his own words, "a scientist--a famous one--would be better than even being on the Central Committee."[41] In earlier years, Tseng had fantasied becoming another Mao. His reason for aspiring to such national prominence is interesting:

> My little brother would follow me . . . He would follow my example.[42]

In other words, Tseng wanted to play father to his younger brother, but in a role much more inflated than the older Mr. Tseng's. Asked why his father's role would have been an inadequate model for his younger brother, Tseng retorts:

> To have been like Mao would be more appropriate. My position would be much higher than my father's.
>
> Question: What if your position were as high as your father's?
>
> Then I would not be important enough.[43]

Thus, by the end of his first year in middle school, Tseng

was bent on becoming a research scientist. The likelihood of superseding his father's political position in a spectacular fashion was diminishing as Tseng came more to grips with reality. To successfully compete with his father, he had to try another direction. His father's job "carried a bit of prestige, but didn't really figure as much."[44] As Tseng states further: "Ha! I wouldn't want to do it myself."[45]

Although his decision to be a scientist was predicated on rivalry with his father, it would only be a logical basis for competition if his father respected intellectuals. Asked about his father's opinion on this matter, Tseng responds:

> He had a lot of respect for intellectuals . . . He felt that intellectuals were a part of the motivating force in society. Without intellectuals, nothing can be done! Not even movements conducted.[46]

Intent upon becoming an intellectual, young Tseng adhered tenaciously to this goal throughout the GPCR. He passively "followed the main tide" and rode out the Cultural Revolution. "They did such and such," he comments, "so I also did it."[47] He says:

> At that time the entire school were Red Guards. They all participated. If I hadn't, I would have been considered really backward.[48]

He began to buck the tide again only after the GPCR by 1969, when school had been resumed. He describes his posture then:

> At that time, I was in middle school. I often came late when they held meetings. I also often did not go. At the start of class, the teacher spoke and criticized me and I said I was individualistic. I didn't go to labor either. I merely made study of primary importance and relegated politics to second place. I put knowledge first and morality and proper attitude second.[49]

Tseng took his criticism well, accepted the fact that he was selfish and "petit-bourgeois," but admits he made no effort whatsoever to change.[50] "As long as I got my [university] education later," he felt, "everything would be all right."[51]

Then, when Tseng K'ai-lao was exposed to numerous intellectual youths and teachers on *hsia-hsiang* in his village, a middle school teacher from Kwangchow living in his home discussed philosophy with him. Tseng was flattered to be accepted in intellectual conversation. His new teacher-friend "persuaded him that it was impossible and unnatural to eliminate the private sector because there would always be selfish people." As Tseng came to neglect politics still more at school, ignore the warnings of his teachers, absent himself from meetings and seek the company of the city intellectuals, he tripped himself up. One day, he saw off some educated city youths, his friends, at their point of flight to Hong Kong. Apparently found out by a villager, he was later subjected to severe criticism in his neighborhood and at school; his father scolded him. He was forced to return to the village for labor. According to Tseng, he felt then that "there was now no longer any way for [him] to make university.[52] He identified his position then with the "hopelessness" of the city-youth on *hsia-hsiang*.[53] In spite of his thinking to himself that "his father might be blamed by the people" were he himself to leave the PRC for a try at an education in Hong Kong,[54] he eventually plunged into the water. The decision to leave the PRC was the ultimate flouting of the system and his father in it.

THE AUTHORITY-SUBMISSIVE, PASSIVE BYSTANDER

Among the Red Guards who participated as followers, only attending meetings and rarely ever speaking out, the reasons for any involvement at all varied. Apart from ties to friendship groups or the psychological need to go along with one's peers, a further motivating factor was simply the reflex response to political campaigns. But such a reflexive reaction among non-red class children, if really sustained, was particularly characteristic of the adolescent accustomed to submitting to authority without question. Obedient to authority in both home and school, he would do what was expected of him in the GPCR, provided no value dissynchronization existed between the two major socializing agencies.

Liang Shu-ming, whose ambition in upper middle school was to study engineering at Tsinghua University in Peking, grew up in a home where neither he nor his older brother dared question the absolute authority of his father. He describes his father as "an old army man" (KMT) who "used strict discipline as an educational method" with his children.[55]

Liang states:

> We were very afraid of him . . . His excuse for beating was love. But I feel one ought not use tyrannical methods too excessively.[56]

In response to the Mao story, Liang states:

> You are resting and your father thinks you are being lazy on the sly and scolds you. Yes . . . There's no need to use the method of jumping in the water . . . If it happened to me, there would be nothing I could do but let him scold me. In the psychology of a child, one must absolutely obey the father. I wouldn't get angry.[57]

Much later, asked about his political attitudes in general and his feelings about Mao in specific, he comments on the leader's political genius and "tyranny with his people." Searching for a more human image of Mao, the interviewer asked: "Didn't other people regard him as a father?" Giggling, Liang adds: "In the tyrannical sense."[58]

Although no politics were ever discussed in his home, Liang Shu-ming cannot conceive of a situation in which any of the members of his household, even his father, could resist the pressures of social authority and abstain from the Cultural Revolution.[59] Indeed, Shu-ming himself, after returning home in June 1966, was pressured in September by a small delegation of *Hung Ch'i* Red Guards, themselves in leadership positions, of good class background, older and relative strangers to him, to go with them to the school and join their unit. Liang comments:

> The main thing for which I ultimately had to criticize myself after the Cultural Revolution was that I didn't care about the Cultural Revolution and had to be ordered to live at school. Because on many issues, they argued that I merely listened on the sideline and did not express an opinion.[60]

But it was in the nature of Liang's personality to take orders and stand on the sideline. Asked a general question about how he would react to an intensely interesting parlor conversation among fellow students only casually known to him, Liang replies: "I'd just listen and in most cases not open my mouth."[61] Activist respondents, asked the same question, gave the opposite answer.

Even in leaving China, Liang was not motivated by defiance of authority, alienation from the social-political system, or the togetherness of a peer group. Noting that he made the decision on the eve of being "sent down" (*hsia-hsiang*), Liang describes his reasoning:

> It was a question of livelihood. Since I felt one couldn't even maintain the most basic livelihood in the village, I decided to leave China. Politics was secondary. If livelihood had been good, then if I didn't do anything bad, I could get by.[62]

If Liang was sucked into the whirlpool of the GPCR, he was now in a current pulling toward Hong Kong. He just paddled along.

ABSTAINING FROM GPCR: VARIATIONS IN THE EARLY ALIENATION OF A BAD CLASS CHILD FROM AUTHORITY

A. Vertical Family Relationship

Evidence from the West suggests that the authoritarian socialization pattern in the home leads to an exaggerated projection of hostility toward father on authority figures in the outer society.[63] A child from a vertical father-son relationship in China was also given to such projections. The "horizontal" adolescent was more capable of effectively ventillating this inter-generational hostility in overt protest against both father and father-surrogate. Even in a "vertical" relationship, given the right circumstances, anger restrained in the home could be redirected in political activity against the authorities. We have seen cases of the adolescent's channeling of such hostility into political activity in a previous chapter.

But for the child in a vertical family who was socially proscribed at an early stage in his maturation, the hostility which he was unable to allow himself to feel against his authoritarian father took the form only of more conscious, though not overtly released, anger toward father-surrogates in the environment. In essence, he blamed the authorities, not only for any oppression he suffered outside the home, but also for the oppression he suffered under his father at home. Already feeling he was beyond the fringe, this sort of alienated youth was unable to immerse himself in a political movement such as the GPCR and overtly express his anger, but he felt it nonetheless. Circumstances had taught him to keep his thoughts to himself. His attitude toward social and political authorities to a great extent seemed to mirror his latent attitude toward authority in the home. In such a context, this natural proclivity to resent authorities, combined with the perceived need to guard against showing one's feelings even when they were sanctioned in a political campaign, contributed still more to the individual's alienation from the social system. Given overt expression, such hostility might have impelled an individual into active and zealous political participation. But for the real "outsider," it was further cause for resistance by "dropping out." Answering a question about how he might cope some day with a disobedient son, Hsu Ta-liang says:

> If you try excessively to force him, he will rise up and resist you as we did in China. The oppression was too great, so we left.[64]

Hsu Ta-liang again makes the same sort of transference from father to political authority in his discussion of Solomon TAT III. He says:

> The father is scolding his son. Like my own father, he is very fierce. The son keeps quiet because that is the way of filiality. The mother is silent because that is woman's nature. Ha! The father looks like Mao--his head.[65]

Suppressed at home and withdrawn on the outside, Huang Yi felt intense hostility for the authorities. Although he was able to cope with the harsh demands of his father, he could not tolerate the restrictions at school. Despite the fact that Huang states that it might have aided his education if his father had spent more time at home, when pressed on the point, he contradictorily declares:

> No, in fact, I do not like someone guiding me. I don't like anyone to have any means of restricting my activity. Possibly, this is related to the

reason for my dissatisfaction with our circumstances in class at school.66

Huang free associates from his resentment of his father to the restrictions at school. Indeed, Huang Yi, only sentences later, deplores the manipulation of students by cadres; he says that he personally made every effort to resist the criticism--self-criticism sessions for this very reason.67

Often unable to admit to themselves at the time their hostility toward an authoritarian father (usually because of their ingrained submissiveness at home but also frequently because they felt threatened on the outside and needed some protection), these individuals first projected their anger on authorities in general. But also prevented by circumstances from overtly releasing this hostility against authorities even in a relatively free-wheeling political campaign like the GPCR, they had to seek other psychological escapes. For some, like Pao Kuo-fu's cousin, such an escape was a psychotic (schizophrenic) breakdown in the village; the cousin took to writing epithets denouncing Mao on the walls, and was totally unaware of what he was doing.68 In his own attempt at diagnosis, Kuo-fu held to the traditional Chinese superstition, in medical metaphor quite sound, that if the *ch'i* (steam) is not released, it will drive you insane.69 But many others in my group of respondents with a similar problem chose another sort of escape--political passivity and their flight to Hong Kong.

B. Horizontal Family Relationship

In cases of a more open relationship between parents and child, a hostile social environment alone, only at times in combination with a parent's real political values or value-image,70 seemed to prevent a child's integration into the system and active participation in a movement of the depth of the Cultural Revolution. Class label and a consistently harsh social reaction to it inhibited the bearer.

Hsieh Ting-teng, a boy from a "class enemy" family, avows an avid interest in politics, but during the GPCR felt too much on the fringe of society to participate. Despite the execution of his Kuomintang-general father when young Hsieh was age eight and the persistent prodding of his mother to be cautious in his social relations and remain politically aloof, Hsieh could not go against the grain of his naturally open personality. In the first two years of primary school, he made friends easily, was accepted by his peers of whatever class background (children especially were unaware of such things as "class label" in the 1950s), and became an informal leader to his coterie of good friends. His agility at sports contributed to his popularity. Hsieh was as enthusiastic about the new political system as he was about his general school environment. He was vaguely aware then of the fact that his father had been executed as a political "enemy" but does not recall ever having borne the political system any malice for his father's death. Yet he struggled to convince himself that his father was a good man and at bottom worthy of his son's continuing respect. In this area, Hsieh's mother provided encouragement. She constantly had her husband's photograph on display and often, as she culled through a collection of old snapshots, would tell her young son stories about his father's camaraderie with subordinate soldiers and of his growing aversion to the corruption of other political and military officers in the Kuomintang. Hsieh feels that he was able to rationalize to himself that his father had just gotten into the political revolution at the wrong stage of history. He hoped to join the Pioneers along with his friends, and buried within himself any suspicions that his father's situation would stand in his way. Asked about his enthusiasm then for politics, Hsieh reflects that he believed that by becoming active himself politically, he only would have been emulating his father and compensating for his error. He even fantasied becoming a general in the People's Liberation Army one day.

However, in Primary three when Hsieh was readying himself for entry into the Pioneers, he suddenly found himself in open confrontation with his father's background. One schoolday, when young Hsieh was behaving mischievously in the back of the classroom, a teacher of "red" class background called him to the front of the room and humiliated the child before his friends. The teacher harshly rebuked Ting-teng for his tomfoolery by recalling former General Hsieh's "crimes" and by drawing attention to the boy's class background. In Hsieh's words:

> [He] scolded me thusly: "Like father, like son!" Scolding me this way, he was saying that such a father would naturally have this sort of son. He did it so that my schoolmates would speak about

me this way. I really hate--[ed. Hsieh begins to
sob here]--Up to the present day, I still hate
that teacher [ed. one more sob, then he recovers
himself].[71]

Henceforth, a strain was omnipresent in Hsieh's efforts
at political participation, in his socialization, and in
his relations with his peers. In Primary five, a gang of
schoolmates goaded him into a brawl by cursing his father.[72]
How did Hsieh feel at the time?

I took it as a sort of insult. I was most afraid
of people bringing up this thing. I disliked most
other persons mentioning this matter. *This was the
thing I hid in my heart. I wanted to accept the
education of the Communist Party. Therefore, this
thing caused a war in my mind.*[73]

Gradually, Hsieh Ting-teng began to accept being on
the "outside" and sought only the company of those whose
class background and/or thinking were consistent with his
own position. Although Hsieh had a few friends of worker
background, these fellows were "good people who would not
discuss anything touchy because they were better than the
others"; most important, they felt compatible with Hsieh,
probably because of their own political delinquency.[74]
Hsieh Ting-teng eventually came to realize that his background
would always mark him as an outcast. When he
needed to prepare a *chen-piao* (detailed personal vita)
for the university matriculation examinations, he did not
have the courage to fill it out. Such a reminder of his
class background was an even more degrading and humiliating
experience for him each time. He explains:

Psychologically, I always felt a sort of pressure
on me that was very unbearable. I knew there was
a difference between me and the other schoolmates.[75]

Asked whether he felt the nation or family was more important,
Hsieh replies:

Most normally, one would say the nation is more
important than the family. But I feel my nation
never regarded me as part of it. Under these
circumstances, my family was more important to
me.[76]

Given his feelings of alienation from society, Hsieh abstained completely from the GPCR, staying away from all demonstrations and declining to join any Red Guard factions. But because of his curiosity about politics, he spent nearly all his time wandering the streets reading the latest *ta-tzu-pao* and following the factional debates with keen interest. He says:

> At that time, I had absolutely no thought of becoming involved in politics. But I thought that if it weren't for my class background being bad, maybe I would have liked to participate . . . I had formerly just stood on the sidelines and watched . . .[77]

Hsieh's alienation from society intensified as he drew his own conclusions about the realities versus the ideals of socialist society.[78] But these intellectual evaluations really seemed to be rooted in his own sense of being a social pariah. Perhaps, the course of Hsieh's long identity struggle, which led to his growing alienation and ultimate decision to leave China, can be summarized best in this one statement:

> [When mother tried to explain father's classification], our thought then (i.e., juvenile years) was much more progressive than hers. Therefore, we suffered an extraordinarily severe inner contradiction. Nor could we provoke an overt clash because of this. We wanted to use our thinking to travel with the times, but there were a lot of questions we were unable to resolve. We put these questions to the side at first and didn't pay attention to them. We hoped that we were mistaken . . . During the long period prior to my graduation from upper middle school, we thought this way. Nevertheless, there were many questions for which there were no means of solution. At this time, we just thought that possibly the lower level policies had been implemented badly and the upper level was correct. We hoped to explain away some problems this way. Nevertheless, after we went to the village (i.e., after the GPCR), we finally discovered that the solution to this problem had never been established.[79]

The reader should note that the first line of defense in upholding the legitimacy of the political system seemed to be the behavior of lower level cadres. Only when it became apparent that the causes for discontent rested not with errors in implementation of policies at the lower levels but with the policies from above, did otherwise loyal individuals tend to lose faith altogether in communist rule.

RETURNING FULL CIRCLE TO THE QUESTION OF CLASS

The children of good class background seemed to enjoy the prerogative of insulating themselves, if not from politics, then from personal, psychological involvement in politics. If their individual interests and chosen avenues for upward mobility lay in other areas, they could get by in the GPCR only by feigning the slightest interest in the movement. Even defiance of authority need not have been spent on the GPCR.

Non-red classers were another breed. They could avail themselves of the GPCR not only as an opportunity to defy authority in adolescence or as a special channel for attaining and testing adult roles but as a means of compensating for class background and as a way to avenge themselves on those good classers who ostracized them in the preceding period. It would not be unreasonable to hypothesize that active participation in the GPCR meant more for the non-red than for the red class youth. Others would abstain, not just out of apathy, but partly because of class-based alienation or a generalized, inexpressible anger at authority, the latter often growing out of an authoritarian home.

Another factor for the reader to consider with regard to non-red youths is that the risk in the end would be greater. Even those non-red youths drawn into passive participation in the GPCR by friends and/or the centripetal pull of this massive political movement could not avoid at some time pondering the possibly dire consequences for bad classers once the movement came to a close. And the very authority-submissive types, like Liang, consistently obeying their elders, could follow the leaders only so far before outside events forced them eventually to withdraw.[80] No matter what the motives and intensity of participation, non-red classers had to beware.

The non-red youths from horizontal family relationships could persist in their autonomous behavior in the political sphere, often even in open rivalry with their parents and authority in general, only until sufficient dissonance from the outer environment did not push them either into identification with their families or complete alienation from the social system.

In the case of even the most active participant, one event or series of events in the outer environment could push the youth to withdraw from the Cultural Revolution, especially in combination with parental and family support for political caution because of class. Although no correlation existed in my pool of respondents between parental "backwardness" and the son's decision to participate or continue participating in the Red Guards, a strong correlation did exist between withdrawal from the GPCR as it progressed and parental caution about the effects of over-involvement for a bad classer. There appeared to be a high attrition rate among Red Guards of non-red class background as the factional strife and armed struggle intensified and as class investigations either seemed to be imminent or were already underway. In this atmosphere, a youth began to listen to his parents' pleas, as often motivated by affection and concern for a child's welfare as by any antipathy to politics or the political system, for caution and disengagement.

From the start, some youths, even the most active and politically zealous, found that their class was an ingrained restraining force in their personalities. Wang, an activist Red Guard and early ad hoc leader, was sufficiently conscious of the possibility, because of his bad class, of later being condemned for current activities to demur from writing more than one *ta-tzu-pao*; indeed he refused to come out against the principal.[81] He began to consider withdrawal when the mass-constituted work team arrived on campus in 1968. Rather than join his mates in the ensuing resistance against the work team (fruitless in the end anyway) he remained silent, afraid of "arousing their revenge and adding to [his] crimes."[82] By that time, he had come to feel that he had already risked his life for nothing. He says: "If we were killed, no one would say we were revolutionary heroes."[83] This shift from zeal to bitter cynicism was accompanied by an overwhelming guilt for not having sided with his "struggled" father by heeding his plea earlier to abstain from the Cultural Revolution. He now began to tell himself that he was afraid further action "would hurt [his] father."[84] Soon afterward, thinking of family and self, he withdrew from the Red Guards and returned with a politically negative attitude. A hostile environment in the end had forced him to fall back on his family identity, and to rely on it as his only protector.

Chou Chung-wang, not clearly rebelling against father or seeking to avenge the suffering of his class, initially sought to *compensate* for his class background by participating rather actively in *Hung Ch'i*. Chou explains the restraining effect:

> My meaning is this. Suppose there is a poor man who goes to a rich man's home. He wouldn't know where to put his hands and wouldn't be able to speak. At the same time, if your class is bad, then you are not prosperous in political capital. Your feeling will be just about the same as that of the man without money.[85]

When Chou felt his "political capital," little as it was for someone of his bad class, completely depleted, he withdrew from factional struggle and Red Guard participation. His older brother, himself a target during the Anti-Rightist Campaign of 1957, cautioned him that "in this sort of situation, [he] had best not participate."[86] As his position in the propaganda department seemed to incite the direct antagonism of the other side and as he began to require *Hung Ch'i* body guards for his safety from those *Tung Fengs* who screamed for his "dog life," Chou admitted to himself that his brother was right in stating that there ultimately would be an "accounting."[87] When his father also urged him to remove himself from the cross-fire of armed factional struggle, Chou returned home.[88]

Therefore, bad class, in many cases an impetus to participation in the Cultural Revolution, could also place a subtle restraint on an otherwise active participant. Moreover, encountering adversity because of his class background, a son, who previously might have disregarded the lessons of older members of his family suffering in earlier political movements, and who had dismissed the cautioning words of his parents as either over-protective or politically "backward," now opened his eyes and ears to his family and returned home to avoid possible retribution. The question remains as to whether such a youth could really accommodate himself to authority again in the long run, or, forced to accept authority, could ever rebel again. Or would the alternative for some be the opportunity to flee China?

7. Concluding Commentary: Changes in Family Relations and the Impact of GPCR in Developing the New Socialist Man

I disagree a bit with Mao Tse-tung's interpretation of Marxism-Leninism . . . He emphasizes everything is for the people and not for oneself . . . He emphasizes other people's interests and denies individual interests.

-- Chai Cheng-li VI-3.

From summer 1966 to early 1967, youths could make the political choice of whether and how to participate in the GPCR. They did not react by letting their emotions run wild, or by being sucked into a typhoon-like movement, carried along by every shift in the wind.

Although various explanations exist--many complementary to one another--for explaining the motivation and behavior of youths during the GPCR, one interpretation which applies to the most militant is inter-generational rivalry between father and son, student and authority. All the active Red Guards in this pool of respondents demonstrated that an animating force behind their political behavior in the Cultural Revolution was a need both to compete with their fathers and to move upward into the adult world. Of course, this finding by no means suggests that all competitive youngsters chose a political outlet for self-expression or even that all militant male Red Guards in China were inexorably driven by father-son competition. We have seen only that the portion of young Red Guard militants examined in this study made clear linkages indicating such motivation and were responding in a personal way to what they perceived to be an official invitation to attack political authorities. The historical fact that the GPCR coincided with the adult role-playing and potentially rebellious phase of maturing young people seemed to be far more than happenstance. Rather, the call to youth to be the vanguard of the GPCR appeared to reflect an intuitive awareness on the part of the leadership of the adolescent's predisposition, universally accepted in the West, to strive for generational succession and to invest great energy in the pursuit or fulfillment of ideals.

Most important is that the behavior of our group of respondents indicates rational response, based on both psychological need and the political means at their disposal, to the Cultural Revolution. Individual behavior in this case then does not have to be analyzed in terms of social or religious movements,[1] nor does it necessarily simply represent an outburst of pent-up hostility in reaction to the sudden delegitimation and removal of authority. If an individual joined in the GPCR at first to fulfill an emotional need, he could also withdraw a while later or change the content of his behavior as much to satisfy another personal need as to avoid what he might come to perceive as the dire consequences for him lying ahead. Moreover, peer affiliation, peer ostracism, and class background (in the Chinese Communist sense) were interactive social factors which affected the political decisions of different types of individuals in manifold ways, depending on the immediate and distal circumstances in both the home and school environments.[2]

But self-directed, rather than explosive, behavior with regard to a movement challenging authority had to be predicated on an individual's ability to express his hostility openly in formative situations in the home; and environmental norms in China would have had to encourage such individual assertiveness in the juvenile years.

NORMS LEADING TOWARD A NEW SOCIALIST MAN

One trend in socialization since the communist revolution in China, and even earlier under the impact of modernizing influences, has been a loosening, not a break, in the father-son relationship. Certain forces have been brought to bear which exacerbate, if not encourage, the generational schism. Among these are the reduction of private ownership and inheritance of property, the introduction of public, state-paid education, and the accompaniment of the parent by the state as partner in the selection of adult work roles for the maturing person; the phenomenon of working parents with little time for their children; emphasis on the comparative ideological purity of the post-revolutionary generation and on the general backwardness in thought and behavior of the older generation; the notion that the child should serve as a political teacher in "struggle" between parent and child; the added stigma of bad class background in formerly Kuomintang, landlord, rich peasant, bourgeois, and even petit-bourgeois (including professional and intellectual) families; the dissipation of guilt over conflict with parents in a horizontal and mutually reinforcing peer group at school; the pull which the peer group itself exerts on the individual; and the environmental enticement to self-initiative in the new society even before the GPCR.

Since the older generation no longer passes on tangible wealth to its scions to the same extent, the younger generation, in a spirit of "do not unto others," may rationalize away its filial obligations. Apart from the impact on the young of the separation of the ownership of the means of production from the individual, the state's role in career selection has also made an inroad on the father-son relationship. In earlier times, the youngster strove to emulate his father, especially if the father's achievements were notable and such continuity would reflect well on the fathers and forbears. And if a peasant wished to provide for his son to become a scholar and bring glory to his family, the child was expected to push himself to comply. But in the new society, both mobility within the educational process and career selection are a function of the individual's relation to the state. A child's climb up the educational ladder is determined by his own efforts and achievements, political and academic, and the recognition of his fitness by the authorities. On the academic side, the school child must take a standardized examination to go on to the next highest level. In earlier days, the father could prepare the child for the examinations because of their sterility of content, their repetitiveness, and the susceptibility to bribes of their administrators; if a child failed, private schools and tutors were available to the wealthy. Nowadays, sometimes even academic expertise is insufficient to insure a student's success over the more politically pure or activist.[3] Recommendations of Party Committees actually have replaced examinations since the GPCR. Much control has been removed from the hands of the father. In the words of one respondent:

> As a father, it is impossible to want his son to do some particular thing . . . If he's a teacher, it is impossible to want his son to be a teacher. Because in order to enter university, the son himself must have government permission. The father himself is unable to act.[4]

Moreover, the old standards and status criteria for choosing a career which will bring glory on the family seem to be changing in the new society. Scholarly endeavors may still gratify a "backwardly" elitist father, but social status and material increments derived therefrom are no longer the same for the young individual. A youth seeking to "get with it" may find his father's career values irrelevant! Furthermore, whereas scholarship in the old society was a prerequisite of political mobility, now it can be the nemesis of either the individual seeking shelter from political involvement or the politically ambitious. In Confucian China, scholarship and absorption of the ideology were complementary; now the act of balancing the two--"redness" and "expertise"--can be precarious for the individual. Mr. Liu, who believes primarily in what is good for himself, states:

Irreverance [for parents]--this is inseparable from the national spirit since Liberation. Since Liberation, over the past ten plus years, I could see just one road for myself. Once you graduate from university, you only make fifty *yüan* or so. Most personnel in academe are promoted rather slowly . . . To be a worker was better . . . so I saw that it was futile to go to a university. *It only amounted to doing work that was a little more cultured and that was all--just an old custom in society.*5

Ironically, the child whose own values are traditionally pro-intellectual, elitist and whose father is a high-status worker (skilled and going back several generations) in today's society can also choose to rebuke a father who now feels quite justified in urging his son to follow in his path. "That was merely his opinion," says the worker's son, commenting on his father's suggestion that he choose a career as a skilled worker, learn his trade, and even depend on his contacts for a good, "red" job. "He certainly didn't prohibit me from study, nor did he have the right not to let me study. That is because the cost of going to university was footed by the nation."6 The three-generation worker's child went to university, and majored in classical Chinese literature.

As a child of this generation pursues his student life, he naturally grows more independent of his family. At the very outset of his school career, he is subjected to a new congeries of influences and role models. According to several respondents, relations with parents, particularly non-red classers, can be rather strained at the primary school level. As one states: "Those whom they [the children] most believe are their teachers and schoolmates, because the children are still innocent and naive then."[7] Subjected to further peer pressures as a maturing juvenile, this same respondent at age ten resented his overprotective mother's visiting him at school, during the economic hardship of 1962, to take him out for lunch:

> I didn't ask her to come, but she came anyway. And my schoolmates' mamas didn't come. Thus, I felt somewhat embarrassed before my schoolmates. I felt that this method was harmful to me . . . So at that time, I was deprived of proper social "steeling." I feel a child is just like a plant . . . it should experience wind and rainstorm. But if you always nurture it . . . when there is a big wind, it will die.[8]

Thus, the school milieu and its concomitant peer and societal value pressures encourage a child of this generation to be autonomous and to sacrifice dependency needs in order to become a self-reliant unit of society.

Before the GPCR, by the time a school boy reached lower middle or upper middle school, he sometimes came to reside in the dormitory.[9] At most, he returned home on weekends for a one-day overnight visit. He became less emotionally dependent on his family. Physically removed from his parents as he matured, this type of student was deprived of a systematic knowledge of his father's personal values at an age when he could be most susceptible to them and certainly mature enough to discuss them intelligently.[10] In a pilot study, interviewing in Hong Kong, Ai-li Chin found that by the time a child entered university, parents played no part in the youth's school life. Not even their signature appeared in student applications or records. Parents normally did not appear on campus, either for visits or graduation ceremonies.[11]

Unlike today's elite children in Taiwan who seem to enjoy a close family life until college,[12] post-revolutionary youths in the People's Republic of China have steadily learned to fend for themselves from an early age onward and, though not necessarily to the exclusion of family affiliation, develop an identity apart from their parents.[13]

> The main thing is that the members of the former family were mutually dependent on one another.

Very possibly, the relationship between the old and the young has changed.[14]

The strength of the child vis-à-vis parents is buttressed by the concept that the post-revolutionary generation is relatively free from the feudal and bourgeois conditions of pre-revolutionary society. To the extent that these influences still exist as a nasty residue, the past generation is the carrier. The elders transmit the bourgeois infection to the younger generation, as if spreading a virus. This notion of the new generation's purity, promoted by the regime, reached a zenith before the Cultural Revolution when youngsters were advised that members of their generation were the vanguard of the revolution and should be attentive to the threat of revisionism. As Lan Wei-ying states:

> . . . in thought and political study we emerged from twenty years of a completely new culture. Therefore, a lot of questions subtly embody politics . . . We rather often discuss theory. Theory is a part of politics. Therefore, generally, our thought awareness is higher than the previous generations's.[15]

For young individuals brought up since the revolution, communist education has been the stuff of their maturation, rather than a postscript to this process, as in the case of their parents. They are being educated, their parents "reformed!" These young people grow up contemptuous of such vestigial cultural traits among their parents as Taoist superstition or Buddhist worship,[16] and this contempt tends to legitimate feelings of generational superiority. Sometimes, lacking any concrete evidence that a father who overtly supports communist values is really "backward," a child nonetheless attributes the appropriate characteristics to his father. In Shih Chi-t'ang's home, the father never once was critical of the communists, said nothing contradictory to communist norms, and encouraged his son's political activism. However, young Shih felt that he himself was more progressive because of his long education in the post-revolutionary school system. He considered the activism the father manifested in his work cell to be insincere. "Most people feel their fathers are backward," he says. "As I gradually grew up, I felt this way."[17]

The older generation has to undergo thought reform--

"cure the illness to save the patient." The new generation starts fresh. One respondent feels that his father only read newspapers to prepare for group study meetings in the evenings, whereas he read out of genuine interest in political affairs.[18] Perhaps there is considerable truth in one respondent's conviction that a student is "more sensitive" to political ideals and finds political study easier.[19]

Young people in China regard members of the older generation as politically passive, logs swept along the rapids of revolution. As Lan Wei-ying sees it:

> In the minds of people of their generation, it was just "let things drift" (*te-kuo-ch'ieh-kuo*); they worked for a couple of bowls of rice or for their families only.[20]

In contrast to the alleged passivity of the older generation, Chinese youths feel they have a vitality which impels them to act or make a stand, one way or the other. In this sense, Chinese youths do not differ from the universal image of adolescents in the West, but certainly represent a departure from the image of the traditional Chinese child, deferential to his elders.

If the new generation has cause to believe it is purer and more politically progressive than its precursors, the children of bad classers are still more acutely aware of the cleavage between generations. As bad class children seeking integration into the new society, they are naturally wary of what their parents might say to them and are on their guard against anything in their own outside behavior that might lead others to conclude, "like father, like son." Even when a bad class parent assumes a role that in large part reinforces the new values which the child has learned in school, as in the case of Chu Nan-po, the child might assume that his father's inner emotions are backward. The reason why Chu Nan-po harbors such a suspicion toward his parent is because his father's former standard of living as a postal clerk in Nationalist China was higher than it is now. With the equalization of socialism, Chu Nan-po supposes that his father's income has been appropriately lowered. "Therefore," the son concludes, "father must retain a sort of residual emotion toward his own past good life."[21]

According to Mao's epistomology, unity is achieved through struggle. Only through dialectical criticism can two or more people achieve unity in a mutual understanding of the truth. Children of all backgrounds are encouraged to be teachers to the older generation, often held to be stubborn about relinquishing feudal social habits. By the traditional standards, teaching a parent or grandparent the correct path to tread is not an entirely unfilial act. Mencius said that a child should do everything necessary to gratify and support a parent except to follow wrong instructions.[22] The *Hsiao Ching* later declared that remonstrance was required of a child in cases of unrighteous behavior on the part of the parents.[23] However, in the past, if a father reacted to this remonstration by protesting and beating his son, a child was supposed to assume an especially submissive posture.[24] Still, the submissive role of the son was essentially unmodified by the cultural ethos in traditional society.

Not quite so in today's China! A child is urged to be unrelenting in pointing out the proper ideological way to his elders. For instance, just before the Cultural Revolution, a rural brigade called on one activist youth to serve as a tutor in her own home; "The revolution should start in the home," they said. Trying first to mobilize her mother, the adolescent girl met with this response: "Studying Chairman Mao's works is good, but isn't it customary for a mother to teach her daughter?" Frustrated, she eventually pleaded with her grandfather who was ideologically backward. His initial response was that at age seventy, he was too old to stay out evenings studying Chairman Mao's works. "Besides," he said, "You're trying to work on me--don't you know from whom you should take orders?" Nevertheless, as the story goes, after cajolingly reading from Chairman Mao, the girl got through to her grandfather.[25]

In non-red families too, a child might attempt to teach his "backward" father. Li Cheng's interpretation of Solomon TAT III is that a son, nurtured under the communist regime, is trying to reason with a father who is unsatisfied with the communists. Man and boy quarrel, and the mother, who feels that in her home father and son should have a relationship of mutual respect, flees the room in tears.[26]

Such ideological struggle need not drive a wedge between parent and child. On the contrary, it is meant to draw them closer together, and it can do so. This was so in the case of Lan Wei-ying, whose father on occasion voluntarily sought his help in interpreting a Central Committee pamphlet in order to prepare for the next day's political study at work.[27] But even when this process of struggle-unity between parent and child is successful, it still elevates the position of the child vis-à-vis parent and indirectly facilitates rivalry in what becomes a more horizontal relationship. When the procedure is less than successful, it seems to be a potential source of strain on the inter-generational relationship.[28]

The expansion of education to include the broad masses, the elimination of tutorial-type education in the elite home, and the pervasion of society with a spirit of camaraderie are facets of the New China which have widened the network of social relationships for the young individual and established the peer group as a cross-pressure on the child, one that might be centripetal to the parental influence, all the more so among those less-guarded non-red children.[29]

According to most respondents who were not harassed at an early age in school for some conspicuous parental act against society, it is probably easier for this generation of youths to make friends. Lo Ping-kok, noting that he "was not restricted by family," puts it this way:

> Formerly, there was a boundary line. Most youths' activities were comparatively narrowly circumscribed. It was not as broad a circle as at present. Now the social activities of most youths are rather broad in scope.[30]

The exposure to peer pressures from primary school onward not only tends to reinforce the norms transmitted at school by the teachers and their supporting group of activist, in-group students, but also allows the child to work out within the peer group his natural feelings of hostility or competitiveness toward a parent.[31] Peers provide a particularly important counter-balance to the vertical-type of relationship between parent and child. Fei K'o-Kuan discusses his own means of coping with the need to withhold the overt expression of hostility toward his father:

> Sometimes to hide it inside yourself was intolerable. You had to search out a schoolmate with whom you could talk it over.[32]

Guilt feelings, generated by anti-filial, political behavior in one's effort at social and political integration, can be rationalized and alleviated within the peer group. For the child who informs on a parent in the *ssu-hsiang chien-t'ao* (written self-examination) he submits at school, the group ameliorates strong guilt feelings. Rationalizing the severe criticism of his parents which he recorded in his *chien-t'ao* during the anti-expert movement, Pao Kuo-fu remarks: "Of course, I was a bit guilty, but everyone wrote in this fashion."[33] Just as a small child in China will sometimes steal fruit or other edibles on the street and not feel any guilt as long as he is in the company of other youngsters, so a child often feels guiltless in diverging from filial loyalties with the sanction of the peer group behind him.[34]

In adolescence as the time of his entry into society approaches, the peer pull becomes crucially important for the young man.[35] As Lo Ping-wen, who feels he no longer has any strong sense of family, states:

> I feel that when an individual comes out into society to work, the family is not too important. I feel what is important is friends.[36]

Compounding the multiple environmental pressures on the filial bond is the ideal that in the new society each person can realize his individual potential even in conjunction with social purposes. This aspiration tends to work against the ingrained adherence to a restrictive and prolonged, vertical father-son relationship. The son is thereby further encouraged to challenge his father's ascendency and is also more likely to feel frustrated if due to family circumstances and his own personality, he continues to remain submissively inactive.

Encouraged to feel they have been raised to be self-reliant, the young people now are subjectively convinced that they are more objective and mature than their counterparts in other societies and different eras. One respondent proudly asserts that in comparing Mainland children to those in Hong Kong, "Our children grow up better." "Most children can speak at age one or so . . . and can work," he tries to assure me.[37] Another feels that his generation is too emotionally mature to express hostility toward father by resorting to rage reaction. He and his ilk allegedly would analyze any given situation "objectively." He would cope with his father by scientifically analyzing the interpersonal problem for him. Seeking reassurance of his maturity from the interviewer, he asks, after a moment's pause of apparent self-doubt: "Do you consider this so as you listen to me?"[38]

Many cling to the belief that a child matures faster in China because he is "steeled" in society at an early age, trained in dialectical analysis, and progresses in growth at a pace commensurate with social progress. It could be then that a child reaching adolescence would feel he has overtaken his father.

Education in the school during the 1950s seemed to encourage individual upward mobility. The child was told he should advance himself politically and balk if those in authority did not acknowledge his progress or were too slow in promoting him to a position of prominence and responsibility. In a 1950s primer, there appears a traditional story of a man who drops packages off a boat and marks the spot on the boat, thinking he can search for the parcels beneath the mark after the boat is in port. The contemporary interpretation of this story is that it provides a lesson about those fools whose vision lingers behind the progressive development of reality. This lesson is illustrated by utilizing the more concrete example of YCL cadres who are remiss in admitting new members because, always "using old eyes to view new youths," they denigrate the progress of candidates for recruitment to the YCL.[39] Such an implicit legitimation of the individual's right to feel frustrated over being held back by authorities at school can feed back into the home, reinforcing the resentment over stoppage of mobility there as well. Also, a child who already feels he is being held at too close a rein by a "traditional" father is indirectly led into making a transference from the restraining parent(s) at home to the obdurate, intransigent authority figures at school. Reminded that he has a right to demand deference to his maturity in the school milieu, he can redirect resentment fostered by a possibly restrictive home environment toward school authorities, and vent his hostility on father-surrogates instead. Both father and father-surrogate are challenged by the environmental sanction against those who obstinately deter the mobility of the young. Both father and father-surrogate came under fire during the Great Proletarian Cultural Revolution.

The move toward individual autonomy receives additional impetus from the individualist elements of the projected communist utopia. From the early Marx, who addressed himself to the alienation of an individual from himself in technical society,[40] to Li Ta-chao, who urged the "liberation of the spirit,"[41] communist ideologies have implanted the idea of a self-fulfilled man, as complementary to the norm of personal sacrifice, in the body of Chinese Communist thought and in the educational program. The individualist dynamic is a viable element of Chinese Communism--in its emphasis on the potential of the individual to transcend his class, the right to disagree with a majority decision, and the interaction of individual and group in the enforced group therapy of "thought reform." So much has been said of the crippling effects on the individual of so-called "totalitarianism" that the possibility of the inversion of the totalist dynamic largely has been overlooked. Although one political stereotype holds that as the nation goes so goes the individual,[42] a "total believer" in our group of respondents says:

> As I see it, although my ideal was individualistic, if it could be realized, it would benefit the nation.[43]

Thus, the believer is also capable of perceiving national direction through the lens of his own self-fulfillment.

In addition to the hardship he is urged to endure for the benefit of generations to come, he is encouraged to believe that he will be fulfilled in his lifetime:

> They [the State] themselves also encourage us to believe that in our socialist motherland, every person has a beautiful future *and can open up his own way*. They all spoke in this manner.[44]

The liberation of the individual inexorably begins in the home. The child is encouraged to strive for self-realization in the service of the larger society.[45] The father does not pose too great a barrier, if only he can be replaced by society's embrace.

MORE OPEN BEHAVIORAL TRENDS IN THE HOME EVEN PRIOR TO GPCR

Fostered by the variegated environmental strains on the filial bond, the positive effects of the strong peer group, and the normative sanction of the young person's autonomy and mobility, the increased stature of this new generation is changing the standards of behavior within the family.

The father now often feels constrained to temper his behavior toward children to accord with the pressures and cues he perceives in the environment. Creatures of the past, parents may seem defensive about their background and tend to limit their own role as socializers of the young in a new, radically changing society.[46] A bad class parent in particular is often afraid to discuss politics. Shih Chi-t'ang interprets his own father's reluctance to discuss political questions in this manner:

> I was young. As I got older, I would receive a communist education. If he were to discuss his inner thoughts with us, we would not be able to get through the education on the Mainland. . .[47]

Apparently, class background or a possibly more widespread feeling of generational obsolescence are not the sole determinants of a father's self-restraint in teaching his offspring. As one respondent views the problem, the father perceives that his own role in the socialization process has been impaired:

> Now parents have no confidence to teach their children because the children seem to belong to the nation. As soon as they are graduated, they participate in manual work and go to the countryside. Most parents merely instruct their children not to fight or learn bad things, and that's all. They all lack the confidence to raise [cultivate] their children.[48]

It seems that, at most, the father's role is supposed to be one of helpmate to the government in the education of a child. "If the government wants your son to go to the village, you must assist the government in persuading your son," says Nieh Li-chih, commenting on the secondary role of his father.[49] Another illustration of the reduced role of the parent in New China concerns a mother, who had divorced her husband earlier when he fled to Hong Kong with the Nationalists' exit, and essentially had been mother and father to her child. Her mischievous little son playfully made a pun of a popular slogan concerning "labor Models" (*lau-tung mo-fan*) by chanting to his primary school seatmate, "Labor Models have nothing to eat" (*Lau-tung mo-fan mei-you fan*; in Cantonese, *mei-you fan* and *mo-fan* sound alike). Confronted by the child's teacher and listening to her complaint, the mother scolded and beat the boy. After the teacher left, the mother admonished the child, emphatically stating: "Hereafter, you are forbidden to say such things; the new society requires orthodox education!"[50]

Whether or not a parent is sensitive and responsive to the new environmental cues, the child becomes aware of them and may use them as reference points for his own family situation and as justification for disobedience to parents under certain circumstances. Ch'iao was critical of his mother (his father had fled with the Nationalists before "Liberation," and his mother had got a divorce) even when he was a small child. "Her bad side was that she received the old education; if children didn't obey, she would punish them," he says now.[51] Although the opinion is retrospective, it indicates some insight into their relationship and self-awareness at the time of the experience. Ch'iao frequently rebelled openly against the strict, early discipline of his mother. Possibly responding to the new environment and/or pressure from her children, "when she saw [he'd] got a bit older, she wanted to give [him] some self-respect,"[52] and suddenly abandoned her role as disciplinarian or authority.

The child in the first post-revolutionary generation in China could also find environmental reinforcement for disobeying an ideologically erroneous parent. Shih Chi-t'ang states:

> Before Liberation, the influence of the family was greater. There was a change in the situation after Liberation. One had to obey Chairman Mao's teaching, *but one didn't necessarily have to obey one's parents* . . . Many parents hadn't been educated the proper way. Educating their children to be like them was incorrect . . . If what the parent says is correct and coincides with the laws of social development, then we ought to obey. But if what the parents say is incorrect and of no use to you later, then you can disobey.[53]

Hence, a breach, or even subjectively perceived breach, in the uniformity of the inculcation of values in home and society can become a justification for disobeying parents. Asked what his reaction would be if his parent had attempted to prohibit him from taking part in the Cultural Revolution, Ch'iao replies:

> If my parent could explain to me concretely, I would obey him. Nevertheless, my own personal experience with this sort of movement and the education derived therefrom would run deeper than what he or she said to me.[54]

Parents in today's China frequently seem to their sons

to be bereft of power. As Ch'iao points out, children need not fear that as a result of "struggling" with their parents "they will be beaten, and bound by a tradition that no longer exists."[55] Ch'iao would even feel justified in arguing outright with a teacher (father-surrogate) if he feels his own position is correct.[56] Often, in cases of conflicting values between home and school, a parent will not react to the opposition of his son; he "will realize that the entire style of society has changed and that society now teaches children this new set of values."[57]

Of course, not all parent-son relationships have become so open. Nearly as many relationships represented in this group remained vertical, two or three rigidly so. But even some of these vertical relationships are characterized by a mutual awareness between father and son of the new environmental perquisites, and a few seem to have been bending toward change. The mere recognition on the part of the child that arbitrarily authoritarian demands from the father are pathological in terms of the new social context is a step toward the breakdown of vertical relationships in the home. It is meaningful that a respondent, who asserts that his father was "very tyrannical and strict," adds the phrase, ". . . and very feudal."[58]

Reflecting an apparent trend toward a more open relationship between parent and child is the notably overt and direct expression of hostility toward parents. From an early age onward, children in the first generation since the communist revolution typically give vent to their anger fairly freely. Varying in form and intensity, hostile reactions to an anger-provoking situation involving parent and child are characteristic of all but two people in the pool of respondents. And not one person is unaware of his anger, even if not always openly expressed. Contrary to other impressions about Chinese people, rage reactions in childhood are seldom totally suppressed. Hence, the outsider's image of rebellion in China, in any social milieu, as the explosion of a pressurized container, seems to be inaccurate.[59]

Anger toward parents is expressed directly, but in various ways. As a small boy, Ch'iao often responded to his mother's scolding by slamming the door or throwing a book.[60] Once, when she blamed him for a quarrel with his older brother when he was not really at fault, he resisted her beating by grabbing hold of her hands.[61] A more passive, but just as direct, form of protest is abstention from eating. Such a form of expression is common, even in vertical relationships. The choice of refusing to eat as a frequent means of expressing hostility toward a mother is interesting.[62] Symbolically, it seems to represent the re-enactment of the infant's pulling away from his mother's breast and thus, even in a vertical relationship, seems to contradict the notion that a child is masochistically submissive in the face of parental punishment. The Chinese child today does not unconsciously respond to parental punishment by regressing[63] to infantile dependency and the merging of selves. On the contrary, he *rejects food!*[64]

Another common reaction to parental punishment is to retaliate against a parent's discipline by leaving home for the night or even a day or two to stay at a neighbor's or friend's home. P'eng once ran away, adamant about not returning until his mother came after him and capitulated first.[65] About five youths state that they would have considered leaving home permanently as young children if their punishment had been frequent and arbitrary or unjust; these youngsters would feel the backwardness of their parents would not be socially condoned.[66]

Among those who do not choose to protest parental punishment directly and overtly, at a given time or because of a permanent personality trait, the typical reaction to an anger-provoking situation involving parent(s) is the *internal* refusal to capitulate (*pu-fu-ch'i*). This attitude is manifested by feigning disinterest[67] or mumbling under one's breath.[68] Such a suppression of overt rage, accompanied by an awareness of one's anger and an internal resistance to the hostility-provoking object, might have been a psychological defense already operative among traditional Chinese as well. But I feel that the willingness and readiness to recall these feelings in later years represents an important departure from the traditional stereotype of the emotionally impassive, repressed, Chinese. The youngest, most neglected, and therefore most manipulative of three brothers in an intellectual household (father, a professor), Huang San proudly states that he was "never as obedient as [his] brothers." How did he rebel against his severe father?

> I'd express it in my mind--like mumbling in a low voice.[69]

But at times he also found himself in open confrontation with either or both of his parents.[70]

The notion that a Chinese child will sacrifice his autonomy in order to masochistically obtain the attention of his father or superordinate does not seem to address itself properly to developmental trends in the personality of individuals brought up since "Liberation."[71] All but one person in my pool of respondents--a worker's son--feel that a father who scolds his child publicly is undermining his "self-respect."[72] This sort of response was elicited from relating to them the famous story, in Edgar Snow's biography of Mao Tse-tung, of the thirteen year-old Mao's reaction to his father's scolding him in front of the neighbors; Mao flew into a rage and threatened to commit suicide by jumping in the pond. Of course, I never told the respondents the name of the character in the story, and only one or two of them had ever heard it before. Under such circumstances, most feel anger is warranted because, as Shih Chi-t'ang puts it, "a thirteen year-old's self-respect is strong."[73]

Dignity, integrity, and self-respect seem to be important to this generation of young Chinese. Young Ch'iao, who balked at his mother's heavy-handed treatment of him when he was a small child, comments on his autonomy by the time he reached Primary six (approximately age thirteen).

> Possibly she [mother] saw that we had gotten a bit older, and she wanted to give us our self-respect.[74]

Commenting on the rage reaction of the thirteen year-old in the Mao story, Ch'iao notes:

> If this had occurred a few decades ago during the feudal-traditional period, one should feel it was strange behavior. But in our era, everything has gone through a lot of change from before. People would not be afraid that because they struggled angrily with their parents, they would be beaten, and bound by a tradition that no longer exists.[75]

If a child feels unduly restrained, he may rebel in small ways. As a pre-adolescent, P'eng was forbidden to use the family bicycle. He had just learned how to ride it. Since no one else used it, he wanted to take it to school. However, P'eng met with resistance:

> Mother wouldn't let me. I lost my temper and afterward surreptitiously rode it to school. The next day, I wrote a letter home explaining myself.[76]

This seems to be a clear assertion of self-autonomy and a defiance of the force seeking to restrain it.

Juvenile or pre-adolescent hostility is not merely characterized by rage reactions or indirect defiance, but can also assume the form of constructive debate between child and parent. Yang feels that in a situation of unjust punishment, he would argue with his father or mother. He recalls that his family superiors often focused on his weak points and ignored his assets, and this made him angry.[77] One respondent's reaction to the Mao story is that he would wait until both he and his father were back inside the house, and then openly confront his parent.[78]

The justification for debating parental demands is found in the environmental sanction of dialectical "struggle." Hence, this reaction to the Mao story:

> If this child wanted his father to stop saying he was lazy, the best method would have been to put more of an effort into what he did later on. If this child had been unjustly accused, he should have argued with his father. *Everyone debate, this is the best method.* If it was in front of others, he should still not be afraid. *Debate--because there is only one truth!* . . . Threatening . . . is very ignorant.[79]

Bolstering the child's self-esteem and giving further psychological support to his individual autonomy is the acknowledgement on the part of some modern fathers of their maturing sons' independent achievements. In contradistinction to practices in a more traditional Chinese society where a child's achievement in school might be answered only by the negative threat of a beating if he doesn't continue to do as well in the future,[80] a father in the People's Republic of China will often celebrate his son's accomplishments and reward him for them. An otherwise strict disciplinarian, Hsu Ta-liang's father bought his son new clothes and took him out to a tea house to celebrate young Hsu's success on the upper middle school matriculation examination. Although he did not use words to compliment his son, the father's pleasure was obvious to his son. One father even went to the extreme--previously considered uncouth--of praising his son outright in front of others.[81] It might also be argued that this behavioral change is a symptom of the father's growing feeling of power-loss and his consequent need to bolster his father-role and credit himself with his son's progress.

Whatever the motivation, this trend away from traditional severity and aloofness serves to strengthen the self-identity of today's youth.[82]

The developmental trend in the relationship between parent and child since the revolution is perhaps best summed up by Li Cheng's words:

> In reality, if [father] respects you, you respect him. If he doesn't respect you, then you don't respect him. This is very realistic and natural.[83]

About forty percent (No. 14) of my total pool of respondents have relations with their parents that can be characterized as open, more-or-less horizontal, and approaching a one-to-one basis.[84] The number is almost exactly equally divided between those of "class-enemy" background (children of landlords, capitalists and KMT) and middle-class parentage (sons of petit-bourgeois businessmen, professionals, and intellectuals); one of the three "reds," a peasant, had a very open relationship with his father, a brigade leader. In contrast, a recent, tentative study on urban elite youths in Taiwan shows that only one respondent in twelve, in a heavily westernized milieu, admits to a situation of interpersonal "give and take" with his father.[85]

The rebelliousness and autonomy of youths in the home must be viewed along a continuum of change. Of course, it should be understood that this study by and large concentrates on an urban center, and that resistance to change might be greater in the more rural areas. But an overwhelming majority of this pool of respondents were sensitive to the environmental cues for this sort of change and made some deliberate attempt at self-assertion. Their success was predicated as much on the attitude of the father toward their autonomy as on environmental support and encouragement. If the father remained intransigently authoritarian, it was a difficult task for a child psychologically to get out from under his thumb without making a total break with him. Even if he chose to defy a father and use political channels for this purpose, the bad class youth could not be assured of obtaining an identity and group acceptance alternate to the family either through entry into the YCL or later through the victory of his faction in the GPCR. Thus, rebellion in a vertical relationship was more uncertain unless a youth could feel assured he was either replacing his father (e.g., Lo Ping-kok) or acquiring a new father-ideal. In more horizontal relationships, a father's encouraging and reinforcing his son's autonomy paradoxically invited his son to grow more competitive with him as the two approached equal status. We should recall that in traditional times a father deliberately removed himself from his son, particularly in the village where father and child worked side by side, at least by the time the child reached the adolescent stage.[86] Now, in a changed horizontal father-son relationship a son feels more capable of replacing his father without offending him and can easily project that interpersonal posture into his social and political behavior.

For the non-red youth in a horizontal father-son relationship, political rebellion served as a further act of defiance, autonomy, and quest for adult succession; at the same time, it was pursued more confidently and steadily because the risk of precipitating a total break with family was low. In fact, one of the shortcomings of this study, along with inadequate attention to the changing position of the mother from a passive figure to frequent role-model and from a mediating influence to a pivotal force for generating father-son competition,[87] was the author's failure to probe more deeply into the ways in which the more resilient father bent to the activities of his son. It may well have been that in addition to a consonance of political values or a respect for his son's autonomous decision-making capacity, the horizontal father's proclivity to compromise with son (already noted in Chapter 4) may have been extended to a vicarious identification with his son's adolescent political behavior.

In the Confucian past, the young person who rebelled against his father and severed his ties with his family was considered to have committed an "act of moral violence."[88] Ironically, it was just such persons who often became leaders and innovators. Characters like young Mao and the rebellious son in the *House of Lim* attained to commanding roles in society. The general spread of youth in today's China seem to be moving in this same direction. No longer in a position of swimming against the mainstream of society, they perhaps are not as free as the alienated rebels of the past. But neither are they as likely to revert to their parents' values as long as an alternate identity is now available to them. The relatively autonomous individual in society can make greater contributions than the dependent follower. As long as a person's identity with the new value system remains unbroken, it does not pose a threat to the equilibrium of the polity and society.[89]

SOME QUESTIONS TO PONDER

One problem the political regime faces is that if inter-generational competition is to be manipulated most effectively for political purposes, the political values of both parents must be brought into line with those taught the child at school. In worker Chai's case, an "intellectual" mother stressed the values of a traditional scholar's education, while playing on the son's latent rivalry with father by deprecating his profession. The school might do well to imprint on both the children and parents the notion that proving oneself within the family can best be reflected in devoted, even if individually degrading, "service" to the nation. As Li Cheng says, "The students at school gave too much thought to making a name for themselves and their families: they had not assumed a plan for being ordinary laborers."[90] The encouragement of contradiction or cleavage between parents and child can only be effective if it achieves the purpose of precipitating the total break of a progressive child from a "backward family" or the resolution of the contradiction through the son's re-educating his parents. The latter purpose, less of an interim design than a goal of permanent change in society, is predicated on the parents' receptivity to the remonstrances of their sons and daughters. They must not respond to such remonstration with a beating (as in traditional times) or an accusation of unfiliality, but with a willingness to open themselves to education in the new values. Perhaps, this sort of re-education will be coordinated through educational institutions like the neighborhood schools, instituted since the GPCR, located near the students' homes, and within easy reach of the parents and parental involvement in the school's educational process.

Class background also can be a serious obstacle to effective channeling of generational competition into political activism. Although the bad or non-red class of most of the respondents in this study might have deterred political participation among the more alienated and cautious, it was also an impetus to political activism in the GPCR. Despite the fact that many "class enemy" children often became alienated and resigned to pariah roles early, and others of the non-red classes possibly were deterred from sustained, active participation in the GPCR because of fear of class-based retribution in the end, the more striking response to class-based ostracism in a politicized environment was growing outgroup resentment and an intensified desire to replace the in-group. Suddenly excluded from political participation just before and/or at the start of the GPCR, many of the non-red children in the schools formed a mass of discontented people, less willing to compromise with the conservative position of the original Red Guards because of their previous exclusion from the political process.

Among my respondents, all the most active *Hung Ch'i* Red Guards, also the most competitive and eager to get ahead, indicated a strong resentment toward the political in-group for excluding them and thereby thwarting their efforts at a crucial stage for upward mobility and social acceptance in adult roles. As rebels against authority in the home and sometimes at school, they were frustrated over this increased blockage to them at school; and once having transferred their rebelliousness from parent to teacher, they were just as apt to project their hostility toward the father-surrogate political elite on to the student elite; most of the latter had been the sons and daughters of those in power whom the ostracized youths perceived to be holding them back.

If their class background had not been a barrier to them, many of the more rebellious and upwardly mobile young people would have gladly joined the political process and would have felt no need to push their way in as outsiders. Still others, like Hsieh, who would have liked to be part of things, would not have been restrained from political activism because of the stigma of bad class background. Many of the non-red class youths questioned the justice of discriminating against children of non-red parents. But perhaps it was also somewhat warranted if a residue "bourgeois" class influence really was to stand some chance of being eliminated from the new society. While it is true that Mao's maxim of each individual's being able to rise above his objective class origins through self-reform was sometimes not properly applied in reality to many eager youths, still other young people had a definite psychological aversion to renouncing their class in specific terms. Hsieh, Lo Ping-kok, Nieh Li-Chih, and others were unable to bear criticism of their class origins, let alone renounce it, because it was inextricably linked psychologically to an identity with their fathers. They refused to "draw a clear line" between themselves and their fathers when the fathers in effect had not changed themselves. Should they not be held to account for their parents' class? One bad class respondent "drew the line" by simply ritualistically criticizing his parents, pretending to behave in a very activist manner and attending YCL classes every Saturday instead of going home for the weekly holiday.[91] Some were even able to chart a safe, middle course for themselves, compartmentalizing their lives at school and in the home, even through the early phase of the GPCR. This was possible in a horizontal family relationship in which the father was both objectively and subjectively "backward" in his political values and yet, because of the father-son relationship he nurtured, would not intrude on his son's outside activities. Nor did every son from an open family relationship have to conform to the father-competitive, activist type. A passive participant like Li Cheng was able to withstand the contradiction between intellectual elitist, "backward," but tolerant parents and his own stance at school, well before the GPCR erupted.

> My teachers said that I was a middle element. I neither demanded very much nor was I very "backward." I said that my parents' influence on me had a good side as well as a bad side. The good side was that they let me go along with the Communist Party . . . the bad side was that their petit-bourgeois thought was rather deep; they emphasized reputation and self-interest; their revolutionary spirit was not strong, and this manifested itself in my own insufficient demand for progress . . . I had no need either to support the middle class or to take the burden of attacking them.[92]

In this manner, at least part way through the GPCR, Li Cheng, politically active even if a bit short of the ideal, could cope with the contradiction between the societal and family spheres.[93]

Of course, apart from any continuance of this negative behavioral syndrome among the children of non-red families, it is quite possible that the leadership, following past patterns and in accordance with its current post-GPCR emphasis on the persistence of the "two class lines" in society, will wish to sustain a contrived class struggle. Its purpose would be to use "class struggle" for generating emotional energies in future political movements. If lines of tension do not continue to exist among the people, then they must be created. Will children in the future be held to account for their parents' class background or misguided political behavior? And as some cynics among those interviewed wondered, what about grandchildren? Indeed, the stigma of bad class background can be overcome. The voluntarist dynamic in Mao Tse-tung Thought makes it theoretically possible for anyone to transcend his objective class and "stand on the proletarian field."[94] However, in actual practice, the requirements for a bad class child to make such a leap have been severe. In the words of one respondent:

> Bad classers have to do something startling to prove themselves. For instance, a landlord's son would have to criticize his father for exploiting the peasantry, and announce that he has cut himself off from his father.[95]

Explicitly, the decision to "draw the line" (*hua-ch'ing-chieh-hsien*) between self and father means going quite far. During each session of political study, everyone is required to reveal his family situation. For example, if there is a person who comes from a landlord background, the YCL Secretary will often try to persuade him to reject any financial aid he might receive from his father in order to demonstrate that he is "drawing the line."[96]

Showing the lengths to which a bad class child must go to attain success, one account states:

> In our school, there was a person, vice-chairman of the Student Association. Her family was "landlord." Her father had been executed by the Communist Party. They followed their mother . . . and lived in their mother's house. Her mother depended for her food on income from rent. She had two daughters . . . Afterward, this daughter said her mother was a landlady and so severed relations with her. She didn't go home to live, but moved to the school and thoroughly drew a line between herself and her family. She didn't use her family's things and didn't take money from them . . . The school gave her a monthly supplement of 12 Yüan on which she was to live. She lived at school; life was bitter. She often undertook jobs at school. On Saturday and Sunday, when there was no class, she helped with work at school. So the school said she was good. Later on, she entered the YCL . . .

And afterward, she was elected vice-chairman of the Student Association.[97]

The psychological force of severing relations with a bad class parent is indicated in the following description of an acquaintance.

> In my younger brother's school, there was a girl who during the GPCR brought the *Chu-yi-ping* herself to search her home. Her mother and father were both very hurt. Her father was *very* hurt. He died the next day. I considered his death a direct result of his anger at his daughter. In addition, he was injured from being kicked.[98]

Regardless of which kick, the physical or psychological one, was the more instrumental in the father's death, the daughter had been induced to wage a personal revolution against her parents. And it was the need to struggle against her own class background that carried her to this extreme. The tragedy of discrimination on the basis of class background, before the Cultural Revolution or at some time again in the future, is that many who "draw the line" but fail to sever the emotional bonds with their family entirely--an especially difficult task for the family-conscious Chinese--are wasted as a result of such policy.

Although my impression is that none of the non-red respondents in my group ever went quite as far as the girls cited above, nearly two-thirds admit trying to rid themselves of the yoke of their family background in some way at various stages of their maturation. One-fifth *seriously* attempted to enter the YCL and made an effort to prove they had "drawn the line." Frustrations of these efforts counterproductively produced or contributed to a sense of social alienation. Chu Nan-po, later to become a Red Guard leader, gave up attending preparation classes for the YCL because a good friend of his had "slaved for a year" and still could not qualify.[99]

Does the young person's need to maintain some emotional tie to parents justify a policy of excluding the children of bad class background from political participation and social mobility because they will not totally divorce themselves from family? Admittedly, they risk being contaminated by their parents and spreading "bourgeois" infection to social organization; but how many years must pass before the non-red youth will be able to count on the same social integration as the red without complete forfeit of family ties? And judging from this study alone, can the leadership be assured that the children of red parentage, like Tseng, are bound to come closer to the socialist ideal than non-reds like Chu Nan-po? One cannot help think that many a bad class child who could serve society well is unnecessarily thrown back on family identification or cast adrift as a consequence of the required radical leap to autonomy from family, the guilt engendered by attempts to make that leap, and the risk of society's closing its portals to him anyway and totally denying him psychological support for his action. Thus, an important condition for rebellion within the family--generational rivalry exacerbated by class struggle--may contain within itself the seeds of a counterproductive alienation of the individual.[100]

Recent reports from China describe a remarkable return to normality in all spheres of life in China since the Great Proletarian Cultural Revolution. Although children of non-red classes were excluded from admission to higher academic institutions before the GPCR, radio reports from Fukien indicate that new children of non-red class origins, as in the period immediately following the Great Leap Forward, are being admitted on a quota basis; more attention is apparently being given to academic performance in the decision to admit children of the exploiting classes.[101]

Despite the return to normality or temporary normality, has the GPCR not left its imprint on Chinese socialization? Apart from the subtle nuances of change, particularly in primary socialization, which we may only be able to detect much later in retrospect, some questions remain for consideration. First, will children in the future be more likely to challenge their teachers in class, defying the traditional good manners of a student's remaining quiet until he is asked to recite? Observers who visited the PRC in 1971 noticed middle school children "talking back" to teachers in class, but others who visited a year later did not witness students questioning teachers at all, except in university. The matter of whether the GPCR had an impact on the institutionalized behavior of young people in school is ground for speculation. Second, does the formation of post-GPCR Red Guard organizations in middle schools, in addition to a reformed YCL at higher level institutions, mean that more youths will be brought into the realm of political decision making and implementation rather than excluded from the political in-group as before the GPCR? Third, how will those young individuals who experienced participation in the GPCR be re-integrated into society? In view of the large and continuing flow of youths to Hong Kong each year in the wake of the GPCR and its implications concerning response to future movements of this type, this question is both immediate and far-reaching and deserves further attention.

If it continues to encourage self-assertion of youth in the home and as the vanguard of political movements like the GPCR, the Chinese communist regime faces a still greater imperative, deriving from human nature, of meeting rising individual expectations concerning responsible participatory roles in adult society and of keeping individual autonomy within bounds. The problem of educating young people toward autonomy and responsible participation and then manipulating increasingly assertive adolescents in such a manner that they consider themselves the vanguard of a major political movement is that it becomes difficult to contain the development of self-esteem and self-importance among individual youths. For political purposes the inflation of the adolescent self must not become so uncontrollable that it cannot be made to submit to authority and withdraw again into a dependent role. Such was the case in the GPCR when adolescent youths often got so out of hand that even "Destroy self" drives coordinated with periodic re-assertions of the military failed to achieve the desired results and made the *hsia-hsiang* of former Red Guards the only realistic approach to unmanageable youths. Although other reasons were apparent for the *hsia-hsiang* movement, Chou Chung-wang's interpretation is relevant in this context.

> Based on what they said, our former education was bad. Therefore, we had to be re-educated again from the start by poor and lower middle peasants . . . This in fact was so. This was the case in reality.[102]

Greater permissiveness in Chinese society, as in our own society, makes adolescents more anxious to take the helm and leads them to expect more as individual members of society. Since the role-testing behavior of adolescents is so erratic, it would not be feasible to place them in very responsible adult positions, even if such positions were readily available.

In the GPCR, many youths were responding to the "world is yours . . ." call. Quoting the "little red book," Red Guard activist Lan Wei-ying observed: "'The next generation comes and still another follows'--this phrase makes sense."[103] Only later did he come to believe, as the Cultural Revolution subsided and normality was restored, that the short clause, ". . . as well as ours," inserted in the statement promising the world to youth, was an equally important element of Mao's famous quotation.[104]

The inflation of the self-esteem of youths during the GPCR was undeniably encouraged. Young people really were led to believe that their skills would be put to use during the movement and afterward in their adult roles. As one of the *Quotations* states:

> The Party organizations should not treat the youth in the same way as everybody else and ignore their special characteristics.[105]

Hence, many suffered dire disillusionment when, at the end of the Cultural Revolution, they were sent to the countryside to work alongside and learn from the peasants. After all, their school education did not really prepare them for the plow. What most zealous young people did not seem to foresee was the extension of the meaning of *integration with the masses* to imply adherence to the commands of those spokesmen embodying the will of the masses (the essence of democratic centralism)--the party or revolutionary committees.

The utilization and manipulation of student mobility in the Cultural Revolution contained an important contradiction evident even during the Yenan period more than two decades earlier; Party discipline and thought reform then had to be promoted to consolidate a re-established and expanding Party organization comprising intellectuals more accustomed to demonstrations than to discipline.[106] How could individual spontaneity, autonomy, and initiative be juxtaposed properly with the ideal of serving the masses? The inflated self searches for emotional satisfaction and continuity in the assumption of adult roles. The activist student Red Guards, who considered themselves at most the rising elite and at least intellectuals who would serve society in roles for which they had been trained, would find it difficult to accept a break in continuity and a resumption of the dependency role vis-à-vis teachers or other authorities. Even if they had not yet succumbed, like the pre-GPCR Youth Leaguers and earlier officials, to the conservatism and arrogance endemically accruing to those in positions of power, these zealots had tasted the power. Now they were forced to accept it as a transitory illusion. Like Lan Wei-ying, they came to realize the importance of the modifying clauses and caveats to the encouraging and inspiring *Quotations*. For instance, after reading through the statement in the "red book" about young people as a "vital force," one comes to this closing sentence:

> Of course, the young people should learn from the old and other adults, and should strive as much as possible to engage in all sorts of useful activities with their agreement.[107]

The dynamic of generational rivalry had been an animating force for adolescent behavior, and ultimately it would have to be brought under control for the sake of restoring social order. The true test of a revolutionary was to advance actively and then accept the will of the leadership in the wake of activity. Of course, none of the possible successes in this process of resolving the contradiction between personal activism and ultimate subjection fled China, much less joined my sample of respondents. But Chou Chung-wang realized the problem which the regime faced:

> Later on, when he [Mao] saw that the rebelliousness of the students had surpassed the desired scope and felt it would develop further, perhaps against himself, he sent all the students down to the countryside (*hsia-hsiang*).[108]

Lan Wei-ying came closest. He felt his Red Guard activity should have constituted a social contribution surpassing his father's but that history had ruled that "objectively this activity [in the GPCR] was not too suitable to the discipline of the development of the movement,"[109] nor apparently to himself.

Once again, the autonomous self, in many cases, apparently outgrew authority when it could not replace the authority itself. In a sense, the post-revolutionary youngster had been variously encouraged all along to assert his autonomy vis-à-vis parents and family and to be self-reliant. If many youths became frustrated in their efforts at self-development, perhaps their disappointment was not so far removed from that of the young adult in our own society who, beginning at an early age in a permissive home environment, is socialized to be an active participant in a "civic culture" and then finds himself essentially excluded from the process of political participation.[110]

But the question still remains whether it is at cross-purposes with human nature to expect youth in China to go through a self-inflating movement like the GPCR and then submit to rigid authority under a "democratic-centralist" system. Can they bear up under the psychological discontinuity of preparing for political, academic, or urban factory careers, playing for awhile at being the elite, and then suddenly being sent down for a lifetime in the countryside? Will their younger sisters and brothers be more reserved, based on the lessons of their older siblings, when and if their time comes to invest their energies in a political movement? Or by that time, will they either make the same misjudgments or throw themselves more zealously into participation, because of an increased proclivity to self-expression and rebelliousness in the home and school or because one never learns a lesson unless he experiences it himself?

NOTES, BIBLIOGRAPHY, INDEX

Notes to the Chapters

CHAPTER 1
Pages 1-12

1. The studies referred to above are Gabriel Almond and Sidney Verba, *The Civic Culture* (Boston: Little, Brown, 1965) and Alex Inkeles and Raymond Bauer, *The Soviet Citizen* (Cambridge: Harvard University Press, 1961). The latter study was based on extensive interviews with Russian emigres in the late 1950s.
2. Peter Blos, *On Adolescence: A Psychoanalytic Interpretation* (New York: The Free Press, 1962), p. 209. A common psychological reaction to the delegitimation of one's consecrators.
3. One common symptom of *identity confusion*, resulting from being kept out of the YCL or later perhaps from frustration in the wake of the GPCR itself, was the sudden development of superstition and faith in a pre-ordained fate. See Shih Chi-t'ang III-18, who first became superstitious when the YCL turned him down. Interviewee Liu and many others suffered similar symptoms after frustration of acceptance and mobility in the GPCR.
4. Of course, the corps of Red Guard propagandists (*wen-tou-tui*) who specialized in the political research necessary for the preparation of newspapers and more sophisticated *ta-tzu-pao* particularly tended to be more cynical about politics and leaders; their own reverence for their leaders at every level receded as they investigated the real-life details about the authorities. See Chou Chung-wang, Pao Kuo-fu, *passim*.
5. Father-surrogates is a term denoting those personalities in the social environment beyond the family who is in the perception of a youth, assume some of the salient aspects of his father's personality, usually because of their authority roles. Because a youth sees his father in such an individual, his behavior toward that individual is influenced by his feelings toward his father.
6. Cf. Neale Hunter, *Shanghai Journal* (Boston: Beacon, 1971), pp. 56-60.
7. *Ibid.*, *passim*.
8. See also Chapter 7 of this study. In fact, I am now in the process of further research which pursues this line of inquiry.
9. Eugene Burdick and Arthur Brodbeck, *American Voting Behavior* (Glencoe: Free Press, 1959), esp. Chapter 22; Angus Campbell, Gerald Gurin and Warren E. Miller, *The Voter Decides* (Evanston: Row, Peterson and Co., 1954), pp. 97-100.
10. Franz Alexander, "Emotional Factors in Voting Behavior," in Burdick and Brodbeck, *op. cit.*, pp. 300-307.
11. A small gratuity customarily is *offered* for each interview.

12. Richard Solomon, *Mao's Revolution and the Chinese Political Culture* (Berkeley: University of California Press, 1971), Appendix V, pp. 541-556.
13. The boundary years of adolescence can only be set arbitrarily. Very generally, "adolescence" is defined here as encompassing those years between puberty and the formation of a sexual love relationship between two partners as well as the attainment of an adult work role.
14. See Fig.1.2., p. 14, N=11. It should be noted that class background is *not necessarily* an index of political behavior during the GPCR.
15. Yang Ying-pu I-6.
16. It should also be noted that many of those who left China did not make their decisions as an immediate response to disillusionment, disorientation or dislocation resulting from the GPCR *per se*. A large percentage of educated youths sent down to the countryside in border areas found themselves in an environment where other educated youths from the cities were leaving for Hong Kong daily and circulating maps of land and water routes. Uncomfortable among the local peasantry (often living apart from them), displeased with the hardship of rural life and most important, finding themselves *sucked into peer groups comprised of other educated youths from the city planning escape*, this alternative suddenly seemed an attractive one. Many of those who made the ultimate decision to leave China had not even considered such a thing prior to their being sent down to a border area.
17. Irene B. Taeuber, "Hong Kong: Migrants and Metropolis," *Population Index*, Vol. 29, #1, January 1963, 3-4.
18. Franz Schurmann, *Ideology and Organization in Communist China* (Berkeley: University of California Press, 1966), pp. 101-102.
19. Kingsley Davis, "The Theory of Change and Response in Modern Demographic History," *Population Index*, Vol. 29, #4, October 1963, pp. 355-356.
20. See, for example, Chou Chung-wang I-30.
21. Yü Ming-li I-12-13.
22. The impression, for example, of Nieh Ching-chih IV-11.
23. Chen II-12.
24. I also used some of Solomon's TATs and my own word association test, both of which proved to be of limited value.
25. The latter, for example, was reflected in the disillusionment of many very committed Red Guards.
26. Harry Stack Sullivan, *The Psychiatric Interview* (New York: Norton, 1954), *passim*.
27. P'eng Te-lai II-17.
28. Nathan Leites, *The Viet Cong Style of Politics* (Santa Monica: Rand Corp. Memorandum RM-5487-1ISA/ARPA, 1969), *passim*.
29. Walter Slote, "Case Analysis of a Revolutionary," Frank Bonilla and Jose Michena, ed. *A Strategy for Research on Social Policy*, Vol. I *(The Politics of Venezuela)* (Cambridge: MIT, 1967), *passim*.
30. Ken Ling, *Revenge of Heaven* (New York: Ballantine, 1972), *passim*.
31. Chai Cheng-li IV-11.
32. See *Daedalus*, "Philosophers and Kings," Summer 1967. A converse approach is to try to correct this weakness by refreshing the respondent's memory for him. (See the introduction to Bennett and Montaperto, *Red Guard*). When the pseudonymous Dai Shao-ai had difficulty recalling specific events and issues in the GPCR, the authors "solved" the problem by sending him back to the library to read up on the Cultural Revolution. The question then becomes: Did the informant refresh his memory or gain new knowledge which was absorbed into his later testimony? Although I could not send my respondents back to

the books, I could have asked leading questions. I tried to avoid this pitfall.
33. E. Walster, "The Temporal Sequence of Post-Decision Processes," in L. Festinger, ed. *Conflict, Decision & Dissonance* (Stanford: Stanford University Press, 1964), pp. 112-128.
34. Yang III-13.
35. Yü Ming-li I-17-18.
36. Lan Wei-ying III-33.

CHAPTER 2

1. For a detailed discussion of the denouement of the GPCR in Kwangchow, particularly in the schools, see Bennett and Montaperto, *Red Guard: The Political Biography of Dai Shao-ai* (New York: Anchor, 1972), *passim;* and Hai Feng (pseud.), *Kwangchow ti-ch'u wen-ko li-ch'eng shu-lüeh* [An account of the Cultural Revolution in Kwangchow] (Hong Kong: Union Research Institute, 1970), *passim*.
2. *Hung Ch'i and Jenmin Jihpao* Edutorial Departments, "On Khrushchev's Phoney Communism," trans. in *Current Background*, #737, July 14, 1964, pp. 32-33.
3. Interview with Edgar Snow, January 1965, in *Washington Post*, February 14, 1965.
4. "On May Fourth Movement," Mao Tse-tung, *Selected Works*, III (New York, International, 1965), p. 17.
5. Mao Tse-tung, *Quotations* (Peking: Foreign Languages Press, 1966), pp. 290-291.
6. *Quotations*, pp. 291-292; a still more explicit statement appears in the companion piece to the original 1939 article. See "Orientation of the May Fourth Movement," *Selected Works*, III, *op. cit.*, p. 10.
7. Chou Chung-wang VII-15. Italics added.
8. Yeh Hen II-14, describing the situation in July 1967.
9. Although one might assume from the start that the Mao faction also *used* the young Red Guards, as it did the army, to smash the Liu-ist Party apparatus, nevertheless the Red Guards' early self-appraisal and interpretation of their roles is a more important indicator of why they participated, and with such zeal.
10. Chou Chung-wang II-39. The "criticism of the 'Three Family Village'" refers to the early criticism in the schools of the Peking writers in May 1966.
11. *Quotations* (1966), p. 288.
12. Wu Kuo-chih V-5.
13. Wang Lok-ch'ao III-6-7.
14. Shih Chi-t'ang IV-4. Emphasis added. Doesn't Shih's cry call to mind the familiar song of the youth culture in the United States-- adolescents convinced the older generation has gone astray and self-righteous about their own vision and rectitude? Of course, Mao encouraged this feeling among the youth in China.
15. Stanley Karnow, *Mao and China* (New York: Viking, 1972), pp. 157-170.
16. *Ibid.*, pp. 170-171; or "Chronology of Important Events Between the Two Lines in the Field of Higher Education," *SCMM* (supp.), No. 18, February 26, 1968, p. 30.
17. See, for example, Yang Ying-pu IV-18. This same dilemma of *horreur de face-à-face* in personal conflicts between individuals on different levels in a French bureaucracy is dealt with very nicely by Michel Crozier, *The Bureaucratic Phenomenon* (Chicago: University of Chicago Press, 1964), *passim*. Crozier also draws our attention to this phenomenon in Japanese culture.

18. Beginning in early June with his praise of Nieh Yuan-tzu and then with the CCRG's recognition of Kuai's protest against the Tsinghua work team headed by Wang Kuang-mei (Liu Shao-ch'i's wife), Mao and the CCRG threw their weight behind the spontaneous-action groups on campus against the work teams. This trend culminated in the Central Committee's "Sixteen Points" on August 8. Bennett and Montaperto, *op. cit.* pp. 60-61; Stanley Karnow, *op. cit.*, pp. 174-175.
19. See, for example, Chu Nan-po I-19.
20. Bennett and Montaperto, *op. cit.*, p. 129.
21. See Yang IV-15; Professor R. Sinha came up with similar figures in a lecture at Columbia University's East Asian Institute in spring 1973 and the point was more generally confirmed in Theodore Chen's *Mao Tse-tung's Educational Revolution* (New York: Praeger, 1974), *passim*.
22. Yang IV-15.
23. Ch'iao Kuo-hsiung IV-18.
24. Ch'iao Kuo-hsiung IV-4-5.

CHAPTER 3

1. "Class enemy" children, as distinct from those who were to be labelled "bad class" at the start of the GPCR, were the sons and daughters of landlords, capitalists, former KMT members or army affiliates, and people targeted in Post-Liberation Campaigns, such as the Anti-Rightist campaign of 1957.
2. Cf. Lucy Jen Huang and Alan G. Hickrod, "Communist Chinese and American Adolescent Sub-cultures," *China Quarterly* (hereafter CQ), No. 22, April-June 1965, 176-180.
   One should question, of course, whether there is ever an ideal uniformity, as the Hickrods contend exists for China, between home and school socialization or smooth continuity between childhood roles and adult roles. Certainly, in our own society, the discontinuities are complex, sharp, and glaring. In my own study, I treat *uniformity* through the perception of the informant. My criteria hinge on his own assessment of sharp contrasts between political education at home and school. Subjectively perceived, however, *sometimes* these abstract contrasts seem to be more fantasy (this is determined by the context of discussion--need of respondent to rationalize unfilial behavior, indications of paranoid sensitivities engendered by bad class stigma, and total lack of supporting examples and evidence of these contrasts) than reality. But the individual's perception is what matters!
3. Fang Yu, "Break Family Ties, Be a Good Child of the Proletariat," *Chung - Kuo Ch'ing - nien*, #21, Nov. 1, 1964 in *Survey of China Mainland Magazines* (SCMM), No. 448, 39. This polemical article appeared at the height of the *Ssu-Ch'ing* movement in 1964.
4. *Ibid.*, 40.
5. See, for example, the interesting case of Shih Chi-t'ang who thoroughly felt on the outside of his peer group and yet saw his father as a negative image because attachment to father would have been counter-productive to his own preoccupation with self-interest. During the GPCR, Chi-t'ang joined his local street Security team (*tiao-ch'a-tui*), a move designed to avoid the GPCR in the schools and the risk it involved, while giving the appearance of activism.
6. Cf. Lucy Jen Huang and G. Alan Hickrod, "Communist Chinese and American Adolescent Sub-cultures," *op. cit.*, 176-180. The authors contend that in contradistinction to the U.S., no adolescent youth subcultures exist in China because of a well-controlled and uniquely

uniform socialization system between home and schoolroom. Although they acknowledge the formation of such a revolutionary youth subculture shortly after the political campaigns of the early 1950s, they argue that the regime seemed to have brought socialization under viable control since then, effectively making the inculcation of homogeneous values a sure thing.

Quite apart from the validity of this generalization for proletarian families (which I tend to doubt on the basis of three case studies), the authors apparently overlooked the matrix for discontinuity in the persisting emphasis on class and class struggle. Even when filiality was promoted in the late 1950s, children of bad classers were still urged to resist and struggle their parents. Yao Yuan-fang, "From Filial Piety to the Treatment of Parents," *Chung-kuo Ch'ing-nien*, #21, Nov. 1, 1956.

7. One-fourth of the parents in my sample were openly critical of their present life and the post-revolutionary government. Of these, only one-half were of "class-enemy" background.
8. Peng Te-lai I-10.
9. Lo Ping-wen VIIB-5. Ping-wen was afraid that his parents "would say something" if they saw his red arm band. (VI-8-9) Their frequent aspersions against the regime led him to this deduction.
10. E.q. Hsieh Ting-teng I-19; Yüan Ching-po, *passim*.
11. Perhaps this impression is partly a distorted one. It is possible that the abortion of such mechanisms could be due in part to the already existing alienated state of many of the youths in question. But others who were not alienated at an early age also speak of the ineffectiveness or limited effectiveness of these devices.
12. See p. 121.
13. Nieh Li-chih IV-12.
14. Lo Ping-kok III-8.
15. "Ho Ch'ing-nien T'an Ku Lun Chin" [Making the Ancient Relevant to the Present in Talking with Youth], ed. Yüan Yu-ming (Peking: Chung-Kuo Ch'ing-nien Ch'u-pan-she, 1956), pp. 11-13.
16. Lo Ping-kok III-4.
17. Ai-li Chin, "A Modern Meaning of Filialism Among College Elite" (Unpublished paper prepared for Seminar on Cognitive and Value Systems in Chinese Society, Bermuda, January 1964), 10. I should qualify this remark by noting such exceptions as private tuition in certain circumstances and also some parents' appearance on campus during the GPCR (an example of the latter phenomenon in the case of respondent Chai).
18. See, for example, Yeh Hen IV-15.
19. *Ibid*.
20. My impression is that these devices were really primarily designed to create *conflict*, rather than either facilitate uniform socialization or smooth the youth's integration into the new society. Such conflict or contradiction would fit into the Maoist scheme, but in reality did not have to resolve itself either in unity (Cf. *On Handling of Contradictions Among the People*) or in a socially positive, rather than negative, polarized decision. Conflict could work for the regime only so long as it was psychologically comfortable for the individual.
21. See Hickrod, "Communist Chinese and American Adolescent Sub-cultures . . .," *op. cit.*, *passim*. Cf. Robert Herriott, "Some Social Determinants of Educational Aspirations," *Harvard Educational Review*, spring 1963, on general role conflict in the U.S.; or Alan B. Wilson, "Residential Segregation of Social Classes and Aspirations of High School Boys," *American Sociological Review*, December 1959, on community-variable role models in the U.S.

22. Lei Feng was particularly regarded as either a contrivance or a fool.
23. This was a famous incident in which rumor had spread that anyone could board this train without permit; the PLA moved in for arrests.
24. Chou Chung-wang V-14.
25. *Ibid.*
26. Chou Chung-wang II-5.
27. Hsieh Ting-teng II-11.
28. Hsu Ta-liang III-8-9.
29. See Chou Chung-wang II-8-9. Chou's group consisted of 12 members, divided into four "progressives," four "mediums" and four "backwards." Activists led the discussion and encouraged "mediums" to join in the attacks on "backwards"; but this could be done in a very impersonal and ritualized fashion.
    Generally, an outline had been prepared beforehand for each meeting's discussion. (Chou Chung-wang II-4).
30. Chou Chung-wang II-10.
31. Yang Ying-pu II-14.
32. One should always bear in mind that these mechanisms were not created for bad classes, but for the proletarian majority in the wider population.
33. See such cases as the Huangs, Liu K'e-chung, Wu Kuo-chih, etc.
34. The "horizontal" father (see next chapter), on the contrary, seemed all the more willing to bend to environmental pressures. In personality, this type, regardless of class, seemed more receptive to both the social and political cues from the environment.
35. All three boys escaped at different times since the GPCR, and all were interviewed.
36. Huang Yi I-4.
37. Huang may have wanted to dismiss his unfilial rebelliousness by sympathizing with his father for the same social pressures, he says, drove him to leave China. Actually, from the time he left for Hong Kong, Huang Yi seems to have been going through a gradual process of self-assertion and defiance of the habits his father taught him when he was a child. These behavioral changes were telescoped in the deepening interview relationship. Stiff, formal, and "proper" at the outset, he later began to march about with his hands deliberately implanted in his pockets and, when I last saw him, had taken to spitting as an expression of anger and disgust.
38. Huang Yi I-3.
39. Huang Yi I-4.
40. *Ibid.*
41. Huang San I-5.
42. Despite obvious feelings of rivalry with their father, Huang Yi and Huang Erh had always been prone to emulate him; belittled, Huang San did not have this option or any other.
    Adult identity is a term coined by Alexander George to denote that period of crisis between childhood and adulthood in the psychological growth of an individual when one seeks to relate earlier traits and experiences to adult roles. See Alexander George, "Power as a Compensatory Value for Political Leaders," *Journal of Social Issues*, Vol. 24, #3, 29-50.
43. Huang Yi IV-2, I-3.
44. Huang Yi I-3.
45. See testimony of Huang San, *passim*.
46. Once she crossed the border dressed in Amah's clothes.
47. Huang Yi II-5-7.
    In her discussion with this interviewer, Mrs. Huang admitted that she had deliberately used this device to persuade her sons; she herself,

she says, felt her husband was naive for continuing to remain in China. Huang Erh, *passim.*, reveals the bitterness his father felt over their leaving.
48. See Chapter 4, p. 99, n. 41.
49. Huang Yi I-4.
50. *Ibid.*
51. Nieh Li-chih I-10.
52. Nieh Li-chih I-4.
53. Nieh Li-chih IV-9-10.
54. Nieh Li-chih III-18-19.
55. Nieh Li-chih III-19.
56. Nieh Li-chih IV-10; also see III-18-19, and II-17.
57. He got into a people's school (*min-pan hsueh-hsiao*) instead of one of the higher grade, elite institutions.
58. Nieh Li-chih IV-3.
59. Nieh Li-chih II-18.
60. Nieh Li-chih III-20.
61. Nieh Li-chih I-7.
62. Nieh Li-chih II-6.
63. Nieh Li-chih IV-7.
64. *Ibid.*
65. Nieh Li-chih IV-15-16.
66. Wu Kuo-chih V-1.
67. Wu Kuo-chih II-3. Some non-red classers got away with early participation in the Red Guards primarily because friendship ties often seemed to obscure proper attention to/or investigation of class. Yang started a *Chu-yi-ping* and later became a major *Hung Ch'i* leader, only withdrawing late in 1967, when he felt a close investigation might reveal the fact that his father (he was living with grandmother) was a KMT in Taiwan. The *extent* of Yang's deception, however, seemed more the exception than the rule.
68. *Ibid.*
69. *Ibid.*
70. Wu Kuo-chih V-3.
71. Shih Chi-t'ang V-2.
72. Shih Chi-t'ang IV-10-11.
73. Shih Chi-t'ang III-2.
74. Shih Chi-t'ang V-16.
75. Shih Chi-t'ang I-8.
76. Shih Chi-t'ang IV-36.
77. Shih Chi-t'ang II-22; II-16.
78. Wei Chau-fan I-13.
79. Wei Chau-fan I-17.
80. Wei Chau-fan I-20-21.
81. Wei Chau-fan III-8.
82. See, for example, Ch'en Ling-ping's assessment, II-4.
83. It is a fact that semi-official pronouncements as early as 1962, in *Chung-Kuo Ch'ing-Nien*, for example, did not seem to indicate this reversal. The uncertainty of the economic situation then may have made it necessary at that time to refrain from singling out the bad classers publicly or by official directive. Townsend does not observe a reversal until at least 1965. He states that pronouncements in print before then seemed to indicate a separation between the *ideal* of class struggle and the real world of relying on the "useful services" the bourgeoisie could render.
Nevertheless, in light of the hindsight testimony of non-red youths regarding that period, one could argue that pronouncements then indicated less of a separation between the ideal and pragmatic than

a *dialectical struggle* between the two approaches. In concrete terms, what this could have meant is that as the *Ssu-ch'ing* pervaded the environment a gradualistic emphasis on class criteria im implementation of academic and YCL admissions was undertaken regardless of the League's ambiguity on these matters. Cf. James Townsend, "Revolutionizing Chinese Youth: *A Study of Chung-Kuo Ch'ing-Nien*, in A. Doak Barnett, ed. *Chinese Communist Politics in Action* (Seattle: University of Washington Press, 1969), pp. 462-465.
84. Nieh Li-chih I-6.
85. See Lo Ping-wen VI-6; Yu Ming-li II-5.
86. I have found that Vogel's hypothesis (in *Canton Under Communism* [Cambridge: Harvard University Press, 1969], pp. 340 ff.) that one of the inducements to students to participate in the Red Guards was the avoidance of *hsia-hsiang* (Down to the country) may have been applicable to the more passive members. As for the activists, they either did not contemplate the matter or, as defeat loomed in their forefront, continued to participate despite the conviction that defeat would lead to doom.
87. Huang Yi I-8.
88. *Ibid.*
89. Yu Ming-li III-7.
90. Chu Nan-po III-8.
91. Lan Wei-ying I-1; VIII-23.
92. See, for example, Wang Lok-ch'ao I-8.
93. Yang Ying-pu I-14-15.
94. Pao Kuo-fu II-9.
95. Wang Lok-ch'ao II-16.
96. In contrast, a "worker," basically sympathetic to those of bad class background, had a more Chinese explanation for the utilization of the class issue (I-12): "In my opinion, your birth status (*ch'u-shen*) should be your own . . . Nevertheless, China is very confusing. In Chinese history, up to the present, if a person commits an error, his sons, wife, father and mother all become 'questionable'(*yu-wen-t'i*)."
97. Harry Stack Sullivan, *Interpersonal Theory of Psychiatry* (New York: Norton, 1953), pp. 252-253.
98. Cf. Seymour Martin Lipset, *The Political Man* (New York: Anchor, 1963), p. 76; pp. 244-247, for analogous discussion of the radicalization through isolation of groups in Western societies with similar points of view (like miners, sheep-shearers and fishermen).
99. Yang Ying-pu IV-15.
100. The freezing of a person's classification was also reflected in the freeze on entry into the YCL, apparently universal at lower levels in practice despite official YCL exhortations to the contrary, for aspirants still hoping to meet the requirements through special study and self-reform. Even Townsend seems to admit that official YCL exhortations to increase recruitment in 1965 may never have gotten off the ground. Cf. Townsend, *op. cit.*, 475.
101. Chu Nan-po III-10.
102. Ch'iao Kuo-hsiung I-2.
103. Ch'iao I-20.
104. Chu Nan-po IV-7.
105. Chu Nan-po III-17. Emphasis added. Note that Chu thought he could only gain from participation, with no threat to an already poor status.
106. Ch'iao Kuo-hsiung IV-24. Emphasis added.
107. Chu Nan-po VII-13.
108. Ch'iao Kuo-hsiung IV-4-5.

109. Ch'iao Kuo-hsiung I-12.
110. Ch'iao Kuo-hsiung IV-17.
111. Chu Nan-po IV-8.
112. Chou Chung-wang I-37.
113. Ch'iao Kuo-hsiung I-13; I-9.
114. Ch'iao Kuo-hsiung I-13.
115. Chu Nan-po III-13.
116. Chu Nan-po I-7.
117. Ch'iao Kuo-hsiung IV-12.
118. Chu Nan-po III-14.
119. Wang Lok-ch'ao II-20.
120. Wang Lok-ch'ao I-30.
121. *Ibid.*
122. Wang Lok-ch'ao II-4.
123. These elite schools, considered the best academically and in terms of university placement, contained a large number of children of cadres and PLA soldiers. Discrimination in admissions against "class enemy" or even "ordinary" class children seemed to increase yearly from 1961 onward.
124. Wang Lok-ch'ao I-14.
125. Wang Lok-ch'ao IV-6-7.
126. Wang Lok-ch'ao I-13.
127. Wang Lok-ch'ao I-19-20.
128. *Ibid.*
129. *Ibid.*
130. See Wang Lok-ch'ao III-21.
131. Wang Lok-ch'ao III-19.
132. Wang Lok-ch'ao I-18.
133. Wang Lok-ch'ao IV-3. He made a futile attempt to qualify for the YCL late in lower middle school, but realized how he was viewed. "To think of reforming is one thing, but in reality it wasn't possible," Wang says.
134. *Min-pan* had evolved as lower level, self-administered, neighborhood schools.
135. Wang Lok-ch'ao II-13. Emphasis added. For further discussion of his humiliation then, see II-15.
136. Wang Lok-ch'ao IV-6-7.
137. Wang Lok-ch'ao II-13.
138. *Ibid.*
139. Wang Lok-ch'ao II-11. Emphasis added.
140. Wang Lok-ch'ao II-15.
141. Wang Lok-ch'ao I-24. Moreover, the rebelliousness he had previously expressed in his horizontal relationship with father was now deliberately suppressed; his family was "as one against the outside." (III-24). Forced to return home in the early days of the GPCR because of the class issue, he became still closer to his father (I-29). Wang rechanneled the anger he now withheld at home toward the authorities outside. Unlike the early-alienated "verticals," Wang was prepared to give overt expression to his re-directed anger. He says: "I would express on the outside the anger I couldn't express at home. For example, when I took part in Red Guard fighting, I thought this was a good way to let off steam." (III-25).
142. Wang Lok-ch'ao I-24.
143. Wang Lok-ch'ao IV-31.
144. Wang Lok-ch'ao IV-30.
145. Wang Lok-ch'ao I-2.
146. Wang Lok-ch'ao IV-15.

147. See also Wang Lok-ch'ao IV-16, for a discussion of his resentment of discriminatory authorities, as well as the good class peers.
148. Wang Lok-ch'ao II-20. For further discussion of Wang's coming of age politically, see III-34.
149. Wang Lok-ch'ao III-23.
150. Wang Lok-ch'ao I-2-3.

CHAPTER 4

1. For further concrete discussion of the new Chinese child, see concluding chapter.
2. See discussion of implications of pecking or ranking orders in Konrad Lorenz, *On Aggression* (New York: Harcourt, 1966), pp. 40-44; for one of many discussions of competition between subordinates and immediate superordinate as the basis for the need for creating organizational counter-measures, see Michel Crozier, *The Bureaucratic Phenomenon* (Chicago: University of Chicago Press, 1964), p. 162 ff.
3. The backwardness even of the older generation proletarian is supported by the notion that "owing to the prolonged rule of the old system, the masses of the people often carry the burden of the old system on their backs (i.e., bad habits)," in An Hsueh-chiang, "We should have Faith in the Masses and the Party," *Hung Ch'i*, No. 1, January 1972, trans. in *Survey of China Mainland Magazines* (hereinafter SCMM), No. 721-722, p. 5.
4. For further discussion and illustration of this point, see later narration of Yüan case on pp. 120-124.
5. Yao Yuan-fang, "From Filial Piety to the Treatment of Parents', in *Chung-Kuo Ch'ing-nien*, #21, November 1, 1956, in *Extracts from China Mainland Press* (ECMM), #65, pp. 21-26. Emphasis added.
6. Wang Lok-ch'ao IV-12-13.
7. *Ibid.*
8. Lan Wei-ying III-37.
9. Wang Lok-ch'ao II-3.
10. One third of the total group falls into the category of vertical-authoritarian relationship. With the exception of worker Chai, all these were of questionable class background. Most were actually "class enemies."
11. Hsu Ta-liang II-6.
12. Chai Cheng-li IV-12.
13. Lo Ping-kok III-12.
14. Lo Ping-kok IV-18.
15. *Ibid.*
16. Lo Ping-kok IV-13.
17. Lo Ping-kok V-A&B-15.
18. Chu Nan-po III-5-6.
19. Chu Nan-po III-5.
20. Organizationally, the Pioneers were structured according to a three-layered pyramid: Squad (*hsiao-tui*), platoon (*chung-tui*) and brigade (*ta-tui*). A *tui-chang* was commander at each level.
21. Chu Nan-Po V-12.
22. Chu Nan-Po IV-3.
23. Yang Ying-pu IV-10.
24. His father was married twice. His first wife, not Ping-wen's mother, died in 1947. One could suppose that the older Lo had concubines as well.
25. Lo Ping-wen II-2.
26. *Ibid.*

27. *Ibid.*
28. Lo Ping-wen II-4.
29. *Ibid.*
30. Lo Ping-wen II-5. The use of the older brother for this purpose not only allowed this son to satisfy his own need to play father to a younger sibling, but was a further means of indoctrinating the younger into conformity. For instance, in Chou Chung-wang's case, whenever he resisted his father, his older brother would admonish him for being impolite (*pu-li-mao:* not following decorum). Chou Chung-wang I-11.
31. Lo Ping-wen III-8. He regarded his mother as socially useless because, confined to the house, she did not seem to him to be engaged in social production.
32. Lo Ping-wen II-5; VI-8.
33. Lo Ping-wen IV-6-7.
34. Lo Ping-wen II-3.
35. Lo Ping-wen II-2.
36. Each respondent was asked to comment on the famous story, related in Edgar Snow's *Red Star Over China* (1938), of the adolescent Mao's defying a father's humiliating reprimand in front of neighbors by threatening to jump in a pond. No mention was made to the respondent that the personality in the story was Mao Tse-tung. The story was simply used to examine the respondent's evaluation of that sort of situation and his own estimate of how he would have reacted in an anger-provoking situation with his father.
37. Lo Ping-wen III-2.
38. Lo Ping-wen III-1-3.
39. Lo Ping-wen III-2.
40. Lo Ping-wen VI-8.
41. Lo Ping-wen II-7.
42. *Ibid.*
43. Lo Ping-wen IV-13.
44. Cf. Huang Yi IV-3 and *passim*. In Lo's case, competition with father revolved around who was more sincere at what they both did. Ironically, Huang regarded his own abstention from politics as more sincere than his father's. To Huang, abstention from politics was a protest against the system in which his own father at first had complete faith; he believed that whereas his father was forcibly proscribed, he *chose* to remain apart from the system. Both Huang and Lo identified with and unconsciously emulated father, but a rivalry still existed beneath the surface. The difference between the cases lies in Lo Ping-wen's *attempt* to separate himself from father as a member of this generation and Huang's effort simply to beat his father at his own game. Huang even went as far as to congratulate himself that he suffered more as a result of his classification than his father would have were he still in school; Huang Yi boasts that he was "targeted" for his "expertise" at school, and that his grades were much better than those of his father, a professor at one of the best universities in China (Huang Yi III-9).
45. The fear of revealing political activity to father, of course, is not acute in value-uniform cases. But even in cases of political non-uniformity between home and school--Chou, for instance--the youth is often able to exist on two levels for some time before falling back on family identification or making the break from family.
46. Lo Ping-wen VI-8-9. Many of Lo's friends also removed their arm bands after school.
47. Lo Ping-wen VII B-5.

48. Lo Ping-wen VI-4-6.
49. Lo Ping-wen V-12.
50. Lo Ping-wen I-4.
51. Lo Ping-wen I-5. Money donated through overseas remittances.
52. Lo Ping-wen I-10.
53. *Ibid.*
54. Lo Ping-wen I-2. The rebel faction opposed to the class "blood line theory" (*hsueh-t'ung-lun*).
55. Lo Ping-wen V-16-17.
56. Lo Ping-wen V-10. Ping-wen spent his leisure time swimming. Illness, either physical or mental, seemed to be a fairly common excuse among my respondents for abstaining from the GPCR.
57. Lo Ping-wen III-15.
58. Lo Ping-wen III-13.
59. Specifically, 1960-1962. During these years there was a retreat from the intensity of the Great Leap and more of an emphasis on expertise than on redness.
60. Timing is an apparently important factor in the reaction to class ostracism. We will see that the intense politicization of the environment came suddenly upon Ping-wen's younger brother as he was entering adolescence and was treated as an impediment rather than as a fact of life. Ping-wen, on the other hand, had apparently resigned himself to bad class identity with all its social ramifications. Moreover, despite the existence of political cliques, he still kept many of his old friends. Although he sympathized with the anti-class stand of the *Hung Ch'i* (*tsao-fan* or rebel) faction, he could not bring himself to do anything about it (see Lo Ping-wen I-2).
61. Lo Ping-kok II-2-3.
62. Lo Ping-kok IV-5.
63. Lo Ping-kok IV-16.
64. Lo Ping-kok II-28.
65. *Ibid.*
66. Lo Ping-kok I-6-7.
67. Lo Ping-kok II-5.
68. Lo Ping-kok II-8-9.
69. Lo Ping-kok II-9.
70. Lo Ping-kok IV-9.
71. Lo Ping-kok III-4.
72. Lo Ping-kok IV-5.
73. Lo Ping-kok I-6-7.
74. Lo Ping-kok II-10. See Sigmund Freud, "Some Reflections On Schoolboy Psychology" (1914), *Standard Edition*, Vol. XIII, pp. 240-245, for a discussion of ambivalence toward father--an admixture of emotions of love and hate.
75. *Ibid.*
76. Lo Ping-kok IV-5.
77. His father had been the owner of the factory before "Liberation," and after the "Five Anti" Movement stayed on as manager.
78. Lo Ping-kok II-5.
79. Lo Ping-kok IV-5.
80. Lo Ping-kok II-15-16.
81. Lo Ping-kok II-12.
82. Lo Ping-kok II-13.
83. In contrast to Ping-kok, elder brother Ping-wen lacked the psychological predisposition to actively attempt a serious break from his father and was more able to accommodate himself to the politicized environment that fell upon him before the GPCR. For Ping-kok, the

curtain of political discrimination was a sudden impediment to his movement. We have seen in the previous chapter that pre-GPCR social ostracism played an important role in radicalizing bad class youths. Indeed, the impact of pre-GPCR group ostracism seems to have been most acute among "competitives," those most overtly trying to prove themselves the better of their fathers, frustrated in their adolescent generational rivalry and quest for mobility because of it.
But age also seems to have been a factor in determining a respondent's reaction to social ostracism before the outbreak of the GPCR. Only two respondents who were age 19 or over at the time the GPCR began participated because of any perceived ostracism; most seem to have become less sensitive to peer approval and/or resigned themselves to their social status by then.

84. Lo Ping-kok II-2.
85. Lo Ping-kok II-16-17.
86. Lo Ping-kok II-12.
87. Lo Ping-kok III-1.
88. *Ibid.*
89. Lo Ping-kok V A&B-1.
90. Lo Ping-kok III-10.
91. Lo Ping-kok II-26.
92. Lo Ping-kok II-17; II-1.
93. Lo Ping-kok IV-1.
94. Lo Ping-kok V A&B-14.
95. Lo Ping-kok III-6-7. See also V A&B-5.
96. Lo Ping-kok IV-3. The reader is referred back to the discussion of the recurrent dreams after father's death (pp. 106-107).
97. Lo Ping-kok I-15.
98. Lo Ping-kok III-28.
99. Lo Ping-kok I-6.
100. Lo Ping-kok I-15.
101. Lo Ping-kok I-13. He adds, upon questioning, that he felt no guilt after this action. Cf. Ping-wen II-7-9, who, on the contrary, felt guilty over unfiliality when he escaped from China. For the first time, he felt he had failed to live up to his father's expectations of success for him.
102. Apart from case-specific indicators, the syndrome of a horizontal father-son relationship consists of such shared factors as lack of arbitrary and harsh discipline in childhood (relative to what seemed to be the norm in my pool of respondents), father encouraging son to express his opinions and taking them into consideration, closeness of father and son (as opposed to father's aloofness), mutual respect, father's encouragement for and praise of son's independent achievements, open debate between father and son over differences.
The category "Horizontal" is, of course, somewhat arbitrary. There is a great deal of variance within this broad category, ranging from slightly horizontal to near equal; in the former, some of the above indicators would not appear or be less pronounced.
103. Horizontal or somewhat horizontal, non-uniform value cases who became Red Guards, some actively so, including Li Cheng, Chou Chung-wang, Yeh Hen, Wang Lok-ch'ao and Mu Chi-jui (two active; two passive, but conscientious about their activity and not just followers; and one passive). Chou Chung-wang and Li Cheng are excellent cases of dual role-playing (see Chapter 7).
Generally, however, most cases of severe value non-uniformity between father and son are in vertical relationships.
104. For a discussion of Dissonance theory, see Leon Festinger, *A Theory of Cognitive Dissonance* (Evanston, Illinois, 1957), *passim*.

218 *Notes to pages 111-122*

105. Pao Kuo-fu I-2.
106. Pao Kuo-fu I-4.
107. Pao Kuo-fu II-9-10.
108. Pao Kuo-fu I-5-6.
109. Pao Kuo-fu I-3.
110. Pao Kuo-fu I-2.
111. Pao Kuo-fu IV-5.
112. Pao Kuo-fu II-9.
113. *Ibid.*
114. Pao Kuo-fu III-2-3.
115. Pao Kuo-fu II-6.
116. Pao Kuo-fu II-7.
117. Pao Kuo-fu I-2.
118. Pao Kuo-fu I-6.
119. Based on Mao's 1957 speech, "On the Handling of Contradictions Among the People."
120. Pao Kuo-fu II-11-12. Emphasis mine. It is interesting to note here also how the GPCR could encourage one to have an inflated perception of his own role in it (last sentence of quote).
121. Pao Kuo-fu III-14-15.
122. Pao Kuo-fu III-2. I have added italics here for the explicit purpose of drawing the reader's attention to the two parallel phrases which seem to represent an equation between his own efforts and his father's type of service to society.
123. *Ibid.*
124. Pao Kuo-fu's III-13.
125. Lan Wei-ying II-15.
126. Lan Wei-ying II-16.
127. Chou Chung-wang II-19.
128. Yeh Hen VI-23.
129. Wei Chao-fan II-17-18.
130. Yang Ying-pu I-5; Pao Kuo-fu II-15.
131. Ch'iao Kuo-hsiung III-26.
132. Wang Lok-ch'ao III-2-3. Emphasis mine.
133. Chou Chung-wang II-22.
134. Secretary of Kwangtung Provincial Party Committee: criticized as elitist and lost formal power at the end of January 1967.
135. Chou Chung-wang VII-16.
136. Chou's father had been a secondary school teacher.
137. Chou Chung-wang IV-20.
138. Lan Wei-ying VI-7.
139. Yüan Ching-po IV-47.
140. Yüan Ching-po I-8.
141. *Ibid.*
142. *Ibid.* Emphasis mine.
143. Yüan Ching-po II-28.
144. Yüan Ching-po I-14-15.
145. Yüan Ching-po III-35-36.
146. Yüan Ching-po II-28.
147. Yüan Ching-po I-5; II-23.
148. Yüan Ching-po II-22. Contrast that filial breach of political honesty over a *ssu-hsiang chien-t'ao* with Lo Ping-kok's behavior, described earlier.
149. Yüan Ching-po II-22.
150. Yüan Ching-po I-13-14.
151. Yüan Ching-po I-9.
152. Private tutoring does exist in China, although not legally sanctioned.
153. Yüan Ching-po I-16.

154. Yüan Ching-po I-9.
155. Yüan Ching-po III-40-41.
156. Yüan Ching-po III-39.
157. Yüan Ching-po III-33.
158. Yüan Ching-po III-34.
159. Yüan Ching-po III-37-39. Yüan uses the expression, "opportunist," twice in separate contexts.
160. Yüan Ching-po II-19-20.
161. Yüan Ching-po II-19.
162. Yüan Ching-po II-17.
163. *Ibid.*
164. Yüan Ching-po III-40-41.
165. Yüan Ching-po III-44.
166. Yüan Ching-po III-43.
167. Yüan Ching-po II-19.
168. Chu Nan-po I-23.
169. Chu Nan-po II-11.
170. Chu Nan-po II-16.
171. Chu Nan-po VI-11.
172. Chu Nan-po I-23-24; VII-1. This represents quite a departure from the parent-son relationships in traditional Chinese society or the overseas Chinese communities in Asia today.
173. Chu Nan-po VI-3.
174. Chu's mother seemed the closer of the two parents during his toddler years; he has little impression of his father then. Later, the situation reversed itself. Father and son became very close (I-22, 23). Contrast to the traditional image of early closeness between father and son and then the father's becoming more aloof later.
175. Chu Nan-po IV-11.
176. Chu Nan-po VII-2.
177. Contrast this phenomenon to the traditional image, particularly apparent in Wolf's Taiwan studies, of the father's conviction that in order to be a teacher to his son he must be severe and maintain a distance from him.
178. Chu Nan-po V-4.
179. Chu Nan-po IV-3.
180. *Ibid.* Please recall that it was a breach of good manners, even in Communist China, to question a teacher, much less quarrel with him, before the Cultural Revolution. The situation seemed to be changing after the GPCR according to reports of visitors in 1971, like David Ho, Ross Terrill and the CCAS Group.
181. Chu Nan-po IV-3.
182. *Ibid.*
183. Chu Nan-po IV-13.
184. Chu Nan-po VIII-1.
185. Chu Nan-po IV-12-13.
186. Chu Nan-po IV-13.
187. Chu Nan-po V-13.
188. Chu Nan-po IV-13-14.
189. Chu Nan-po IV-15; II-5.
190. Chu Nan-po V-6.
191. Chu Nan-po VI-12.
192. Chu Nan-po VII-3.
193. *Ibid.* Nan-po always had taken political study very seriously throughout school (see V-13).
194. Chu Nan-po VIII-2.
195. Chu Nan-po I-9.
196. Chai Cheng-li I-18-19.

197. *Ibid.*
198. Chai Cheng-li I-25.
199. Chai Cheng-li I-21.
200. *Ibid.*
201. Chai Cheng-li II-6.
202. *Ibid.*
203. Chai Cheng-li II-8.
204. *Ibid.*
205. Chai Cheng-li II-7.
206. *Ibid.*
207. Chai Cheng-li I-24.
208. Chai Cheng-li I-20.
209. Chai Cheng-li I-24.
210. Chai Cheng-li III-9.
211. Chai Cheng-li III-10-11.
212. Chai Cheng-li III-12.
213. Chai Cheng-li I-25-26.
214. Chai Cheng-li I-25-26.
215. Chai Cheng-li I-26.
216. Chai Cheng-li III-4.
217. *Ibid.*
218. *Ibid.*
219. Chai Cheng-li III-16. Perhaps, the Chai case also points up the dangers for a uniform communist education inherent in a marriage between two people of different educational backgrounds and social values.
220. Chai Cheng-li VI-6.
221. Chai Cheng-li VI-6.
222. Chai Cheng-li IV-16.
223. Teams composed of PLA, workers and peasants.
224. Chai Cheng-li VI-11.
225. Authority figures in school and society.
226. It is still not clear to what extent father-son competition might have been a submerged current in still earlier generations of Chinese, but unobservable or disguised to the anthropologist or outside observer.
227. Actually, of the entire body of eleven militants, the two respondents who did not indicate competition with parents were orphans; one of them, Ch'iao, places great emphasis on what he perceives to be his own feeling of inner-directedness (see IV-11; 30). Orphans constituted the majority of the elite "August 31" group of militants in Kwangchow, a shock force in the January 1967 "seizure of power." They were free from both parental restraints and the fear of retaliation against their family.
228. The discrepancy here between the number of clearly indicated "horizontals" and "verticals" on the one hand and the *total* number of respondents on the other is due to the fact that some of the respondents presented a murky picture, according to criteria already listed, of the structure of their relationships with their father. As we have seen, class was an important variable in participation for this group of respondents, but it did not necessarily impede participation in the GPCR. Thirty-four percent of the "class enemies" participated in the Red Guards (six out of seventeen), despite their natural predisposition to early social alienation in a hostile environment. Of the three proletarians I interviewed (not really valid as a control group), one abstained from the GPCR, and two were passive participants for only a short while.
229. For Lo Ping-wen's reaction to leaving China, see Lo Ping-wen II-8-9.

230. In families where the mother is the only parent, a son will identify with the mother or, more often, the image she depicts for her son of his father, if it is a positive one. In some cases of a serious cleavage between the two parents, the son may sympathize strongly with his mother and her aspirations for him. But there is no evidence that a son will depart so radically from his father's path that his father cannot perceive him as a competitor.

CHAPTER 5

1. In traditional society, and to a great extent today, no one ever met a stranger without proper introduction.
2. Ch'en I-12.
3. Ch'en Ling-ping VI-6.
4. For a general discussion of theoretical formulations concerning the correlation between trust/mistrust in an authoritarian family history in Western society, see Fred Greenstein, *Personality and Politics* (Chicago: Markham, 1969), pp. 104-106; See also G. Almond and S. Verba, *The Civic Culture* (Boston: Little, Brown, 1963), p. 334, for a discussion of trust as a formative value of democratic political culture.
5. See, for example, Ch'iao Kuo-hsiung III-19.
6. See Pao Kuo-fu, *passim*.
7. Later, however, as the situation became more chaotic and armed factional struggle erupted, the attrition rate was high. E.g., Yü Ming-li III-31; Lan Wei-ying VII-24-25. About half the participants in the sample had withdrawn by the time of the second armed struggle.
8. Chu Nan-po VI-33.
9. Lan Wei-ying IV-12; VIII-33-34. The atmosphere became more restrictive and unhealthy, according to Lan, by the time the factional fighting broke out.
10. Chou Chung-wang VI-9.
11. Lan Wei-ying V-3; Yü Ming-li V-26.
12. Yü Ming-li VI-13.
13. Wei Chau-fan II-20.
14. Yü Ming-li discovered only in pre-adolescence that his class background was non-red. Until then, his father had made him believe that he had served with the Red Army during the revolution. Only late in his childhood did young Yü discover that his father had defected from a KMT-controlled local self-defense corps less than three years before Liberation.
15. Yü Ming-li III-37.
16. Yü Ming-li III-24-25.
17. Yü Ming-li IV-7.
18. Yeh Hen IV-3; see also V-8.
19. *Ibid*.
20. *Ibid*.
21. Yeh Hen V-6-7; III-1.
22. Yeh Hen III-1.
23. Yeh Hen V-8.
24. See Peter Blos, *On Adolescence, op. cit.*, p. 206. In the West, clothing is a well-known part of the adolescent phenomenology of gangs and social groups. As Blos states: "These self-chosen clothing styles give expression to the adolescents' changing body and self-image besides serving the social purpose of establishing a group identity . . ." In Yeh Hen's case, we see that besides preserving a group-social identity, his adherence to the dress style

advocated by his mother reflects no attempt at assertion of his own personality and autonomy in this area.
25. Yeh Hen V-8.
26. Yeh Hen VI-12.
27. I have found that several respondents despaired of being taken seriously and therefore made no attempt to be politically active or acceptable. They feared over-zealousness would be mistaken for sheer hypocrisy by the authorities and in-group. But in this instance, I got the impression that the individual's negative social affiliation could be as much cause as effect of a decision to cling to a politically negative position.
28. Yeh Hen III-9. Even if Yeh was also using this line as a defense against being excluded, it only served to reinforce his need to rely on his group affiliation.
29. Yeh Hen III-6.
30. Yeh Hen IV-7.
31. Yeh Hen VI-7.
32. Chu Nan-po V-2.
33. Lan Wei-ying V-12-13.
34. See Chapter 4, pp. 104-105.
35. Lo Ping-kok III-5.
36. Friends who became buddies in armed combat with the opposing faction. Sometimes, these friends, as closely tied as possible to one another emotionally, only knew each other by nicknames. One such buddy of Lan Wei-ying's wore conspicuous glasses and was known by everyone as "Old Big Eyes" (Lan Wei-ying V-5).
37. Chu Nan-po VII-16.
38. Lo Ping-kok III-18.
39. Lan Wei-ying V-15.
40. Chou Chung-wang VI-7.
41. Ch'iao Kuo-hsiung VI-11; Chou Chung-wang VI-9.
42. One important study of the complexity and importance of countervailing social pressures in community conflicts is James Coleman, *Community Conflict* (New York: Free Press of Glencoe, 1957), *passim*.
43. See Chapter 2 for a discussion and diagram of the organizational structure of factions which eventually developed in the schools by the end of 1966.
44. Yang Ying-pu IV-12.
45. Lan Wei-ying VII-26.
46. Ch'iao Kuo-hsiung IV-29.
47. Ch'iao Kuo-hsiung VI-7.
48. Lan Wei-ying VII-24-25, III-19-21. This was before the formal division into factions with city-wide command headquarters.
49. Lan Wei-ying VII-25.
50. Lan Wei-ying V-8.
51. Lo Ping-kok I-2.
52. Pao Kuo-fu II-3.
53. Ch'en Ling-ping I-18.
54. Fei K'o-kuan I-3.
55. Fei K'o-kuan II-8.
56. Fei K'o-kuan II-4.
57. Fei K'o-kuan II-3.
58. Yüan Ching-po I-16.
59. Yüan Ching-po I-17.
60. Yüan Ching-po I-19.
61. Yüan Ching-po III-35-37.
62. Yüan Ching-po III-37.
63. Yüan Ching-po III-37-38.

64. Pao Kuo-fu II-1.
65. It will seem that in this group, it is difficult to differentiate between the effects of the oppressive stigma of bad class and oppressive family socialization. I agree that the overwhelming practical implications of being of non-red class or "class enemy" background must have been extremely important in influencing basic attitudes. I am merely trying to suggest that socialization could have played a complementary role in this process. An an indication that socialization is definitely an operative variable here, one "class enemy" showed a fair level of trust, two moderately bad classers had a fair level of trust, and the "worker" with the authoritarian father indicated extreme mistrust! The former had horizontal types of home socialization.
66. Huang Yi I-15.
67. Huang Yi I-8.
68. *Ibid.* In the 1950s, children were encouraged to make politics the foundation of their peer friendships, rather than other criteria like common interests or having fun. (See, for example, Kao Hsü-yang's article in *Kung-jen jih-pao*, April 24, 1958).
69. Huang Yi I-8.
70. Nieh Li-chih III-1-2.
71. Nieh Li-chih III-1-2. Ezra Vogel, "From Friendship to Comradeship: The Change in . . . ," *China Quarterly*, No. 21, January-March 1965, 46-7. Vogel argues that the new camaraderie generally exists only on this superficial level. But has the author checked the findings against the class background or family upbringing of the respondents? In recent years at least, most of the younger refugees available to scholars for interviewing have been of non-proletarian background. I should think this factor might make a considerable difference in any generalization about how the individual relates to others.
72. Nieh Li-chih I-2.

CHAPTER 6

1. Cf. Robert Hess and David Easton, "The Child's Image of the President," *Public Opinion Quarterly*, XXIV (Spring 1960), pp. 632-644.
2. See discussion of Chu Nan-po in Chapter 4 or Wang Lok-ch'ao to follow on p. 158, n. 22.
3. These schools were established during the Cultural Revolution for the purpose of re-educating political and administrative cadres in revolutionary purpose and "mass line" and stripping them of any bureaucratic encrustation.
4. Lan Wei-ying IX-11.
5. See Margery Wolf, *Women and the Family in Rural Taiwan* (Stanford: Stanford University Press, 1972), p. 168; or Marian Levy, Jr., *The Family Revolution in Modern China*, Part II: Traditional Family (New York: Atheneum, 1958), p. 174.
6. Lan Wei-ying VII-2.
7. Lan Wei-ying VIII-28-30.
8. Lan Wei-ying I-3; III-22.
9. Lan Wei-ying I-9-11. This statement seems to contradict the conventional interpretation of the YCL's anxious effort to recruit again in 1965 (see Townsend, *op. cit.*, p. 475, and "Revolutionization of Chinese Youth," *China Quarterly*, #30, April-June 1967, 62-67. But even Townsend questions whether this recruitment drive, so heralded in *Chung-kuo Ch'ing-nien*, really ever got off the ground.

224 Notes to pages 156-159

10. Lan Wei-ying V-9.
11. Lan Wei-ying IV-2.
12. Lan Wei-ying VIII-24.
13. *Ibid.*
14. Lan Wei-ying IV-18; I-4.
15. Lan Wei-ying IX-7.
16. Lan Wei-ying II-18-19. Cf. case of Mr. Fei, I-3; I-10; I-6; I-11. I have created the category "transitional horizontal" for cases in this first generation after the communist revolution in which *both* father and son seem to be experiencing a need to re-adjust their relationship in terms of new norms but the father is not fully able to resolve the contradictions with his own personality-upbringing and is often in a quandary as to how to treat his son. Fei was a more acute case of transitional father-son relations (i.e., in less of a progressed state) in which the father, in order to cope emotionally with power deflation in his role, withdrew entirely from his son. Thus, father evaded possible impending rivalry. Ai-li Chin, *op. cit.*, 17, discusses a similar phenomenon in her sample of young students in Taipei, where families have been subjected to the Westernizing-modernizing influence.
    The gradual move toward a horizontal relationship necessarily creates strains and demands various temporary adjustments.
17. Lan Wei-ying V-7.
18. Lan Wei-ying II-7.
19. Lan Wei-ying II-7-8.
20. Lan Wei-ying II-23.
21. Lan Wei-ying II-10.
22. Lan Wei-ying II-13. The reader should compare the phrasing to the quotation concerning the incident with his father on the previous page; in both instances, Wei-ying seems to be preoccupied with his being too old to tolerate abuse to himself by superordinates.
    I would also like the reader to contrast this youthful reaction to a blow to one's self-respect to the "morally masochistic" youth stereotype in Lucian Pye, *The Spirit of Chinese Politics* (Cambridge: MIT, 1968), p. 74.
    For another good example of youthful rebellion against a teacher even before it became acceptable in the GPCR, see Wang Lok-ch'ao III-5-6. In a quarrel over criticism received during training class for "steeling" (*tuan-lien*) in the village, Wang "stood up, shoved the desk and swore at the teacher." Class was discontinued. He remarks, "Before the Cultural Revolution, to dare to stand up and scold a teacher, one could say was a very rare occurrence at school." Wang's father had been consistently permissive and Wang would not tolerate frustration of his maneuverability outside the home. Wang also became a militant Red Guard and, like Wei-ying, let his father see his hand gun.
23. Lan Wei-ying II-10-11.
24. Lan Wei-ying VII-6. Chou Chung-wang V-13, also generalizes: "My schoolmates were very regulated before the GPCR. They sat in the classroom without making a sound."
25. Lan Wei-ying I-12.
26. Lan Wei-ying III-19.
27. Lan Wei-ying III-18.
28. Lan Wei-ying VI-12.
29. Lan Wei-ying: Notes from Session I, unrecorded section due to tape defect.
30. Lan Wei-ying VI-12.
31. Lan Wei-ying IX-1.

32. *Ibid.*
33. See, for example, Robert N. Bellah, "Father and Son in Christianity and Confucianism," *Psychoanalytic Review*, Vol. 52, #2, summer 1965, 110, or Lo Ping-kok's relationship with his father; the more the young son protested, the more his father beat him.
34. Tseng K'ai-lao I-27. Cf. Marion Levy's discussion of the deliberate lack of affect on the part of a father toward his son in traditional Chinese rural society, in Levy, *op. cit.*, pp. 172-173.
35. Tseng K'ai-lao I-11-12.
36. Tseng K'ai-lao III-23-24.
37. Tseng K'ai-lao III-23-24.
38. Tseng K'ai-lao III-10-11.
39. Tseng-K'ai-lao I-31-32.
40. Tseng K'ai-lao II-12-13.
41. Tseng K'ai-lao II-3.
42. Tseng K'ai-lao I-37.
43. Tseng K'ai-lao I-37-38.
44. Tseng K'ai-lao I-36.
45. *Ibid.*
46. Tseng K'ai-lao III-47.
47. Tseng K'ai-lao I-6.
48. Tseng K'ai-lao III-43.
49. Tseng K'ai-lao III-14-15.
50. Tseng K'ai-lao III-33.
51. Tseng K'ai-lao III-15.
52. Tseng K'ai-lao I-4.
53. Tseng K'ai-lao III-12.
54. Tseng K'ai-lao I-23.
55. Liang Shu-ming I-1.
56. Liang Shu-ming I-2.
57. Liang Shu-ming I-5-6.
58. Liang Shu-ming II-19.
59. Liang Shu-ming III-19.
60. Liang Shu-ming III-13.
61. Liang Shu-ming II-11.
62. Liang Shu-ming II-14.
63. See T. W. Adorno, Else Frenkel-Brunswik, Daniel Levinson and R. Nevitt Sanford, *The Authoritarian Personality* (New York: Harper, 1950), *passim*.
64. Hsu Ta-liang II-23.
65. Hsu Ta-liang III-23.
66. Huang Yi II.
67. Huang Yi II-12, and *passim*.
68. Pao Kuo-fu IV-*passim*.
69. *Ibid.* Cf. Margery Wolf, *Women and the Family in Rural Taiwan* (Stanford: Stanford University Press, 1972), p. 70.
70. See case below in which the positive *image*, sustained by the mother, of a liquidated KMT father seemed to create some psychological conflict for the child in his deliberate effort to integrate with the system. Were the father still alive, it is quite likely that such a conflict would not present itself; the father might have encouraged, or at least tolerated, such efforts.
71. Hsieh Ting-teng I-6.
72. Hsieh Ting-teng I-15.
73. *Ibid.* Emphasis added.
74. Hsieh Ting-teng I-5-6.
75. Hsieh Ting-teng I-5.
76. Hsieh Ting-teng II-9.

77. Hsieh Ting-teng II-2.
78. Hsieh Ting-teng III-1.
79. Hsieh Ting-teng II-1.
80. Liang Shu-ming II-4.
81. Wang Lok-ch'ao IV-39.
82. Wang Lok-ch'ao IV-29.
83. *Ibid.*
84. *Ibid.*
85. Chou Chung-wang IV-13.
86. *Ibid.*
87. Chou Chung-wang I-22.
88. Chou Chung-wang II-18; III-18-19.

CHAPTER 7

1. Cf. Anthony Wallace, "Revitalization Movements," *American Anthropologist*, LVIII (April 1956), *passim*; Seymour Martin Lipset and Philip G. Altbach, eds. *Students in Revolt* (Boston: Beacon Press, 1970), *passim*.
2. For comparison, the reader is referred to a very interesting, earlier survey-study of the effect of mother dominance in family socialization, peer ties, and formal school education on the various political interests of adolescents in Jamaican society. See Kenneth Langton, *Political Socialization* (New York: Oxford University Press, 1969), *passim*.
3. See Chapters 2 and 3.
4. Lo Ping-kok III-20. However, according to many of the visitors to China since the GPCR, parents who are cadres do seem to have the influence to get their children into better schools and positions. One wonders how much of the past GPCR educational reform effort is wasted because of the persistence of an elite with self-replicating tendencies.
5. Liu K'e-chung II-3. Emphasis mine.
6. Chai Cheng-li III-6.
7. Lo Ping-kok II-11. Richard W. Wilson found in his study in Taiwan that children there also tend to place more credence in their teachers than in their parents during the first three years of primary school; afterward, the influences of home and school seem to balance out. *Learning to be Chinese* (Cambridge: MIT, 1970), pp. 139-140.
8. Lo Ping-kok II-13-14.
9. Since the GPCR, neighborhood schools have been instituted in the city with the apparent possibility now of greater cooperation between home and school.
10. Ch'en Ling-ping V-4.
11. Ai-li Chin, *op. cit.*, 10. One should qualify this assertion by noting that during the GPCR many "red" parents visited their children residing on campus.
12. *Ibid.*, p. 13.
13. Only a good thing if the older generation's influence is considered to be hampering the youth's emotional autonomy or pernicious to the social and political values he acquires.
14. Lo Ping-wen VI-14.
15. Lan Wei-ying III-14-15.
16. Wu Kuo-chih I-3 and Yang, *passim*. Many a parent is also critical of life since the communists came to power.
17. Shih Chi-t'ang IV-3.

Notes to pages 180-184 227

18. Lo Ping-wen VI-2.
19. Lan Wei-ying III-14.
20. Lan Wei-ying III-15.
21. Chu Nan-po V-1. From this remark about his father, the question of who is more bourgeois, father or son, in this case remains open.
22. Mencius, Book IV, Part A, Chapter XXVII.
23. *Hsiao Ching* (Classic of Filial Piety), trans. by James Legge, the *Sacred Books of the East*, ed. F. Max Müller, Vol. III, Part I (Delhi: Motilal Banarsidass, 1966), pp. 483-484.
24. Quoted from *Li Chi* (Book of Rites) by Robert N. Bellah, "Father and Son in Christianity and Confucism," *Psychoanalytic Review*, Vol. 53, #2, Summer 1965, 110.
25. "Massively Develop an all Red Family . . . ," *Hung-wei-pao*, formerly *Yang-ch'eng Wan-pao*, Kwangchow, Kwangtung, December 8, 1966. The counterpart in the adult political culture of educating superordinates is when peasants are urged to be the "master of the house" and correct cadres' shortcomings. See article in *Nan-fang Jih-pao*, November 14, 1964, *SCMP*, #3361, December 21, 1964, 4-6.
26. Li Cheng III-46.
27. Lan Wei-ying VII-32.
28. One might compare this situation to the apparent ill-effects of an aborted political study or thought reform session. In the group, the technique of unity-struggle-unity is also utilized in criticism and self-criticism. However, many respondents report that emotions and animosities between individuals often work against the process and impede unity.
29. Also see my comment on Vogel's hypothesis, p. 151, n. 69 concerning friendship.
30. Lo Ping-kok IV-14.
31. See Peter Blos, *On Adolescence*, pp. 211-221. The group gradually fills a vacuum for needs the family cannot fulfill.
32. Fei K'o-Kuan I-9.
33. Pao Kuo-fu III-6.
34. Generally, guilt can be expunged or reinforced by the group. See F. Redl, "Group Emotion and Leadership," *Psychiatry*, Vol. V, p. 582. In a shaming culture, other-directed behavior is very common indeed. The father, father surrogate, or group serves as the *external* embodiment of reward and punishment. The child relies heavily on cues from the environment. See Erik Erikson, *Childhood and Society* (second rev. ed.; New York: Norton, 1963), pp. 34-36; Lucian Pye, *The Spirit of Chinese Politics* (Cambridge: MIT, 1969), pp. 94-96; Hu Hsien-chin, "The Chinese Concept of Face," *American Anthropologist*, 46 (1944), *passim*.
35. The influence of the peer group on adolescent political behavior was discussed at length in Chapter 5.
36. Lo Ping-wen VI-13.
37. Lo Ping-wen IV-22 C.
38. Ch'iao Kuo-hsiung III-9.
39. "Ho Ch'ing-nien T'an Ku Lun Chin" (Making the Traditional Relevant for Today in Discussion with Young People), ed. Yüan Yu-ming (Peking: Chung-kuo Ch'ing-nien Ch'u-pan She, 1956), pp. 11-13. Many of these stories are specially interpreted versions of common pre-school stories. See Lo Ping-wen VII A-5.
40. Karl Marx and Friedrich Engels, "The German Ideology" (1846), trans. Lewis B. Feuer, *Marx and Engels: Basic Writings* (New York: Doubleday, 1959), pp. 251-261. For a complete translation, see International Publishers' edition (1947, last printing 1968), ed. R. Pascal. For further presentation and discussion of Marx's early

writings, see *Karl Marx*, ed. T. B. Bottomore [with forward by Erich Fromm] (London: Watts, 1956), *passim*.
41. Li Ta-chao, "Ching-shen-ti-chieh-fang" (Liberation of the Spirit), *Hsin Ch'ing-nien*, February 8, 1920, in *Selected Works* (Peking, 1967), pp. 303-304.
42. Hannah Arendt, *The Origins of Totalitarianism* (second ed., New York: Meridian, 1958), Part III, *passim*.
43. Wu Kuo-chih IV-3.
44. Chai Cheng-li V-25.
45. The inherent contradiction here of individual fulfillment and service to the state has remained a problem unresolved in the GPCR. Although the CCRG at first encouraged spontaneity and a "seizure of power," its response to over-zealousness in factional strife was "Destroy self, uplift collective" (*P'o-ssu-li-kung*), first advocated in *Chieh-fang Chün-pao* and JMJP editorials from January through March 1967, and reiterated sporadically thereafter (including Lin Piao's Ninth Party Congress address).
46. An impression largely based on youth's own perceptions. For the most part, parents were not interviewed. I only interviewed one mother, and she supported this contention of the youths.
47. Shih Chi-t'ang I-4. Another fine example of this syndrome is Lan Wei-ying's parents' deliberate effort to keep any dissatisfaction with the political system or life in general to themselves (See Lan Wei-ying I-7).
48. Wu Kuo-chih I-5. This is probably more valid for the urban areas. Based on the limitations of the pool of respondents, it would be difficult to judge whether the role of the father has been similarly affected in this negative way in rural areas. Using Tseng as an example, one could hypothesize that the father might be more influential in the countryside, but one can also speculate that the homogeneity of collective village life may bring the father under greater pressure politically as well as socially in his treatment of his children.
49. Nieh Li-chih III-12. Please note that I am discussing here environmental restraints on the father, but by no means wish to imply that a considerable degree of non-uniform socialization is not still present in China, at least in my pool of respondents.
50. Ch'iao Kuo-hsiung II-9.
51. Ch'iao Kuo-hsiung II-8.
52. Ch'iao Kuo-hsiung II-10. "Older" was age thirteen or so.
53. Shih Chi-t'ang IV-33.
54. Ch'iao Kuo-hsiung VI-15.
55. Ch'iao Kuo-hsiung III-2.
56. *Ibid.*, 4-7.
57. Shih Chi-t'ang IV-34.
58. Liang Shu-ming I-3.
59. Cf. Hypotheses expressed in Lucian Pye (*Spirit of Chinese Politics* Cambridge: MIT Press, 1968), *passim*.: Richard Solomon, *Mao's Revolution and the Chinese Political Culture* (Berkeley: University of California Press, 1971), pp. 103-104; also 140-141, 150-153.
60. Ch'iao Kuo-hsiung III-15-16; II-10.
61. Ch'iao Kuo-hsiung III-15-16.
62. Yüan Ching-po I-15.
63. Regression is not necessarily psychopathological, can be partial and ritualized.
64. Cf. Pye, *op. cit.*, p. 44 and *passim*. for the converse observation and deductive hypothesis, based on orality, about the Chinese child. Please note that a father comes to substitute for the infantile

"other self" or mother in most situations, though he does not replace her entirely. See Wolfenstein, "Some Variants in the Moral Training of Children," in Mead and Wolfenstein, eds. *Childhood in Contemporary Cultures* (Chicago: University of Chicago, 1955), p. 365.
65. P'eng Te-lai I-5.
66. See, for example, Lo Ping-kok A&B-1; Pao Kuo-fu. Most others were simply equivocal about whether they would ever leave.
67. Yang Ying-pu I-3-4, who forced his elder brother (father replacement) to beat him until he made a superficial promise.
68. Huang San I-9.
69. Huang San I-9.
70. *Ibid.*, 10. The peculiar aggressiveness of the youngest son might be related to sibling sequence and concomitant variations in Socialization. See Brian Sutton-Smith and B. G. Rosenberg's *The Sibling* (New York: Holt, Rinehart and Winston, 1970), pp. 67-68; 108-155. G. William Skinner is also investigating the effects of sibling sequence among overseas Chinese.
71. Cf. Pye, *op. cit.*, p. 74.
72. Yüan Ching-po I-15; Shih Chi-t'ang I-1; Pao Kuo-fu I-6 et al.
73. Shih Chi-t'ang I-14.
74. Ch'iao Kuo-hsiung II-10.
75. Ch'iao Kuo-hsiung III-2. It is interesting that Ch'iao makes this contrast with "feudal" China. Is this what he was taught?
76. P'eng Te-lai I-8-9. The letter to mother, apart from the guilt it obviously represents, also seems to indicate a degree of *horreur de face-à-face* consequential to conflict with authority. See p. 46 for a discussion of the possible occurrence of this phenomenon in the GPCR.
77. Yang Ying-pu I-7.
78. Shih Chi-t'ang I-14-15.
79. Li Cheng I-4-5. Emphasis added.
80. Margery Wolf, "Child Training and the Chinese Family" in Maurice Freedman, ed., *Family and Kinship in Chinese Society* (Stanford: Stanford University Press, 1970), p. 44.
81. Shih Chi-t'ang II-14. Cf. Margery Wolf, *Women and the Family in Rural Taiwan* (Stanford: Stanford University Press, 1972), p. 168. "A mother said . . . you cannot let children know you approve of them; if they know that you praise them, they won't try to improve."
82. I should qualify these remarks by adding that just as many fathers are still unwilling to praise or celebrate their children's successes. The evidence I present, however, does seem to suggest a new trend.
83. Li Cheng I-5.
84. This descriptive category is based on such indicators as the free exchange of opinions between parents and child, lack of arbitrary and especially severe punishment, and a relatively permissive atmosphere in the home.
85. Ai-li Chin, *op. cit.*, 17-18.
86. Martin C. Yang, *A Chinese Village* (New York: Columbia University Press, 1945), pp. 57-59. Contrast with case of Tseng K'ai-lao.
87. Chai case.
88. Margery Wolf, *House of Lim* (New York: Appleton-Century-Croft, 1968), pp. 46-47.
89. The above statement presumes integrative change between individual and society. Cf. Robert Jay Lifton, "On Psychohistory," in Robert Holt and Emanuel Peterfreund, eds., *Psychoanalysis and Contemporary Science*, Vol. I (New York: MacMillan, 1972), *passim*.
90. Li Cheng IV-48.

91. Liang Shu-ming I-8-10; III-12.
92. Li Cheng III-37.
93. Unlike others (Cf. case of Yeh Hen, pp. 142-145) who really could not tread the "middle" course really because of their strong identity with authoritarian and "backward" parents, Li Cheng did not suffer sufficient dissonance to be forced to one extreme or the other before the GPCR got underway. Li was drawn into the GPCR as much by a previous history of playing the political game as by strong peer ties.
    Given the tolerance of the socializing agent(s), an individual could learn to live with internalized cultural contradictions. Both Dr. Sullivan (*Inter-Personal Theory* . . . , *op. cit.*, p. 207) and David Riesman (*Individualism Reconsidered* [New York: Free Press, 1954], p. 420) note that a person can bring to bear various defenses against embracing a total identity of one sort or another in the most rigid of systems; he can live with contradictions. And yet we can see that anything short of total political commitment was at cross-purposes with the Maoist vision of the new socialist youth, capable of educating his parents and surpassing them in socialist ways.
94. See Mao Tse-tung, *On Practice, passim*. For further discussion of this point, the reader may refer to John W. Lewis, *Leadership in Communist China* (New York: Cornell University Press, 1963), pp. 35-39; Franz Schurmann, *Ideology and Organization in Communist China* (Berkeley: University of California Press, 1966), pp. 45-53; and William Hinton, *Fanshen* (New York: Vintage, 1968), pp. 183-187.
95. Nieh Li-chih II-9.
96. Chou Chung-wang III-6.
97. Liu K'e-chung II-13. It should be noted parenthetically that in rural areas such financial severance is unpermissible.
98. Wang Lok-chao II-22. The coincidence that both these outstanding cases of renouncing parents, as well as Lifton's example in the early 1950s (*Thought Reform and the Psychology of Totalism* [New York: Norton, 1963] pp. 344-345, 377), involve female children suggests a further area of investigation. What peculiar aspects of the early socialization of girls might account for possibly more acute rebelliousness toward parents? Has the home socialization of girls since "Liberation" changed too radically or lagged too far behind?
99. Chu Nan-po III-6.
100. See Chapter 3.
101. Tillman Durdin, *New York Times*, July 9, 1973.
102. Chou Chung-wang I-23.
103. Lan Wei-ying VI-13.
104. *Ibid*.
105. Mao Tse-tung, *Quotations* (Peking: Foreign Languages Publishing House, 1967), p. 290.
106. Lifton, *op. cit.*, p. 379; Mark Selden, "The Yenan Legacy: The Mass Line," in A. Doak Barnett, ed., *Chinese Communist Politics in Action* (Seattle: University of Washington Press, 1969), pp. 101-108.
107. Mao Tse Tung, *Quotations, op. cit.*, pp. 290-291.
108. Chou Chung-wang VI-11.
109. Lan Wei-ying IX-13.
110. This is a projection on current American Society of a theme discussed in Almond and Verba, *The Civic Culture* (Boston: Little, Brown, 1965), p. 334.

Bibliography

BOOKS AND MONOGRAPHS

Adorno, Theodore W.; Frenkel-Brunswik, Else; Levinson, Daniel J.; Sanford, R. Nevitt. *The Authoritarian Personality*. New York: Harper, 1950.
Almond, Gabriel and Verba, Stanley. *The Civic Culture*. New York: Little, Brown, 1965.
Arendt, Hannah. *The Origins of Totalitarianism*. 2nd ed. New York: Meridian, 1958.
Barnett, A. Doak, ed. *Chinese Communist Politics in Action*. Seattle: University of Washington Press, 1969.
Baum, Richard and Teiwes, Frederick. *Ssu-Ch'ing: The Socialist Education Movement of 1962-1966*: China Research Monographs, No. 2. Berkeley: University of California Press, 1968.
Benedict, Ruth. *Chrysanthemum and the Sword*. New York: Meridian, 1967.
Bennett, Gordon and Montaperto, Ronald. *Red Guard: The Political Biography of Dai Shao-ai*. New York: Anchor, 1972.
Blos, Peter. *On Adolescence: A Psychoanalytic Interpretation*. New York: Free Press, 1962.
Bonilla, Frank and de Silva Michena, Jose, eds. *The Politics of Venezuela. A Strategy for Research on Social Policy*. Vol. I. Cambridge: MIT, 1967.
Bronfenbrenner, Urie. *Two Worlds of Childhood: U.S. and USSR*. New York: Pocket Books, 1973.
Campbell, Angus; Gurin, Gerald; and Miller, Warren E. *The Voter Decides*. Evanston: Peterson, Row and Co., 1954.
Chen, Theodore H. E. *Mao Tse-tung's Educational Revolution*. New York: Praeger, 1974.
Chiang, Yee. *A Chinese Childhood*. New York: Norton, 1963.
Christie, Richard C. and Jahoda, Marie, eds. *Studies in the Scope and Method of "The Authoritarian Personality."* New York: Free Press, 1954.
Coleman, James S. *Community Conflict*. New York: Free Press, 1957.
_____. *The Adolescent Society*. New York: Free Press, 1961.
Crozier, Michel. *The Bureaucratic Phenomenon*. Chicago: University of Chicago Press, 1964.
Festinger, Leon, ed. *Conflict, Decision and Dissonance*. Stanford: Stanford University Press, 1964.
_____. *A Theory of Cognitive Dissonance*. Stanford: Stanford University Press, 1957.
Feuer, Lewis S., ed. *Marx and Engels: Basic Writings on Politics and Philosophy*. New York: Doubleday, 1959.

Freedman, Maurice, ed. *Family and Kinship in Chinese Society*. Stanford: Stanford University Press, 1970.
Freud, Sigmund. *Civilization and its Discontents*. Translated by James Strachey. New York: Norton, 1961.
Greenstein, Fred I. *Personality and Politics*. Chicago: Markham, 1969.
Hai Feng (pseudonym). *Kwangchow ti-chu Wen-ko Li-ch'eng Shu-lüeh* ("A Narrative Account of the Cultural Revolution Process in the Kwangchow Area"). Hong Kong: Union Research Institute, 1971.
Hinton, William. *Fanshen*. New York: Vintage, 1968.
_____. *Hundred Day War: The Cultural Revolution at Tsinghua University*. New York: Monthly Review Press, 1972.
Horney, Karen. *New Ways in Psychoanalysis*. New York: W. W. Norton, 1939.
Huang, Sung-k'ang. *Li Ta-chao and the Origin of Marxism in Modern Chinese Thinking*. The Hague: Mouton, 1965.
Hunter, Neale. *Shanghai Journal*. Boston: Beacon, 1971.
Hsiao Ching (Classic of Filial Piety), translated by James Legge. *Sacred Books of the East*. Edited by F. Max Müller. Vol. III, Part I. Delhi: Motilal Banarsidass, 1966.
Karnow, Stanley. *Mao and China: From Revolution to Revolution*. New York: Viking, 1972.
Kenniston, Kenneth. *The Uncommitted*. New York: Dell, 1965.
Kessen, William, ed. *Childhood in China*. New Haven: Yale University Press, 1975.
Lang, Olga. *The Chinese Family and Society*. New York: Archon Books, 1968. (Reprint from 1946 Yale edition).
Langton, Kenneth. *Political Socialization*. New York: Oxford University Press, 1969.
Lasswell, Harold. *Psychopathology and Politics*. New York: Viking, 1960.
Leites, Nathan. *The Viet Cong Style of Politics*. Santa Monica: The Rand Corporation, Memorandum RM-5487-i-ISA ARPA, May 1969.
Levy, Marion J., Jr. *The Family Revolution in Modern China*. New York: Atheneum, 1968.
Lewis, John Wilson. *Leadership in Communist China*. Ithaca, New York: Cornell University Press, 1963.
Li Ta-chao. *Hsuan-chi* . . . (Selected Works). Peking, 1962.
Lifton, Robert Jay. *Thought Reform and the Psychology of Totalism*. New York: Norton, 1963.
Ling, Ken (pseudonym). *Revenge of Heaven*. Translated by Ivan London. New York: Ballantine, 1972.
Lipset, Seymour M. and Altbach, Philip G., eds. *Students in Revolt*. Boston: Beacon, 1970.
Lorenz, Konrad. *On Aggression*. Translated by Marjorie Kerr Wilson. New York: Bantam, 1967.
Mao Tse-tung. *Quotations of* . . . Peking: Foreign Language Publishing House, 1966.
_____. *Selected Works of* . . . Four English-edition Volumes. New York: International, 1954.
_____. *Selected Works of* . . . Vol. IV. Peking: Foreign Language Press, 1961.
Marx, Karl. *Selected Writings*. Translated by T. B. Bottomore. New York: McGraw-Hill, 1964.
Marx, Karl and Engels, Frederick. *The German Ideology*. Translated by R. Pascal. Parts I and III (1846). New York: International, 1947.
Mead, Margaret and Wolfenstein, Martha, eds. *Childhood in Contemporary Cultures*. Chicago: University of Chicago Press, 1955.
Mencius. Translated by James R. Ware. New York: New American Library, 1960.

Munro, Donald J. *The Concept of Man in Early China*. Stanford: Stanford University Press, 1969.
Pa Chin. *The Family (Chia)*. Translated by Sidney Shapiro. Peking: Foreign Language Press, 1964.
Pruitt, Ida. *A Daughter of Han: From the Story of Ning Lao T'ai-t'ai*. Stanford: Stanford University Press, 1967.
Pye, Lucian. *The Spirit of Chinese Politics*. Cambridge: MIT, 1968.
Pye, Lucian and Verba, Sidney, eds. *Political Culture and Political Development*. Princeton: Princeton University Press, 1965.
Rice, Edwin. *Mao's Way*. Berkeley: University of California Press, 1972.
Riesman, David. *Individualism Reconsidered*. New York: Free Press, 1954.
Schram, Stuart. *The Political Thought of Mao Tse-tung*. Rev. ed. New York: Praeger, 1963.
Schurmann, Franz. *Ideology and Organization in Communist China*. Berkeley: University of California Press, 1966.
Selden, Mark. *The Yenan Way in Revolutionary China*. Cambridge: Harvard University Press, 1971.
Sidel, Ruth. *Women and Child Care in China*. New York: Hill and Wang, 1972.
Snow, Edgar. *Red Star Over China*. New York: Random House, 1944.
Solomon, Richard H. *Mao's Revolution and the Chinese Political Culture*. Berkeley: University of California Press, 1971.
Sullivan, Harry Stack. *The Inter-Personal Theory of Psychiatry*. New York: Norton, 1953.
_____. *The Psychiatric Interview*. New York: Norton, 1954.
Sutton-Smith, Brian and Rosenberg, B. G. *The Sibling*. New York: Holt, Rinehart, Winston, 1970.
Townsend, James R. *Political Participation in Communist China*. Berkeley: University of California Press, 1969.
Waley, Arthur. *Analects of Confucius*. New York: Vintage, no date of publication.
Wilson, Colin. *The Outsider*. New York: Houghton-Mifflin, 1956.
Wilson, Richard W. *Learning to be Chinese*. Cambridge: MIT, 1970.
Wolf, Margery. *House of Lim*. New York: Appleton-Century-Croft, 1968.
_____. *Women and the Family in Rural Taiwan*. Stanford: Stanford University Press, 1972.
Yang, C.K. *Chinese Communist Society: The Family and the Village*. Cambridge: MIT, 1959.
Yang, Martin C. *A Chinese Village*. New York: Columbia University Press, 1945.
Yüan, Yu-ming, ed. *Ho Ch'ing-nien T'an Ku Lun Chin* ("Making the Ancient Relevant to the Present in Talking with Youth"). Peking: Chinese Youth Press, 1956.
Yung Mao Tse-tung Ssu-hsiang Chien-she Kung-ch'ing-t'uan ("Use Mao Tse-tung's Thought to Establish the Communist Youth League"). Peking: People's Publishing House, 1971.

ARTICLES, ESSAYS AND UNPUBLISHED PAPERS

Adcock, C. J. and J. F. Ritchie. "Intercultural Use of Rorschach." *American Anthropologist*, #60 (1968), 881-892.
Alexander, Franz. "Emotional Factors in Voting Behavior." *American Voting Behavior*. Edited by Eugene Burdick and Arthur Brodbeck. New York: Free Press, 1959.
An Hsueh-chiang. "We Should Have Faith in the Masses and in the Party." *Hung Ch'i*, #1 (January, 1972).

Appleton, Sheldon. "The Political Socialization of Taiwan's College Students." *Asian Survey*, X, #10 (October 1970), 919-923.
Bellah, Robert N. "Father and Son in Christianity and Confucianism." *Psychoanalytic Review*, Vol. 52, #2 (Summer 1965), 110.
Bridgham, Philip. "Mao's Cultural Revolution: Origin and Development." *China Quarterly*, #29 (January-March 1967), 1-35.
Chao Sheng-hui. "How Shall We Treat Parents and Relatives Who are Landlords and Counter-Revolutionaries?" *Chung-kuo Ch'ing-nien*, #22 (November 16, 1956), in *ECMM* #65 (November 16, 1956), 12-16.
Chen, Theodore H. E. and Chen, Wen-hui. "Attitudes toward Parents in China." *Sociology and Social Research*, XLIII, No. 3 (January-February 1959), 175-182.
_____. "Recent Social Changes in China," *Sociology and Social Research*, Vol. 32, No. 5 (May-June 1948), 831-841.
Ch'i Yung-hung. "Further Strengthen the Party's Centralized Leadership." *Hung Ch'i* #1 (January 1972), in *SCMM* #721-22, 32-35.
Chin, Ai-li (in collaboration with Robert Chin). "Modern Meaning of Filialism Among Taiwan's College Elite." Unpublished Paper Prepared for Seminar in "Cognitive and Value Systems in Chinese Society," Bermuda, January 1964.
Chüeh Tsai. "Ai fu-mu." *JMJP*, December 24, 1956.
Davis, Kingsley. "The Theory of Change and Response in Modern Demographic History." *Population Index*, Vol. 29, #4, October 1963, 355ff.
Fang Yu. "Break Family Ties, Be a Good Child of the Proletariat." *Chung-kuo Ch'ing-nien*, #21 (November 1, 1964), in *SCMM*, No. 448, 36-40.
Freud, Sigmund. "Some Reflections on Schoolboy Psychology" (address at 50th anniversary of his middle school Alma Mater). *Standard Edition*, Vol. XIII, 240-245.
George, Alexander. "Power as a Compensatory Value for Political Leaders." *Journal of Social Issues*, Vol. 24, #3, 29-50.
Herriott, Robert. "Some Social Determinants of Educational Aspirations." *Harvard Educational Review* (Spring 1963).
Hess, Robert D. and Easton, David. "The Child's Image of the President." *Public Opinion Quarterly*, XXIV (Spring 1960), 632-644.
Hickrod, Lucy Jen Huang and Hickrod, G. Alan. "Communist Chinese and American Adolescent Subcultures." *China Quarterly*, No. 22 (April-June 1965), 171-181.
Hu Hsien-chin. "The Chinese Concept of Face." *American Anthropologist*, 46 (1944), 45-64.
Huang, Lucy Jen. "A Re-evaluation of the Primary Role of the Chinese Communist Woman: The Homemaker or the Workers." *Marriage and Family Living*, Vol. 25, No. 2 (May 1963), 162-166.
Kau Han-ying. "Oppose Wine and Meat Friends." *Kung-jen Jih-pao*, April 24, 1958.
Kwong, Peter. "The Red Guards in Peking, December 1965-March 1967." Unpublished East Asian Institute Essay, Columbia University, 1970.
Li Ta-chao. "Liberation of Spirit." *Hsin Sheng-huo* (February 8, 1920). *Selected Works*. Peking, 1962, 309.
Lifton, Robert Jay. "On Psychohistory." *Psychoanalysis and Contemporary Science*, Vol. I. Edited by Robert Holt and Emanuel Peterfruend. New York: MacMillan, 1972.
_____. "The Struggle for Cultural Rebirth," *Harpers*, April 1973, 86-90.
"Massively Develop an 'All Red Family' and Promote Study in the Entire Brigade." *Hung-wei-pao*, Canton, December 8, 1966.
McClelland, David C. "Motivational Patterns in Southeast Asia with Special Reference to Chinese Case." *Journal of Social Issues*, XIX, #1 (January 1963), 6-19.

Raddock, David M. "Innocents in Limbo." *Far Eastern Economic Review* (April 29, 1972).
Redl, Fritz. "Group Emotion and Leadership." *Psychiatry*. Vol. V.
Sandler, Joseph and Rosenblatt, Bernard. "The Concept of the Representational World." *The Psychoanalytic Study of the Child*, Vol. 17, 1962, 128-145.
Selden, Mark. "The Yenan Legacy: The Mass Line." *Chinese Communist Politics in Action*. Edited by A. Doak Barnett. Seattle: University of Washington Press, 1969, 99-151.
Slote, Walter. "Case Analysis of a Revolutionary." *A Strategy for Research on Social Policy* Vol. I. Edited by Frank Bonilla and Jose de Silva Michena. Cambridge: MIT, 1967.
"Sum up Experience in Strengthening Party Building." *Hung Ch'i*, [*JMJP*, *CFJP* joint editorial], October 30, 1971.
Taeuber, Irene B. "Migrant and Metropolis." *Population Index*, Vol. 29, No. 1 (January 1963), 3-12.
"Tai-fang fu-mu pu-neng wei-fan Kuo-chia li-yi." ("Care for Parents Can't Conflict with Interest of the State"). *Chung-kuo Ch'ing-nien*, #4 (February 16, 1957), 8.
Titiev, Mischa and Hsing Chih-tien. "A Primer of Filial Piety." *Papers of the Michigan Academy of Science, Arts and Letters*, Vol. XXXIII (1947), 259-266.
Townsend, James. "Revolutionizing Chinese Youth, A Study of *Chung-kuo Ch'ing-nien*." *Chinese Communist Politics in Action*. Edited by A. Doak Barnett. Seattle: University of Washington Press, 1969.
_____. "Revolutionization of Chinese Youth." *China Quarterly*, #30 (April-June 1967), 62-67.
Vogel, Ezra F. "From Friendship to Comradeship: The Change in Personal Relations with Communist China." *China Quarterly*, No. 21 (January-March 1965), 46-60.
Wallace, Anthony. "Revitalization Movements." *American Anthropologist*, LVIII (April 1956).
Walster, E. "The Temporal Sequence of Post-Decision Processes." *Conflict, Decision and Dissonance*. Edited by Leon Festinger. Stanford: Stanford University Press, 1964, 112-128.
Weakland, John H. "Orality in Chinese Conceptions of Male Genital Sexuality." *Psychiatry*, XIX (1956), 237-247.
Wilson, Alan B. "Residential Segregation of Social Classes and Aspirations of High School Boys." *American Sociological Review*, December 1959.
Wolf, Margery. "Child Training and the Chinese Family." *Family and Kinship in Chinese Society*. Edited by Maurice Freedman. Stanford: Stanford University Press, 1970, 37-62.
Wolfenstein, Martha. "Some Variants in Moral Training of Children." *Childhood in Contemporary Cultures*. Edited by Margaret Mead and Martha Wolfenstein. Chicago: University of Chicago Press, 1955, 349-368.
Yao Yüan-fang. "From Filial Piety to the Treatment of Parents" in *Chung-kuo Ch'ing-nien*, #21 (November 1, 1956), *ECMM*, #65, 21-26.

Index

Academic performance, 66-67, 79, 85-86, 120-121, 132, 176, 199
Adolescence (*ch'ing-nien*) defined, 206
Adolescent phenomenology, 118, 143, 221-222
Adult identity, 1-2, 10, 67-68, 72, 117-119, 122-124, 128, 138, 154, 174-175, 193, 195, 200-203; defined, 210
Adult succession, 193. *See also* adult identity
Age, as variable, 8, 216-217
Almond, Gabriel, 1
Alexander, Franz, 9
American voter studies, 9
Ambivalence, 6, 216. *See also* father-son relations, ambivalence in . . .
Anomie, 18
Anti-Rightist Campaign, 65, 67, 88, 150, 173
Arendt, Hannah, 77
Authority, attitudes toward, 4, 127-128, 153
Authority-dependent, 5-6, 101, 120-124 (Yüan case), 154, 163-165, 171, 183
Authority-figures. *See* father-surrogates

Bauer, Raymond, 1, 16-17
"Blood-line" question (*hsüeh-t'ung-lun*), 50, 51-53, 80, 107

Central Cultural Revolution Group (CCRG), 45, 51-52, 55, 208, 228
Chai Cheng-li (respondent), 24, 94, 130-134, 174, 194; biographical sketch, 28-29
Chang Hsin (respondent), biographical sketch, 29
Chao Tzu-yang, 118
Ch'en Ling-ping (respondent), 21, 149; biographical sketch, 29
Chen-piao (personal vita), 169. *See also ssu-hsiang chien-t'ao* and *tang-an*
Chen Po-ta, 52
Chiang Ch'ing, 52, 56
Ch'iao Kuo-hsiung (respondent), 52-53, 78-82, 118, 187, 188, 190; biographical sketch, 29-30
Chinese Communist Party (CCP), 41, 52
Chou Chung-wang (respondent), 42, 43, 63, 117, 118-119, 140, 173, 200, 202, 205; biographical sketch, 30
Chu Nan-po (respondent), 78-83, 95, 96, 125-130, 136, 140, 145, 146, 180, 198, 19°; biographical sketch, 30.
Ch'uan-lien, 3, 18, 48, 51, 101, 114, 140, 147, 148
Civic Culture, 1, 203
Class background, general effects of, 196-199;

[237]

stigma of, 7, 11, 14, 50-60, 70, 72-74, 75-89, 101, 103-106, 121-122, 150-152, 167-169, 171-173, 175, 194-199; attempt to compensate for, 81, 168, 171, 173; political emphasis on, 50, 73-76, 80-83, 100; as defense, 105-106; and privilege, 80.
"Class enemy," definition of, 208
Confucian family system. See traditional family
Cultural Revolution Committee, 45
Cynicism, political, 2, 100-101, 108, 172

Dai Shao-ai, 50, 206
Davis, Kingsley, 18
"Destroy Four Olds" (*ta-p'o-ssu-chiu* or *p'o ssu-chiu*), 47-48, 50-51, 79, 86, 123, 127, 134
"Destroy Self, Uplift Collective" (*P'o-ssu-li-kung*), 200, 228
Dissonance-reduction, 15, 22, 27-28, 171-172
Dormitory, 143, 178
Dreams, 106-107, 124. See also fantasies

Ego: autonomy, 5, 102-103, 112, 118, 120, 126, 128, 129, 137, 145, 155, 158, 175, 184, 185, 189-193, 201-203; defenses of, 26, 64, 66-67, 100-102, 136, 155, 222, 230 (see also suppression); inflation of, 42-44, 48, 81, 96, 108, 116-119, 129-130, 200, 201, 202-203
Elite middle schools, definition of, 213
Elitism (social and political), 41-44, 49-50, 52-53, 82, 226
Exchange of Experiences. See *Ch'uan-lien*

Fanshen, 16
Fantasies, political: in childhood, 93, 118, 161, 168; in adolescence, 100-102, 161
Father, role and behavior of, 4-6, 65-66, 137, 175-182; identification with, 66, 85-86, 92-97, 100, 105-111, 120-124, 195; image of, 68-69, 112-113, 177, 179
Father-son relationship, 4-5, 10; Vertical (See vertical relations); Horizontal (See horizontal relations); rivalry and competition in, 6, 83-87, 90-137, 154-160; ambivalence in son's rivalry in, 6, 104, 106-111
Father-surrogate, 2, 5-6, 66, 91, 108, 126-128, 134, 154, 158-159, 165, 184, 189, 199, 205, 224; defined, 205
Fei K'o-kuan (respondent), 149, 182; biographical sketch, 30.
Feng Chih-hsiang (respondent), biographical sketch, 31
Filiality, 5, 69, 90, 92-97, 99, 122-123, 127-128, 136, 157, 166, 176-177, 180, 182-183, 185
Food, as symbol, 189
"Four Olds" (*P'o-ssu-chiu*). See "Destroy Four Olds" Campaign
Freud, Sigmund, 28, 57, 77, 90
Friendship, 51, 138-141, 145-146, 182, 222, 223. See also peers

Great Leap Forward (*ta-yüeh-chin*), 73-74, 103
Great Unity. See *Ta-lien-ho*
Guilt, after perceived defiance of father, 106-108, 111, 115-116, 124, 136, 182

Hong Kong, 17-19, 67-69, 110, 134, 149, 167, 183
Horizontal family relations, 5-6, 10-11, 91, 111-116, 125-130, 135, 138-139, 154, 165-167,

171-173, 182, 192, 193, 196, 210; defined, 217; transitional, 224
Horreur de face-à-face, 46, 207, 229
Hostility, 5, 10, 102, 121-123, 155, 158-160, 165, 166, 167, 175, 182, 188-191, 213
House of Lim, 193
Hsia-hsiang ("Down to the Village" movement), 124, 134, 165, 200, 202, 212
Hsiao Ching ("Classic of Filial Piety"), 181
Hsieh Ting-teng (respondent), 167-171, 195; biographical sketch, 31
Hsu Ta-liang (respondent), 63, 94, 166, 191; biographical sketch, 31
Hua-ch'ing chieh-hsien ("Draw a Clear Line" between self and family), 68-69, 104, 195-199
Huang Erh (respondent), 66-67, 88, 136; biographical sketch, 32
Huang San (respondent), 66-67, 88, 136, 189; biographical sketch, 32
Huang Yi (respondent), 65-67, 88, 136, 150-151, 166-167; biographical sketch, 31-32
Huang Yung-sheng, Gen., 55
Hunter, Neale, 8

In-groups, 77-83, 117, 151-152, 195, 222
Inkeles, Alex, 1, 16-17
Interpersonal psychoanalytic theory, 22-23; application in interviewing in this study, 23-26

Ko-ming Ta Ch'uan-lien. See *Ch'uan-lien*
Kuai Ta-fu, 47
Kuang Ch'ing (respondent), biographical sketch, 32-33
Kuo-Te-en (respondent), biographical sketch, 33

Labor models, 186
Lan Wei-ying (respondent), 93, 117, 119, 140, 145, 147, 154-160, 179, 180, 181, 201, 202; biographical sketch, 33
Legitimacy of political system, 170-171
Lei Feng, 210
Li Cheng (respondent), 181, 192, 194, 196; biographical sketch, 33-34
Li Ta-chao, 184
Liang Shu-ming (respondent) 163-165, 171; biographical sketch, 34
Lin Piao, 228
Liu K'o-chung (respondent), 177; biographical sketch, 34
Liu-ist (adhering to principles of Liu Shao-ch'i), 53, 207
Lo Ping-kok (respondent), 61-62, 94, 97, 102-111, 136, 146, 192, 195; biographical sketch, 34-35
Lo Ping-wen (respondent), 60, 97-102, 136, 143, 155, 183; biographical sketch, 35

Manipulation (political), 9, 41-44, 167, 194, 201
Mao Tse-tung, 41-44, 49, 81, 91, 166, 167, 174, 180, 181, 187, 193, 202, 208; Mao Tse-tung thought, 42, 44, 115, 144, 195, 197; *Quotations*, 42-44, 201, 202; and story about threatening father, 98, 112, 120, 122, 164, 190-191; reading about, 100; and loyalty and emulation of, 116-117, 160, 161
Marx, Karl, 184
May Fourth Movement, 41-44, 129
May 7 Cadre Schools, 155, 223
May 16 Circular, 45
Mencius, 181
Min-pan schools, 85-86, 211, 213
Mother, 79, 112-113, 132-134 (in Chai case), 157, 166, 168, 178, 181, 188, 190, 193, 194, 215, 219, 221
Mu Chi-jui (respondent),

biographical sketch, 35

Narcissism, 2
Neighborhood schools, 194. *See also min-pan* schools
New socialist man, 68, 175-185
Nieh Li-chih (respondent), 60-61, 68-72, 151, 186, 195; biographical sketch, 35
Nieh Yüan-tzu, 47

Officialdom, desire for, 94-97
Orality, 228-229
Orphans, 220
Ostracism (peer group), 3, 7, 11, 48-51, 57-58, 77-87, 105, 144, 149, 151-152, 175, 194-195
Outgroup, 3, 7, 77-83, 149, 151-152, 195
Outsider, 117, 142, 144, 166, 169-170. *See also* outgroup

Pan-kan, 8, 51, 71, 145
Pao Kuo-fu (respondent), 76, 111-116, 118, 136, 140, 145, 147, 148, 150, 167, 183, 205; biographical sketch, 36
Peers: in adolescence, 3, 7, 11, 51, 66, 71, 77-83, 101, 105, 138-153, 163-165, 169, 175, 178, 182; in childhood, 65-66, 93, 138-140, 142-143, 169, 206
Peng Chen, 45
Peking University, 41, 47
People's Liberation Army (PLA), 51, 53, 69, 73, 93, 156, 168, 210
P'eng Te-lai (respondent), 60, 189, 190; biographical sketch, 36
Permissiveness, 200-201. *See also* socialization, horizontal relations
Pioneers (*Shao-nien hsien-feng-tui* or *Shao-nien-tui*), 60, 71, 91, 93, 95, 103, 132, 155, 168, 214
Political study (*cheng-chih hsüeh-hsi*), 60, 70, 97-98, 129, 142, 149, 155-156, 181-182, 196, 197, 210, 227
Production brigade, 181, 192
Propaganda teams (*hsüan-ch'uan-tui*). *See* work teams
Pu-fu-ch'i ("refusing to capitulate internally"), 98, 189
Psychositic reaction, 167

Radicalization (of non-reds), 51-55
Rage reactions, 98, 183, 188-191
Red Guards: activist category, defined, 14-15; passive category, 14, 16, 141; abstainer category, defined, 14, 16; and factionalism in, 51-56, 79-82, 86, 101, 113, 115, 118, 125, 141-142, 146-147; and "five kinds of red," 49-50, 78, 80; *Mao Tse-tung Ssu-hsiang Chu-yi-ping*, 11, 49, 55, 71, 78, 80, 81, 82, 86, 134, 198; *Tung Feng* faction, 55-56, 72, 141, 142, 146, 147, 148, 156, 173; *Hung Ch'i* faction, 53-56, 79, 80-86, 114-115, 125, 140, 141, 142, 144, 146, 147 (. . . *wei ping*), 148, 164, 195; armed struggle (*wu-tou*) in, 81-83, 108, 115, 117, 128, 142, 173
Red Guard newspapers, 3
Regression, 189, 228
Religious movements, 175
Revolutionary heroes, 93, 210
Revolutionary successors, 2, 41-44, 91, 96

Schurmann, Franz, 18
Security brigade (*tiao-ch'a-tui*), 72
Self-esteem. *See* Ego, or trust, or horizontal family relations
"Self-expose" movements, 75, 84
Sex, 8-9, 140, 147, 230
Shaming culture, 227
Shanghai, 53

Shih Chi-t'ang (respondent), 44, 71-72, 179, 186, 187, 190; biographical sketch, 36
Siblings, 16-17, 97-111 (case of Lo brothers), 161, 229
Smith, M. Brewster, 6
Snow, Edgar, 41
Snow-balling technique, 12-13
Social Environment, 6-7, 22, 66-72, 88-89, 91, 136, 146-148, 150, 165-166, 172, 175-193, 228
Social equilibrium, 193
Socialist Education Movement, 14, 47, 73-76, 78-79, 88, 104, 149, 156
Socialization: in family, 4, 11, 22, 58-65, 97-101, 106, 111-113, 120, 125-128, 130-131, 138-139, 150, 164, 176, 179, 185-191; at school, 58-64, 126-127, 169, 178-179, 183-186, 194; uniformity and non-uniformity in, 58-64, 73, 87-89, 137, 163, 180, 187-189, 194, 196, 208-209, 215, 230; in Confucian China, 177, 189, 193, 194
Solomon, Richard, 14, 21-22; thematic apperception tests of, 166, 181
Soviet Citizen, 1
Ssu-ch'ing Movement ("four clean-ups"). *See* Socialist Education Movement
Ssu-hsiang chien-t'ao (self-examination), 60-61, 71-72, 103-104, 121, 182-183
"Steeling" (*tuan-lien*), 41, 44, 178, 183
Student Association, 49, 51, 197, 198
Struggle (*tou-cheng*), 62
Superstition, 205
Suppression, 5, 90, 154, 166, 188, 189

Ta-lien-ho ("Great Unity"), 55, 81
Ta-p'o-ssu-chiu. *See* "Destroy Four Olds" Movement

Ta-tzu-pao. *See* wall posters
Taiwan, 178, 192
T'an Li-fu, 52
T'ang Nai-chang (respondent), biographical sketch, 36-37
Tang-an ("dossier"). *See Ssu-hsiang Chien-t'ao*
Teachers, question of struggling, 114-115, 123
Teng T'o, 45
Thought reform (*Ssu-hsiang kai-tsau*), 98, 99, 179-180, 185, 227. *See also* political study
"Three Family Village," 43, 45, 207
"Totalitarianism," 77, 185
Traditional Chinese family relations, 90, 92, 97, 159, 178-181, 188, 189, 190, 191, 193, 219, 224
Transference, 90, 166, 195
Trust, 6, 66, 88, 138-139, 150, 152, 223; indicators for, 139
Tseng K'ai-lao (respondent) 160-163, 199; biographical sketch, 37
Tsinghua University, 47, 49

Upward mobility, 8, 77-79, 83-88, 117-118, 126, 156, 171, 186, 193, 195

Values: parental, 6, 88, 91-94, 99-100, 103, 120-121, 128, 129, 130-133 (clash in), 135-137, 154-155, 177, 178, 217, 220; social-political, 91-92, 128, 137, 157, 177
Verba, Sidney, 1
Vertical family relations, 5-6, 10-11, 91, 93, 94, 96-111, 120-124, 130-134, 135, 139, 154, 165, 167-171, 182, 183, 188-189, 192, 214
Wall posters (*ta-tzu-pao*), 3, 45, 70, 80, 127, 140, 147, 159, 170, 172
Wang Kuang-mei (Mme. Liu Shao-Ch'i), 208
Wang Lok-ch'ao (respondent), 44, 83-87, 88, 93, 118, 172; biographical

cal sketch, 37
Wei Chao-fan (respondent), 117; biographical sketch, 37
Work teams (*Kung-tso-tui*): at start of GPCR, 47, 52, 83, 208; at end of GPCR in schools, 134, 172
Wu Kuo-chih (respondent), 70-71; biographical sketch, 37-38

Yang Ying-pu (respondent), 15, 64, 78, 118, 147, 191; biographical sketch, 38

Yeh Hen (respondent), 43, 63, 117, 142-145; biographical sketch, 38
Yenan period, 201
Youth League (YCL), 2-3, 45, 49, 51, 71, 72, 76, 79, 84-85, 91, 93, 99-101, 113, 126, 128, 132, 156, 184, 192, 196, 197, 198, 199, 202, 212
Yü Ming-li (respondent), 18-19, 140-142; biographical sketch, 39
Yüan Ching-po (respondent), 24-26, 60, 93, 120-124, 136, 149-150; biographical sketch, 39

WITHDRAWN
From Bertrand Library

DATE DUE			
APR 13 1982			
1982			
GAYLORD			PRINTED IN U.S.A.